ETERNAL GUILT?

Forty Years of German-Jewish-Israeli Relations

ETERNAL GUILT?

Forty Years of
German-Jewish-Israeli
Relations

MICHAEL WOLFFSOHN

Translated by Douglas Bokovoy

COLUMBIA UNIVERSITY PRESS
New York

Columbia University Press
New York   Chichester, West Sussex
Copyright © 1993 Columbia University Press
Originally published in Germany as:
Ewige Schuld? 40 Jahre deutsch-Judisch-israelische Beziehungen.
Copyright © R. Piper GMBH and Co., 1988.
All rights reserved

Library of Congress Cataloging-in-Publication Data

Wolffsohn, Michael.
[Ewige Schuld?   English]
Eternal guilt? : forty years of German-Jewish Israeli relations /
Michael Wolffsohn   ;   translated by Douglas Bokovoy.
p.   cm.
Includes bibliographical references.
ISBN 0-231-08274-6
1. Germany (West)—Foreign relations—Israel.
2. Israell—Foreign relations—Germany (West.
3. Holocaust, Jewish (1939–1945)—Public opinion.
4. Public opinion—Germany (West).
5. Public opinion—Israel.
6. Jews—Germany (West)—Politics and government.
I. Title.
DD258.85.I75W6613   1993
943'.004924—dc20
93–837
CIP

∞

Casebound editions of Columbia University Press books
are printed on permanent and durable acid-free paper.

Printed in the United States of America

c 10 9 8 7 6 5 4 3 2 1

Contents

Preface

Eternal Guilt has remained a kind of bestseller in Germany. The book was published in April 1988 and within a year three editions were sold out. My various comments on German television during the Gulf War, especially concerning its implications for German-Jewish and also German-American-Jewish relations, increased interest in the book's topics and its author as well. Thus, a fourth edition was published in early 1991, and a fifth edition appeared in 19993. Personally I was able to realize the truth of what I had said again and again: Germany is a splendid market for books dealing with Germany's recent past. Germans devour books that try to explain their past and present problems with their history—i.e., with themselves.

Eternal Guilt was presented to the German public on April 20, 1988, which is a symbolic date in modern German history: *Führers Geburtstag:* Hitler's birthday. It was my suggestion to publish on this day because it allowed me to show that we have won, despite the terrible and cruel losses of 6 million Jews and more than 50 million other people who died during the Second World War. We? We the Jews. And we the civilized part of humanity, Germans and non-Germans, Jews and non-Jews.

How did I come to write this book? The answer is simple. German-Jewish-Israeli relations are part of my research and also part of my biography. I was born in Tel Aviv in 1947. I came to Germany in 1954, where I received my formal education at high school and university. Between 1967 and September 1970 I served in the Israeli Army and then returned to Germany.

Contrary to many Diaspora Jews I supported Israel not only by words but also by deeds. I gave Zionism a fair chance: I went to Israel and tested my Israeliness, the hard way. I came to realize that I was and wanted to remain a Diaspora Jew—a German Diaspora Jew. A Diaspora Jew with respect to my Jewish as well as my German identity. To make things worse (for some critics, Jews and non-Jews alike): I have identified with this identity, with these identities. I cannot (and no longer wish to) separate my Jewish from my German identity. German-Israeli-Jewish relations are, in other words, an integral part of my personality. Like any person and personality I am and must be an object of criticism.

Sometimes, the criticism is as unfair as it is unrealistic. Some Jews consider my identification with the new and democratic Germany (originally West Germany, of course) as a betrayal to Jewishness and Israel. My answer: "I did it my way," the hard way: I dedicated three long years of my life to the collective and sometimes dangerous effort of building and defending the Jewish State—one that I support wholeheartedly but not uncritically. With broken hearts, my Israeli friends have accepted my decision. Like me, they have realized that despite my outspoken Jewishness and my cosmopolitan outlook I feel at home where my home stood during the formative years of childhood, adolescence, and general education—in Germany.

Others, fellow-Jews, criticize my rational analysis and criticism of Diaspora Jewish representatives, such as the late German Jewish leader Heinz Galinsky and Edgar Bronfman of the World Jewish Congress. We should not identify these Jewish representatives with all (or even the majority of) Jews, let alone with Judaism. Jews and Judaism are too important and multidimensional to leave them exclusively to Jewish representatives. As political representatives they have to be measured by universal standards that apply to all human beings. Moral measurement by origin could be compared with racism. *Ahavat Israel* (i.e., love for Israel, Jews, and Judaism) is not calculated by the measure of consent to Jewish representatives who are as good or bad as any other non-Jewish representative.

Some non-Jews ask: Why Germany—of all places? My answer is contained in this book, as far as Germany's effort to "overcome" or to cope with its terrible past is concerned. Moreover, Germany has, of course, been a Western democracy for more than forty years. Why not live in one? Recent manifestations of xenophobic, as well as anti-Semitic sentiments cannot be denied, of course. Unfortunately, they are not limited to Germany. They can be observed in other Western and more so in Eastern European countries. Germany opened its gates to roughly 500,000 foreigners in 1992; Britain and France to less than 50,000. Quantities sometimes determine the quality of a problem. I do not underestimate recent manifestations of anti-Semitism in Germany or elsewhere. But, as a historically conscious Jew (a Jewish historian and a history professor) I profess that I do not have to be reminded of the dangers of anti-Semitism. Sheer survival instincts make it impossible to overlook them.

Considering recent events and developments in Germany we should ask: Is *Eternal Guilt* too optimistic as to the New Germany? I do not think so. This is my answer. And this is my explanation: As before, the vast majority of Germans are tolerant, democratic, liberal, and by no means anti-Semitic. But because of revolutionary changes in and around Germany the minority has turned more militant. It has been able to dictate the agenda of German politics. This is a new problem between majority and minority. But it does not jeopardize the proportions. On the other hand: Fundamental changes have rarely been initiated by majorities. Therefore, we have to watch developments carefully—but not hysterically. After all, the so-far silent majority of Germans broke its silence in late 1992. Its "chain-of-lights" demonstrations against racism and anti-Semitism are silently eloquent symbols of light, determination, and hope.

Munich, January 1993

Archives

Thanks to the generous support of the Volkswagen Foundation it was possible to gain access to the material on German-Jewish-Israeli relations in the following institutions and archives:

IN THE FEDERAL REPUBLIC OF GERMANY: Bundesarchiv (Federal Archives) Koblenz, Politisches Archiv des Auswärtigen Amtes (Archive of the Foreign Ministry), Archiv für Christliche-Demokratische Politik, Archiv der Friedrich-Ebert-Stiftung, Archiv für Christlich-Soziale Politik, Archiv der Friedrich-Naumann-Stiftung, Stiftung Bundeskanzler-Adenauer-Haus, Ludwig-Erhard-Stiftung, Archiv der Evangelischen Kirche in Deutschland, Bayerisches Hauptstaatsarchiv, Staatskanzlei München, Landesarchiv Berlin (West), Senatskanzlei Berlin (West), Stadtarchiv München, Deutscher Gewerkschaftsbund, Deutscher Sportbund, Deutscher Städtetag, Deutsch-Israelische Gesellschaft, Nah- und Mittelostverein, Archiv Bund Freiheit der Wissenschaft (Bonn), Archiv Notgemeinschaft für eine freie Universität (Berlin). The Deutsch-Arabische Gesellschaft refused access to its materials.

IN ISRAEL: State Archives, Archive of the World Zionist Organization, Histadrut Archive, Ben-Gurion papers at Sde Boqer, Weizmann Institute, and the archives of the following parties: Israeli Labor Party, Cherut, Mapam, Ahdut Haavoda.

IN THE UNITED STATES: National Archives, Institute for Jewish Research (New York), John Foster Dulles papers (Princeton) and the following presidential libraries: Truman, Eisenhower, Kennedy, Johnson, Nixon, Ford, Carter.

IN GREAT BRITAIN: Public Record Office, Institute for Jewish Affairs (London).

IN FRANCE: Archive du Ministère des Affaires Etrangères (Quai d'Orsay), Archive Nationale, Archive du Parlement, Archive de l'Armée de Terre.

Among other materials, the chief newspapers and news magazines appearing in East and West Germany, Israel, the United States, Great Britain, France and Austria as well as the daily records of the West German Bundestag and the Israeli Knesset were evaluated for the period 1949 to 1987.

ETERNAL GUILT?

*Forty Years of
German-Jewish-Israeli
Relations*

1

WITHOUT HITLER—NO ISRAEL?

The Historical Dimensions of the Founding of the State of Israel

If it hadn't been for Hitler there would be no Israel. If there had been no Holocaust there would be no Jewish State today. How often this line of reasoning is used! Even the German-British writer Sebastian Haffner, who is undoubtedly above suspicion, repeats the argument several times in his book *Amerkungen zu Hitler*. And even the late president of the World Jewish Congress, Nahum Goldmann, echoed the claim that without Auschwitz there would be no Israel. Others less ideologically immune to the brown bacillus are fond of making the same argument for their own particular purposes.

But constant repetition does not improve the quality of the reasoning. The claim remains a legend. The mass-murderer of the Jews was not the midwife of the Jewish State. As though one legend were not enough, the argument is also advanced that if it had not been for the roles played first by Great Britain as the mandatory power in Palestine, then by the United States and the Soviet Union in the United Nations, the declaration of independence on the part of the State of Israel on May 14, 1948, would "never" have come to pass. As this legend would have it, the Zionist goals were achieved with the aid of an unlikely coalition of powers and personages cooperating unintentionally and with immeasurable ill-will but apparently with great effect: Hitler and Himmler, Chamberlain and Churchill, Attlee and Bevin,* Roosevelt and Truman and, last but not least, Stalin. The claim is not only grotesque, but also ascribes to Hitler a role to which he is neither morally nor historically entitled.

■

It is superfluous to comment on Hitler's relations with the Jews. But the without-Hitler-no-Israel legend also revives the controversy over the so-called "Transfer Agreement." Negotiated between Nazi Germany and Zionist organizations in the summer of 1933, it permitted limited Jewish immigration from Germany to Palestine and was intended as a means of rendering Germany *judenrein* (literally: "clean of Jews"). Jewish wealth was confiscated as the price of an exit visa and Hitler thus had no need to soil his hands with Jewish blood at an inopportunely early date. Hitler, together with his Foreign and Economics Ministries, hoped to polish Germany's international image, which had been considerably tarnished in consequence of the boycott of Jewish businesses proclaimed on April 1, 1933. The hope was that an improved image would lower the psychological barriers to German exports abroad. Convinced of the "omnipotence of World Jewry," Hitler sought to deflect the counter-boycott of German products being organized by both Jews and non-Jews in Western countries.

For their part, the Zionists agreed to this pact with the devil for two reasons: First, individual persecuted Jews and, second, the Zionist cause in Palestine would be served by the skills and capital that the Jewish immigrants would bring to Palestine.

The Transfer Agreement functioned smoothly up to 1937 and only haltingly thereafter until 1939. From the start, however, it was an object of controversy within the Zionist movement. It is noteworthy that the agreement was concluded by the left-leaning Zionist majority

*Translator's note: Clement Attlee was Prime Minister in England's postwar Labour Government (1945–1951). Ernest Bevin was his Foreign Secretary.

under the leadership of David Ben-Gurion. From the very beginning, the Revisionists of the rightist Zionist opposition rejected any form of cooperation with Hitler and demanded a total boycott of Nazi Germany. The consequences of this disagreement were to prove far-reaching. When, in January of 1952, the Ben-Gurion government was preparing to initiate restitution negotiations with the Federal Republic of Germany as the recognized legal successor of the German Reich, Menachem Begin accused Ben-Gurion of once again making a compact with the German devil.

The Transfer Agreement of 1933 did not prevent the Holocaust, the vast majority of the victims of which were Eastern European Jews, who had always displayed more enthusiasm for the Zionist cause than their assimilated co-religionists in Western Europe and America.

It is here that we come to the heart of the without-Hitler-no-Israel legend. The key contention is that only in the wake of the Holocaust was Zionism propelled into political legitimacy. Had Zionism not achieved majority support as a direct result of the Holocaust, so the argument goes, the Zionists would have remained what they had been before: an embattled minority movement among the numerous organizations of the Jewish Diaspora. By this logic, the Holocaust—as horrible as it was for the individual victims—thus performed a collective service for the survivors—and for the Zionists in particular. What is more, it is even claimed that the Zionist leadership under Ben-Gurion had deliberately chosen to remain silent when knowledge of the Holocaust first reached Palestine and the West in November of 1942. Allegedly, the Zionist politicians did nothing in order to be able to later cite the catastrophe as proof for the accuracy of Zionist warnings concerning the dangers of anti-Semitism.

In chapter 3 we will take a closer look at the actual and the presumed functions of the Holocaust in the political-historical arena in Israel. But could the Zionist leaders really have been not only so cynical but also so stupid as to stand by while their greatest reservoir of potential supporters, the Jews of Eastern Europe, were annihilated in order that these same politicians could later erect a Jewish State based on the watered-down Zionism of the Western Jews? What is more, like Ben-Gurion himself, the Zionist leadership in Palestine had its roots—not to speak of family and friends—in Eastern Europe. The accusations leveled against Ben-Gurion and his Zionist compatriots are clearly neither politically nor personally tenable.

Immediately following Hitler's assumption of power there were a few Zionists here and there, including Germans, who, like Kurt Blumenfeld in April 1933, thought that the anti-Semitism of the National-Socialist regime would serve to win over new adherents to Zionism among the Jews of Germany, who had previously maintained a cool distance from the Jewish national movement. Blumenfeld quickly recognized his error and realized that National Socialism was directed against all Jews, Zionists as well as non-Zionists, and could never be instrumentalized to serve any Jewish purpose.

In general, both the Zionist right and left quickly recognized German National Socialism for what it truly was: an extremely dangerous threat to Jews. But the deadly nature of that threat was discerned with hesitancy and not until late in 1942.

■

According to the legend, after the Holocaust the world was no longer able to say no to the creation of a Jewish state. The fact, however, is that after 1945 the world not only could but actually did say no. Most important, Great Britain as the mandatory power in Palestine opposed the foundation of a Jewish state. The British kept the door to Palestine shut tight for Jews, including Holocaust survivors, seeking to immigrate there. Great Britain did so in order to curry favor with the Arabs and with the goal of erecting an Arab, not a Jewish, state in Palestine.

Zionism had no need of the Holocaust as testimony to its legitimacy and necessity. From the time of the Old Testament prophets the Jewish understanding of history has been shaped by the assumption that the Jewish Diaspora and the persecution of Jews are two sides of the same coin, that the history of the Jews is the history of their persecution. Seen in this light, the so-called "battle of the historians" (*historikerstreit*), the controversy that began in 1986 among historians in Germany over the presumed historical uniqueness of the Holocaust is, for a tradition-conscious Jew, as un-Jewish as it is ahistorical. In the long history of the sufferings of the Jewish people the Holocaust does not represent a wholly singular event.

As developed in the late nineteenth century, the basic presumption of Zionism—that Jews always have been and always will be persecuted—is merely a modern, secularized variation on the millennia-old Jewish perspective of the world and its history. Not that this presumption formed a common ground on which secularly oriented Zionists and religious traditionalists were able to agree. Even after the Holocaust, Jews drew differing conclusions. In the face of persecution, only a minority of Jews, whether religious or not, desired to immigrate to the Jewish State. The majority of nonreligious, assimilated Jews did not view anti-Semitism as a lethal threat and did not promote a Jewish state as either a political or geographic alternative. Religious Jews combatted Zionism, which they regarded as an attempt to interfere with God's will as manifested in the history of the Jewish people and thus in the history of salvation.

■

The without-Hitler-no-Israel legend also overlooks the simple fact that Zionism was an active force in Palestine long before Hitler's advent and had grown considerably in strength after 1929. It is certainly true that the great increase in immigration did not occur until 1933, but this wave included far more Polish than German Jews. Of the approximately 217,000 Jewish immigrants to Palestine between 1932 and 1938, 47 percent were from Poland and only 18 percent from Germany. Since Poland had regained its independence in 1918/19, the Jews of that nation had been made the scapegoat for the numerous difficulties of both the new Polish state as well as its predecessors and were subjected to steadily increasing harassment. Since the United States had closed its doors in the 1920s, increasing numbers of Polish Jews fled to Palestine.

More important, these Polish Jews had already found themselves in dire straits in the two decades preceding the Holocaust. The steady increase in anti-Jewish militancy in Poland brought many Jews to the point where they were prepared to resort to more violent means themselves. Many sympathized with Yabotinski's opposition rightist-Zionist Revisionists and joined the Revisionists' military arm, Ezel, beginning in 1937. The Jewish immigrants from Poland were determined to make Palestine into more than the mere "national home for the Jewish people" promised by the British government in 1917 or the Jewish "community" which the ever moderate majority socialists did not demand until 1942. The goal of the Revisionists was a Jewish state, to be attained by all necessary means, including force. The political-military infrastructure of the small Jewish community which was either already present in Palestine before Hitler's rise to power or had immigrated there without his involvement strove unerringly toward this goal. The day of the impatient and the militant dawned in 1944 with the rebellion led by Menachem Begin against the British authorities.

■

If we view the rise of the Jewish State in the global historical context of the process of decolonization, it is hard to see why, if there had been no Hitler, such a determined Zionist community would have shown any less willingness to struggle for its independence than any other colonial people. If, with all due respect, such states as Ruanda and Burundi, or even Kuwait, proved capable of achieving independence, why should the Zionists have been unable to do so?

One might respond: If it had not been for Hitler and the Second World War he plunged the world into, there would have been no decolonization and therefore no Jewish State. Such a line of reasoning, however, ignores the fact that the process of decolonization had begun long before Hitler came to power. As starting points we could take the American Declaration of Independence in 1776 or the independence movement in Latin America in the first decades of the nineteenth century. A prime example for the direction of developments in the closing decades of the nineteenth century was Britain's most important colony, India, where the Congress Party was founded in 1885. The establishment of the World Zionist Organization in 1897, following the immigration of an (albeit small) number of Jewish pioneers to Palestine from 1882 on, falls into the same time frame. The Second World War—and Hitler—thus served as unwitting catalysts in the acceleration of trends already well established.

After having pledged "a national home for the Jewish people" in 1917, the British government was, by the late 1930s, attempting to block the transformation of Palestine into a Jewish homeland. In response, the Zionist groups were organizing political and military resistance. The Second World War and the Holocaust were therefore events which, rather than intensifying, actually forced a suspension in the Zionists' anti-British struggle for independence.

In 1944, with an Allied victory over Hitler but no change in course with regard to Great Britain's pro-Arab policy in Palestine in sight, Menachem Begin's Ezel proclaimed "rebellion" against the British. Although not ruling out the use of force if necessary, Ben-Gurion decided to pursue the struggle on the political and diplomatic fronts and counted on receiving support from the United States.

By 1947 Israel's founding fathers had succeeded in—quite literally—bombing the British out of Palestine. Their targets, however, had been predominantly military rather than civilian in nature. In February 1947, the British government threw in the towel, dumping the unresolved problem of Palestine into the lap of the United Nations. On November 29, 1947, the General Assembly of the United Nations passed a resolution calling for the partitioning of Palestine into an Arab and a Jewish state.

As so often in the history of Israel, here, too, we find fact intertwined with legend: this time the legend of the historical significance of the UN vote. It is claimed that the bad conscience of the majority of the UN member states for not having done enough to save the Jews from the Nazi threat played a decisive role in the outcome of that vote. Accordingly, the chief function of the UN General Assembly resolution was to lend international legitimacy to the founding of the State of Israel. There can be little doubt, however, that the Jewish State would have been proclaimed sooner or later, with or without the sanction of the United Nations. The die had been cast in February of 1947 with the British decision to give up the Palestine mandate.

■

What was the role of the United States, upon which Israel's founding father, Ben-Gurion, was counting? The events surrounding the Holocaust had not left the United States morally unblemished, as it cannot be said that America had laid out the welcome mat for Jewish refugees from National-Socialist persecution. Especially disturbing was the turning back of the *St. Louis*, a ship laden with German Jews, in May of 1939. Unable to find any country willing to take in its cargo of refugees, the *St. Louis* returned to Europe, dispersing its passengers to France,

Holland, Belgium, and Great Britain. Only those refugees who entered Britain were spared the way to the gas chambers after 1940.

Repeated requests by Jewish and Zionist leaders that the U.S. bomb Auschwitz and the other extermination camps, or at least the approaches to this inner circle of Nazi hell, were rejected by the Roosevelt administration, specifically by Deputy Secretary of War John McCloy. The arguments for this inaction were anything but convincing. Making "restitution" in the form of support for the founding of a Jewish state would thus not have been inappropriate—if one were to argue that a moral obligation existed "because of Hitler."

In addition, a "Zionist lobby" was highly active in the United States and, from the 1930s on, the "Jewish vote" was one of the pillars of support for the Democratic administrations under both Roosevelt and Truman.

Nevertheless, from the Zionist point of view, the support coming from the U.S. left much to be desired. In February of 1945 (shortly before his death) President Roosevelt expressed broad sympathy for the Arab position in Palestine to Saudi-Arabian King Ibn Saud. This despite Roosevelt's supposed dependence on the Jewish vote. Roosevelt promised that his administration would not adopt any measures with regard to Palestine without first consulting the Arabs. Saudi Arabia represented the first significant political and economic stronghold for the U.S. in the Middle East and Roosevelt had every intention of building up that bastion.

As Roosevelt's successor, Truman sought to avoid conflict with the British over Palestine, but entered the fray nevertheless when polls began forecasting serious trouble for the Democrats in the approaching 1946 Congressional elections. Truman underwent a pro-Zionist "conversion" in October of 1946 when he called on the British government to suspend its virtual ban on Jewish immigration to Palestine in order to permit the entry of 100,000 Holocaust survivors. President Truman's pronouncements in favor of the partitioning of Palestine— and thus in favor of the creation of a Jewish state—were the object of considerable controversy within the administration. Both the State and Defense Departments actively opposed the President's position. Working together, the two departments succeeded in imposing a strict embargo on the export of U.S. weapons to the Middle East in December 1947, an embargo that hit primarily at Israel.

In early 1948, State and Defense again imposed their will when the Truman administration retracted its position of the previous November in favor of the partitioning of Palestine and supported instead a proposal for a United Nations Trusteeship over the territory. But Ben-Gurion and his followers were determined to proclaim the independence of Israel immediately upon the final British withdrawal on May 14, 1948. It was only the continuing U.S. arms embargo that hurt Israel badly.

■

In the meantime, however, another source of arms supplies had become available: the Soviet Union. On May 15, 1948, one day after Israel's Declaration of Independence, the armies of the new nation's Arab neighbors attempted to turn back the clock of history and to destroy the Jewish State. It was with Soviet arms that Israel defended its existence in the 1948–49 War of Independence.

For decades, Zionists had been accustomed to harsh criticism from Moscow. According to the traditional line of the Communist Party of the USSR, Zionism represented a bourgeois-reactionary force. But to the surprise of many, not least of all the Zionists themselves, from early 1947 on the Soviet Union pursued a recognizably more pro-Zionist and pro-Israel policy.

The sudden pro-Zionist shift in course was justified with reference to the Holocaust: After all that Hitler had done to the Jews, they could no longer be denied their long hoped-for state. But such noble and moral sounding tones merely served to cover the real motives.

Moscow's turnaround was in response to Britain's retreat from Palestine. The Soviet Union hoped to be able to step into the ensuing political vacuum. This proved a miscalculation, as Israel's founding fathers, despite their predominantly socialist views, were not inclined to allow Israel to be used as Moscow's stepping stone into the Middle East.

Stalin's policy toward Israel maneuvered the Soviet leader into an embarrassing domestic dilemma he had apparently overlooked. Soviet aid to the Jewish national movement in the Middle East generated Zionist enthusiasm among Soviet Jews and strengthened their sense of group identity in 1947–48. Such a national renaissance among an ethnic group within the Soviet Union threatened to upset the delicate balance of the entire Soviet nationalities policy.

Stalin thus initiated countermeasures in the winter of 1948–49. The arrest of Zionist activists in the USSR clouded and, in the early fifties, ultimately poisoned Soviet-Israeli relations. In February, 1953, shortly before Stalin's death, the Soviet Union broke diplomatic relations with Israel.

■

The creation of the State of Israel was primarily the political, economic, social and military achievement of its founders. Of course, they had allies, but—and this is decisive—the alliances were shifting and unreliable. One figure, however, was never the Zionists' ally, neither subjectively nor objectively: Adolf Hitler.

To argue otherwise is to attempt to reverse the course of history, as Israel was well on its way toward statehood before the Holocaust took place. One—albeit unintended—consequence of such a slanting of history is a partial exculpation of Hitler. Contributors include not only unredeemable disciples of the past seeking to whitewash their Führer's image, but even such totally unimpeachable witnesses as Nahum Goldmann, British Chief Rabbi Jakobovits, or the German-British writer Sebastian Haffner.

In the late 1970s and early 1980s the without-Hitler-no-Israel legend was given a new twist in West Germany. At the same time it became acceptable in polite society, having been repeatedly uttered by Federal Chancellor Helmut Schmidt himself. The extended line of argument went: Without Hitler there would be no Israel. Without Israel there would be no Palestinian refugees. Being thus indirectly responsible for the plight of the Palestinians, Germany is thus at the least obligated to render a form of political restitution, i.e., support for the rights of the Palestinians to self-determination and statehood.

The legitimacy of these rights was and is a subject of heated controversy, including the public argument between Helmut Schmidt and Menachem Begin. What is not debatable, however, is the fact that Germany is not the author of the sufferings of the Palestinian people and

Israel's responsibility for this suffering is not an outgrowth of German-Jewish history.

Knowingly or unknowingly, the adherents of this dubious theory of Germany's "indirect responsibility" have ventured onto the path leading back to Germany's direct responsibility: From 1936 to 1943 the Palestinian National Movement under the leadership of Amin el-Husseini cooperated with Adolf Hitler and offered its assistance in carrying out the "final solution." In 1991, additional documents were discovered which document that the Arab role went beyond tacit and passive agreement to include *active* cooperation with Hitler's murderous campaign against the Jews. This only increases German guilt for the fate of the Jews. One cannot, however, speak of German guilt toward the Palestinians when the latter were not victims but accomplices of the German perpetrators. Their politically understandable motives explain but do not exculpate the Palestinians' guilt.

2

GESCHICHTSPOLITIK

Phases of German-Jewish-Israeli Relations

The existence of Israel represents a stumbling bloc not only to German foreign policy but also to German politics in general. Israel confronts the Germans with their national, most especially with their National-Socialist history. The conduct of normal policy, of a pragmatic policy based on present-day and future interests, is encumbered and sometimes rendered impossible by the continuing presence of the past.

The policies of states can also differ with regard to their relationship with the past. They can attempt to ignore history and instead orient policy toward the pursuit of present interests. In German, this is called *tagespolitik*, i.e., day-to-day or routine policy. Alternatively, states can posit their actions on historical experience. The German term for this is *geschichtspolitik*, literally: the politics of history. We speak of *geschichtspolitik* when political decision-making strives to deal with the continuing presence of the past, which is not to imply historical continuity. The historical frame of reference can apply to domestic as well as foreign policy and can form a significant determinant in the representation and identity of the state as well as its citizens.

1. Restitution, 1949–1955

In the first years of its existence, the Federal Republic of Germany was confronted with its past in the form of financial burdens for indemnification and restitution. In terms of foreign policy these burdens brought the new West Germany a measure of dignity. The standing of the young republic and its Chancellor, Konrad Adenauer, rose in no small degree because this restitution was pledged voluntarily and without pressure from the United States.

The admittance of the Federal Republic of Germany into the fine club of Western nations in the 1950s was a consequence of the Cold War—not a result of West German restitution to Israel and the Jews. Although its restitution payments cannot be regarded as a price of admission, West Germany's willingness to atone for the past certainly eased the atmosphere.

The Federal Republic of Germany did not enter the refined society of the international community with the bowed posture and clothing of the penitent. Let us briefly review the aspects relevant to Israel and to Germany's *geschichtspolitik*: In January and March 1951, Israel presented the four Allied powers diplomatic notes stating its demands for material restitution from Germany, both east and west. Israel rejected any direct negotiations with either German state.

The Soviet Union gave no official reply to the notes. The Western powers referred Jerusalem to Bonn. In their desire to see Germany rehabilitated first morally, then militarily, the Western powers did not hesitate to offend Israel's historical sensibilities.

In the following two years leading to the signing of the Luxembourg Restitution Agreement and its ratification by the West German Bundestag on March 18, 1953, the government of the Federal Republic was able to maintain an upright posture in its dealings with the representatives of Israel and the Jewish Diaspora. Before, during, and after the protracted and difficult negotiations, the interest and involvement of the Western media and public were minimal, to say the least. Conversely, West Germany's standing both before and after the treaty with Israel was so high, and the West so in need of the new Germany, that the restitution agreement cannot be regarded as having been a necessary condition for the acceptance of the new German republic by the Western nations.

The historical legend, nurtured by a strange coalition of German and Arab opponents of restitution and by Israeli as well as a number of Diaspora historians, puts forth the opposite claim: Supposedly it was the United States that had pressured the West Germans into yielding to Israel's demands. This is simply untrue. Washington was well aware that rearmament and restitution would cost the West Germans a great deal of money. If Bonn were unable to come up with the necessary sums, the United States would have had no other choice but to make up for the difference, and the American administration sought to avoid such a situation. As it appeared then, rearmament *and* restitution were not feasible. The United States viewed rearmament as the higher priority and thus resisted Israel's insistent and repeated pleas to apply pressure in Bonn.

■

In order to obtain sorely needed funds for its nation-building effort, Jerusalem was left with no other choice but to respect the wishes of the Western powers and to negotiate directly with Bonn. As a precondition to direct contacts with the Germans, the Ben-Gurion government insisted on a public acknowledgment of guilt on the part of the Federal Chancellor. What is more, Adenauer was expected to acknowledge the collective guilt of all Germans for the Holocaust. On September 27, 1951, Chancellor Adenauer gave an address before the Bundestag concerning German responsibility for the Holocaust. It contained no mention of collective guilt.

For weeks, Israelis and Germans had haggled behind the scenes over nearly every word of Adenauer's declaration. The Chancellor had consistently refused to even mention, much less to recognize, the principle of collective guilt, and he had his way.

The principal sources of the massive, in part polemical, criticism of the restitution agreement in Germany were not to be found among the ranks of the parliamentary opposition, as the Social Democrats (SPD) supported Adenauer's position without reservation. It was the Chancellor's coalition partners in the conservative Bavarian Christian Social Union (CSU), the both liberal and nationalist Free Democratic Party (FDP) and the conservative, nationalist German Party (DP, *Deutsche Partei*), that were more than merely reserved. The objections centered mostly on the limited financial resources of the new republic: The needs of the day, *tagespolitik* rather than *geschichtspolitik*, dominated the discussion. Restitution *and* rearmament *and* repayment of foreign debts, it was argued, were more than the new Germany could afford. Finance Minister Fritz Schäffer (CSU) contended in a cabinet meeting early in 1952 that rearmament and the settling of the foreign debt issue were the higher priorities, not just from the domestic but also from the foreign policy viewpoint.

It was thus possible to deliver a polemic against restitution to Israel and yet stand historically on the sunny side of the street. Under the cloud of the intensifying Cold War, the historically unencumbered Western powers called for the rearmament of West Germany and preferred to see the funds of the West German treasury flow west rather than east to Jerusalem. This they freely admitted, both to the Germans and to the Israelis.

In an April 10, 1951 meeting with Henry Byroade of the State Department's German Desk, Israeli Finance Minister Horowitz stated that "the question was whether the Israeli people should be kept on a level of starvation so that the Germans might be permitted to contribute to Allied security." Byroade replied coolly that "there was a question of priorities," emphasizing that "he was sympathetic to the logic of the Israeli position, but . . . also acutely conscious of the practical difficulties arising out of the nature of the world in which we live today."

■

A closer look at the arguments of the opponents of restitution allows us to better recognize Adenauer's achievement. Like Finance Minister Schäffer, Justice Minister Dehler (FDP) had succeeded in keeping his shirt spotlessly white in brown times. Nevertheless (or perhaps for this very reason?), Dehler had his doubts about preferential treatment for Jews and Israelis. Restitution, in Dehler's opinion, ought to take all claims into account, both Jewish and non-Jewish. In the February 26, 1952, cabinet meeting Dehler argued using the example of a farmer whose land had been appropriated by the Nazis and who had been compensated with "aryanized" land. Dehler claimed that it would not be proper to punish the farmer a second time by taking away the formerly Jewish property in the name of restitution.

What he lacked in political sensitivity, Finance Minister Schäffer made up for in terms of imagination in his opposition to the restitution agreement. On March 7, 1952, Schäffer told Franz Böhm (SPD), an energetic and combative supporter of restitution and later the chief of the German delegation at the restitution negotiations, that, since no budget resources were available, restitution to Israel could be financed only by floating an international dollar loan. The chances were "not bad," according to Schäffer. Since the American Jews were being subjected to all sorts of pressure tactics to extract "voluntary contributions" for building up the Jewish State, the Finance Minister argued that U.S. Jewish circles might be willing to organize a loan for the purpose of financing West German restitution payments to Israel in order to thereby limit Israel's direct claims on their generosity.

The geopolitical motives soon degenerated into pure financial horse-trading. In the presence of Chancellor Adenauer on April 5, 1952, Hermann Josef Abs, who led the German delegation to the London Conference on Germany's external debt, stated that it was necessary to make clear to the Israelis that "no more than ten to fifteen million dollars" in annual payments could be considered—not the two hundred million expected by Jerusalem. Abs added that a bitter disappointment was only being put off, but ultimately could not be avoided.

Vice Chancellor Blücher of the FDP came out in favor of restitution to individuals but not to the State of Israel. The sum of ten billion marks would be necessary "just for the Jewish problem." For Blücher, restitution represented only one—and certainly not the most important—of the numerous financial demands West Germany had to face and, as he argued in the May 20, 1952, cabinet meeting, these demands could not be met without unleashing inflationary forces. Pointing to the "danger of a new anti-Semitism" which he saw looming over the horizon, the Vice Chancellor regarded restitution not as atonement for, but rather as a new trigger for anti-Semitism. Finance

Minister Schäffer argued along the same lines in the June 17, 1952, cabinet debate.

Polls taken in West Germany at the time revealed that the supporters of the then nationalistically and conservatively oriented FDP strongly rejected restitution, and it is thus to be presumed that Blücher's stance was related to that of his political clientele. While 44 percent of all West Germans regarded restitution as "unnecessary," 57 percent of those who sympathized with the FDP expressed this opinion.

■

Transport Minister Seebohm, a representative of the German Party (who later joined the CDU) was also thinking of his supporters. His "yes, but" position exhibited an admixture of international politics, anticommunism, local interests, policies articulated by the organizations of German ethnic groups expelled from the former eastern territories, a willingness to make amends, careful attention to the interests of his own clientele and a lack of sensitivity with regard to other peoples. Most especially it was hard and fast *realpolitik*. Seebohm's own roots were in the Sudetenland, the German-speaking region included in the Czechoslovak state after the First World War, seized by Hitler's Germany in 1939, and returned in 1945 to Czechoslovakia, which then proceeded to expel the remaining German population.

In a letter written to Böhm in May, 1952, the transport minister supported in principle the "necessity of sufficient German restitution to the Jews of the world, including the State of Israel, but also other Jewish individuals and organizations." Seebohm even promised to devote "all available energy" to this goal, but added that he considered the "fulfillment of such a moral duty" to be justified only "if sacrifices of a similar nature" (what could he have meant by that?) were not imposed on others. "The question of the possibility of fulfilling the German obligation towards the Jews is, in my view, closely related to the task of securing our people and thus Europe against a further advance of the Bolshevist-Asiatic tendency. Wherever the fulfillment of this task is endangered, the moral duty of restitution ends." Put in plain words: rearmament rather than restitution.

After linking the issue with his overriding political goal, Seebohm brought in the interests of the Germans of the Sudetenland: "If I am prepared at the present time to recognize the moral duty of making restitution to the Jews, I can only do so if the other powers in the world are prepared to fulfill their moral duty to make restitution to the Germans expelled from their homeland. . . . For me, freedom, the dignity of man and the right to a homeland are of absolutely equal rank. . . . Whoever violates or takes away these rights commits the worst crime that can possibly be committed . . . , and it makes no difference if the final result of a robbery is the extinction of a physical existence, which is not as important as the will to destroy these unconditional prerequisites of unconditional humanity for an individual or a group of persons. The methods employed against the Jews by the National-Socialist leadership, which we all bitterly condemn, are thus fully the equal of the methods employed against the German expellees."

Seebohm thus equated the Holocaust with the expulsion of the Germans from their homelands after the Second World War, rhetorically reducing the sufferings of the one group by weighing them against those of another.

■

On July 11, 1952, by a margin of only five votes to four, the Bonn cabinet approved the sum of 500 million marks to meet the claims of the various Diaspora organizations represented by the Claims Conference. Besides Schäffer, Bundesrat Minister Heinrich Hellwege (German Party), Justice Minister Dehler (FDP) and the Minister for All-German Affairs Jakob Kaiser (from the left wing of the CDU) were opposed.

Chancellor Adenauer attempted to convince the skeptics and opponents of restitution, the opposition within the government, with moral and what amounted to economic arguments. The Jews of the world, especially the American Jews, argued Adenauer, possessed enormous economic influence. Their good will could be of great benefit to German exporters. This train of thought is to be found again and again in the protocols of meetings of the cabinet and of other political decision-making groups in Bonn.

When, in the cabinet session of June 17, 1952, Finance Minister Schäffer pointed out to Chancellor Adenauer that the politics of restitution were not popular and could cost the Union (of Christian-Democratic parties) votes, Adenauer ignored this warning concerning the domestic political atmosphere and turned the discussion to international political issues, including the attitude of the United States, which, it must be added, demonstrated much more reservation than the Chancellor claimed.

The polls prove that restitution was, indeed, an extraordinarily unpopular issue. Only 11 percent of the West Germans polled responded favorably; nearly half were opposed. The picture is made more complete when we recall that at that time about 10 percent of the West Germans still considered Hitler a great German statesman.

Adenauer was willing to take on domestic political risks that he was under no foreign pressure to assume. Of course, he had no intention of allowing either himself or the German people to be humiliated or condemned by sweeping generalizations. Adenauer's *geschichtspolitik* toward Israel and the Jews can be characterized as a mixture of self-confidence and a willingness to atone for the past. This is illustrated by his actions before the signing of the Luxembourg restitution agreement. The original planning had called for speeches after the formal signing. The evening before, the Chancellor received a copy of the text of the statement Israeli Foreign Minister Sharett intended to make. According to Adenauer's confidant Herbert Blankenhorn, the Chancellor found Sharett's speech too "old-testament-like" and called for changes, which were accepted. In the end, however, it was agreed not to give any speeches at all.

■

As late as August 22, 1952, the Bonn cabinet apparently did not think it necessary to even consider any balancing measures in German Near East policy in consequence of the impending treaty with Israel. Both proponents and opponents of restitution were in agreement that a contribution for the "Arab refugees from Palestine" was "inopportune." But just one week later, Vice Chancellor Blücher raised "serious doubts about the repercussions of the treaty among the Arab States" with the Chancellor. More than any other coalition partner, Blücher's FDP voiced the interests of West Germany's export industry.

Similar cautionary notes were sounded by other representatives of the ruling coalition, including von Brentano (CDU), Schäffer (FDP) and Merkatz (German Party), at the decisive cabinet meeting on September 8, 1952, just two days before the planned signing ceremony.

Adenauer and his Deputy Foreign Minister Hallstein pushed these warnings aside and, in the end, only Finance Minister Schäffer and Employment Minister Storch (of the left wing of the CDU) voted against the agreement.

No, the opposition within the West German government to the restitution agreement was neither unwilling to consider atonement nor anti-Semitic. Granted, the opposition was sometimes virulent, often lacking in historical sensitivity, Germanocentric at best, and sometimes reminiscent of the bluster of the Wilhelmenian era. We recall Seebohm's equating of the Holocaust with the expulsion of the Germans from Eastern Europe after the war and Blücher's call for restitution also for "non-Aryans" (sic!).

The criticism centered mainly, however, on doubts concerning West Germany's ability to finance and carry out the Chancellor's good intentions. It was both Adenauer's strength and weakness that he disregarded financial considerations. The strongest verbal opponent of the restitution agreement, Fritz Schäffer, avoided any appearance of servility to the Arabs as well as any reference to "traditional" German-Arab friendship. Other opponents were less consistent, and after the signing of the agreement, Bonn attempted to secure Arab good will by dispensing economic aid.

■

Beginning in October 1952, the Arab states launched a major effort to prevent the ratification of the Luxembourg Agreement in the Bundestag. The attempt was sorely misguided because the Arabs failed to recognize the historical dimension to Adenauer's frame of mind. Suspecting that the Chancellor's self-confidence masked a familiar German defiance of the West, they (like many Germans and non-Germans then and today) assumed that Adenauer had been pressured into offering restitution to Israel by the Americans. Behind the scenes, the Arab League delegation dispatched to Bonn repeatedly reminded their hosts of aspects of a common German-Arab past that were no longer politically opportune in the new West Germany, among them that both Germany and the Arabs had been on the losing side of the recent world war. Indirect but unmistakable references were made to purportedly mutual anti-Jewish resentments.

West German Foreign Ministry internal records unambiguously document how Deputy Minister Hallstein, acting on behalf of Chancellor and Foreign Minister Adenauer, in effect showed the Arab delegation out the door. These documents also indicate the self-imposed limits of the new republic's policy toward the Middle East and illustrate the first problems that relations with Israel presented for the overall conduct of West German foreign policy.

2. Tagespolitik *and* Geschichtspolitik, *1955–1965*

In May 1955 the Federal Republic of Germany achieved what amounted to nearly full sovereignty. In the years leading up to the assumption of diplomatic relations between Bonn and Jerusalem in 1965 the interweaving of the day-to-day with the historical dimensions of policy became ever more complicated. During this period, diplomatic relations with Israel would have jeopardized Bonn's claim to be the sole legitimate representative of Germany (the so-called Hallstein doctrine). In the event of the establishment of formal relations between Bonn and Jerusalem, the Arab states threatened to in turn recognize the East German regime—and to impose a trade boycott on West Germany.

Complicating matters was the following delicate situation: During the 1950s the influence of the United States, Great Britain, and France had been steadily eroding in the Arab world. In order to prevent Western influence from disappearing altogether, West Germany's allies strongly urged the Federal Republic to maintain the best possible relations with the Arab states and not to place its good contacts at risk by assuming diplomatic relations with or otherwise demonstrating preferential treatment for Israel. It was supposed that because of "traditional German-Arab friendship," Bonn was well-suited to represent Western interests in the Arab region.

An ironic twist of history: With the approval of the Western Allies, who had fought the Second World War to defeat Hitler, West Germany was to assume its place under a brightly shining political sun on the basis of the dark side of its past, the one-time collaboration between (chiefly Palestinian) Arabs and Hitler's Germany.

This whitewash by the Western powers provided legitimation in Bonn for the advocates of a greater German engagement in the Arab world, which by necessity and intention had to come at the expense of Israel. The pro-Arab officials, most of whom were to be found in the Foreign Ministry, were soon engaged in a prolonged struggle with Chancellor Adenauer, who sought to prevent any change in his policy. From 1957 on, Adenauer even maintained a secret military relationship with Israel, but without establishing formal diplomatic ties. His successor, Ludwig Erhard, also attempted to continue this policy, which had nearly succeeded in squaring the circle, but Erhard lacked Adenauer's fine touch and good luck.

■

The Suez crisis of 1956–57 once again demonstrated that Israel represented a potentially disruptive factor for West German foreign policy. Despite Soviet and U.S. insistence, Israel for months steadfastly refused to withdraw from the territory it had conquered in its 1956 Suez campaign. In order to raise the pressure on Jerusalem, the U.S. imposed certain sanctions on Israel and Secretary of State Dulles contributed to the increasingly intense public debate on further, possibly U.N.-sponsored, sanctions. The prospect of West Germany joining in with a suspension of restitution payments until such time as Israel agreed to pull back from the occupied lands was also discussed.

For his part, Konrad Adenauer firmly dismissed any such action. In his view, the German restitution agreement was a fundamental issue (*geschichtspolitik*) and Israel's occupation of the Sinai a transitory issue (*tagespolitik*). In order to preserve his basic policy toward Israel, Adenauer was prepared to stand up to pressure from Germany's most important ally and his personal friend, John Foster Dulles. Chancellor Adenauer continued steady on his historical-political course, even though sailing with the currently prevailing winds could have brought political and economic advantages. This was certainly to Adenauer's credit. In pragmatic terms, however, it confirmed Israel's role as a source of potentially serious conflict in the formulation of German foreign policy.

■

For a time, the shadows of the German-Jewish past receded under the warm sun of day-to-day political relations. They began to reemerge in 1959 with the debate over the role played by West German cabinet minister Oberländer in a murderous episode during the Second World War. Soon afterward, political rowdies, many of whom—but certainly not all—we now know were in the pay of the East German regime and the USSR, began desecrating Jewish cemeteries and painting swastikas throughout the country. In the rest of the world, people began to wonder if the new West Germany was maybe not so new after all.

Unexpected aid came from, of all places, Israel. To anyone willing to listen—and many in Israel were not—Prime Minister Ben-Gurion publicly declared his faith in the new Germany, despite the current campaign by old-German political painters. In January 1960, Ben-Gurion was even prepared to appear together with Adenauer on radio and television.

West German Foreign Minister von Brentano, however, counseled the Chancellor against putting in such an appearance. Von Brentano, who feared that such a media event would darken relations with the Arabs, argued that the swastika campaign was already receding. The foreign minister considered the potential damage to relations with the Arabs to be more significant than the historical burden in relations with Israel. Once again, Adenauer attempted to square the circle. Declining the media appearance, the Chancellor met unannounced with Ben-Gurion in the Waldorf Astoria in New York on March 14, 1960, thus obtaining the Israeli Prime Minister's seal of approval. Adenauer's historical-political investment had thus clearly begun to yield interest. The pragmatic lesson, as applicable today as it was then, is that atonement for the sins of the past is not merely a burden. It can also bring future comfort and relief.

Of course, this support from Israel was not entirely without its price. The two elder statesmen did not limit their exchange in New York to formal niceties. Both Ben-Gurion and Adenauer were in agreement that West German financial aid and the deliveries of military goods that had been secretly negotiated two weeks before by German Defense Minister Franz Josef Strauss and Israel's Deputy Defense

Minister Shimon Peres would make Israel more secure and would thus be in harmony with Germany's obligations to the Jewish State. In 1962, with the active encouragement of the United States, a comprehensive but informal verbal agreement on arms deliveries was concluded.

Adenauer's *geschichtspolitik* and not von Brentano's *tagespolitik* ultimately yielded greater benefits. The new Israeli seal of approval soon proved most useful, as just two months after the Adenauer–Ben-Gurion meeting the past once again threw a dark shadow over German-Israeli relations. Israel's capture of Adolf Eichmann in May 1960 set off a renewal of both the German domestic and the German-Jewish debate over the German past. After the initial, involuntary attempt at confronting the past, at the insistence of the Allies beginning in 1945, there now followed a renewed confrontation with the brown burdens of German history.

Although stimulated by external events, this discussion was undertaken voluntarily, with greater intensity and less self-pity than before. The Nazi era could now be analyzed with greater objectivity and with less inclination to whitewashing and self-exculpation. Court proceedings, the "Auschwitz trial" as one example, were now undertaken with a sense of urgency. In 1963 the theater world was confronted with Hochhuth's *Der Stellvertreter* ("The Deputy," dealing with the conduct of Pope Pius XII and the Catholic Church with regard to the Holocaust) and in 1965 with Peter Weiss's *Die Ermittlung* ("The Investigation," a dramatization centering on the Frankfurt Auschwitz trial).

Ben-Gurion's recognition of the accomplishments of the new Germany were most helpful, as it contradicted the argument of the old and new disciples of yesteryear that no matter what Germany did, it would never be enough for Israel and the Jews. In fact, the good relations between the two old men, Ben-Gurion and Adenauer, helped to overcome a number of difficult obstacles. Among these were Eichmann's abduction from Argentina by Israeli agents in May 1960, his subsequent trial in Jerusalem in 1961, and the public clash over the (private) activities of German rocket engineers who were reported working in Egypt in 1962.

As before, the German Chancellor's role was not that of the penitent but a self-confident German. Adenauer publicly expressed his disapproval of Eichmann's abduction by Mossad and showed his displeasure at Jerusalem's decision to try Eichmann in Israel. The Chancellor steadfastly refused to bow to Israel's demands for legislation to force the German rocket experts to return from Egypt, explaining that the government of a free and democratic country cannot pass laws regulating where its citizens may or may not work and reside.

■

In 1963 the two grand old men both departed from the political stage, but the problem of the German rocket technicians in Egypt remained and Ben-Gurion's successor, Levi Eshkol, issued what amounted to an ultimatum demanding legal measures. Eshkol brandished history as an argument, claiming that German weapons experts were once again endangering Israel's security.

In the midst of the overheated atmosphere of 1964, Germany was faced with the highly sensitive decision of how to deal with the statute of limitations on National-Socialist crimes. In addition, Jerusalem was clamoring ever more insistently for the establishment of diplomatic relations and an extension of the German restitution payments. Still another hot issue arose in the wake of President Johnson's request to Chancellor Erhard in July to increase the export of German weapons to Israel and to include tanks in the deliveries.

Return of the rocket scientists, extension of the statute of limitations, weapons, restitution, diplomatic relations—Israel demanded more and more, ever more insistently. Moreover, after Ben-Gurion's resignation the tone turned ever more harsh and irreconcilable. In October 1964, the *Frankfurter Allgemeine Zeitung* (West Germany's most influential daily) reported that Israel was "dissatisfied with Bonn" and on October 20 Prime Minister Eshkol questioned the "moral foundation" of German policy.

There are many indications that in 1964 Israel had raised the ante too high. Someone's patience broke. To this day it is still not clear who leaked details of the German arms exports to Israel to the *Frankfurter Rundschau* and the *New York Times* in late 1964. What is clear is that the deliveries of military hardware could not remain clandestine, as they had until then. It does not seem likely that the source of the indiscretion was in Israel, as disclosure could serve only to hinder or prevent altogether the procurement of important military equipment. There are signs that the Bonn Foreign Ministry in particular regarded Israel as an impediment to German foreign policy and was especially incensed by the tone of the Israeli demands. We must also keep in mind that this was a phase of increasing self-assertiveness in West Germany, and the we-are-somebody-again mentality was amply demonstrated by the Bonn Chancellery in the 1965 election campaign.

Despite all the signs, open questions and contradictions still remain with regard to the actual source of the leak, and not all relevant documents are available. The official spokesman of the Bonn government, von Hase, had little precise information to offer in a background briefing given editors of CDU-friendly newspapers on February 18, 1965, but he placed the source of the indiscretion in the Middle East, arguing that, since Bonn had intended to terminate the arms deal in any case, Jerusalem may have been attempting to "force" a continuation of the deliveries. The disclosure was aimed at exposing Bonn to the Arabs and thus bringing about a "break with the Arab world." This, according to von Hase, would have prepared the way for Germany to openly provide Israel with the desired military hardware.

On the other hand, von Hase also considered the possibility of an Arab attempt at blackmail: a Cairo effort to literally capitalize on the threat of extending official recognition to the East German regime in retaliation for Bonn's arms deliveries to Israel. In a background briefing for editors from the ARD television network on February 22, Chancellor Erhard himself categorically excluded even the possibility that the leak might have originated in Bonn.

Wherever or whoever the source, in late October, 1964, newspaper readers learned what they could have read between the lines at a much earlier date but, like the majority of politicians, probably did not want to know, namely that the young Federal Republic of Germany had long lost its innocence in terms of providing arms to global hot spots. In connection with (accurate) rumors about arms shipments to Israel in late 1957, the West German government had publicly professed that its policy was not to deliver military goods to any parties in regions of crisis. Since then, however, the government had, in fact, clandestinely done otherwise.

In late 1964 the tangle of problems briefly degenerated into chaos. The Erhard government appeared preoccupied with patching up one breakdown after another rather than formulating its own policy with regard to the Middle East. Members of the cabinet and government appeared to be trying to pull the rug out from under the Chancellor, who was steering a wild course rather than a steady line. In contrast, Foreign Minister Gerhard Schröder knew exactly what he wanted: no more arms for, no diplomatic relations with Israel.

To all appearances, Israel seemed to achieve all of its aims. The missile experts were lured back to Germany with attractive job offers. The statute of limitations on National-Socialist crimes was extended. Diplomatic relations were established between Bonn and Jerusalem. Further military equipment was provided by the United States. Germany offered the Jewish State low-interest loans. But all of this took place in an atmosphere that had become so poisoned even Konrad Adenauer felt the aftereffects during his 1966 visit to Israel, where he was rudely treated, and not only by Prime Minister Eshkol.

■

In October 1964 a decisive, long-term shift in the historical-political climate set in, but it was hardly noticed then. The growing German we-are-somebody-again mentality was less willing than ever to let anybody kick sand in its face.

The tones of short-term discord could hardly be overheard in 1964–65. In private, von Hase described Israel's reaction to Bonn's expression of its desire to end the arms exports as "disappointing on the whole and with little understanding of our situation" vis-à-vis the Arab world. Even the good-hearted and well-disposed Ludwig Erhard did not entirely succeed in concealing his anger, at least in the already mentioned background conversation with the ARD-network editors: "If Mr. Eshkol thinks that we have a moral obligation to the people of Israel that cannot be fulfilled by a single delivery of arms, then he is absolutely right. . . . But we do not have a perpetual obligation to supply arms to Israel."

In early 1965, with the help of CDU parliamentary leader Rainer

Barzel and CSU chief Franz Josef Strauss, both of whom backed Erhard's policy toward Israel but were otherwise conniving at his downfall, the Chancellor pushed through the decision to establish diplomatic relations with Israel. This was done over the strong objections of Foreign Minister Schröder, who argued that, while Germany's behavior toward the Jews must always "follow moral principles" because of the past, the country's "most important human and moral task," as Schröder reminded no one less than the President of the Evangelical Church in Germany, Kurt Scharf, in December 1964, was the "policy of reunification in freedom."

One reason why Ludwig Erhard kept his reaction off the record on February 22 was that only a few days before David Ben-Gurion had publicly defended the German Chancellor against the massive recriminations being hurled against him in Israel. As long as Adenauer's policy was continued, Ben-Gurion's faith in the new Germany would remain unaltered. The former Prime Minister forcefully reminded his skeptical countrymen that Ludwig Erhard was "not Hitler."

3. The Shift to "Normality," 1965–1973

The exchange of ambassadors marked a new chapter, which began with irritations over West German Ambassador Rolf Pauls's past service in the *Wehrmacht*, but because of the Ambassador's sensitivity as well as his personal charm and charisma soon turned into something of a honeymoon. The advantage of hindsight reveals that in the summer of 1966 Pauls first began to redirect the focus of the political dialogue between Bonn and Jerusalem from the past to the present and future, that is, toward what soon thereafter was cautiously and still very reticently termed "normality."

The caution of the West German government, the hope that Israel would show understanding for Bonn's admittedly opportunistic policy with regard to the Arabs, and the aim of achieving normalization via neutrality became abundantly clear at the outbreak of the Six Day War in June 1967.

At that time a Grand Coalition was in charge in Bonn: Kurt Kiesinger (CDU) held office as Chancellor and Willy Brandt (SPD) as Foreign Minister. In imitation of Adenauer's style, the coalition attempted to square the circle, but this time with considerably more contradictions. Brandt spoke in turn of the necessity of Germany remaining neutral and of the impossibility for Germans to indulge in "neutrality of the heart" toward Israel.

Germany's politicians were neutral, and then again they weren't. They pursued the dictates of the day—*tagespolitik*—and pretended to be attending to the requirements of history—*geschichtspolitik*. In contrast, the polls showed that, for the first time, the West German populace stood solidly and with conviction on the side of the Jewish State (see chapter 6).

Both Adenauer and Erhard had long tried to guide the Germans toward a historically grounded pro-Israeli course—with little success. But in 1967 this goal was reached, and now the politicians began to steer in the other direction, albeit barely noticeably at first.

The cautious course was abandoned by the coalition between the social-democratic SPD and the liberal FDP under Chancellor Willy Brandt (SPD) and Foreign Minister Walter Scheel (FDP) which came to power in October 1969. In view of the coalition's dramatic symbolic and political gestures of reconciliation with Eastern Europe and with the Jews—Willy Brandt kneeling at the monument in the Warsaw Ghetto is probably the most well-known visual image—this fact is often overlooked.

In 1971 Walter Scheel openly pursued the goal of achieving "normality." He became the first West German Foreign Minister to visit Israel. Willy Brandt was the first West German Chancellor to visit the Jewish State while in office. Much to the distress of official and unofficial Israel, Brandt attempted to market the commodity "normality" on the German-Israeli exchange. There were no buyers. Using her home-court advantage, Prime Minister Golda Meir virtually read Chancellor Brandt the riot act, and, in Israel, the Chancellor's normalization initiatives met with a much fainter echo. Back on home turf, the coalition was able to maneuver with greater assurance, but its course was still unsteady. For some, the demonstrative attempts at normalization went too far, for others not far enough, and Willy Brandt vacillated between both positions. This could be clearly seen during the Yom Kippur War in October 1973.

4. The Breakthrough to Demonstrative "Normality," 1973–1984

"In the middle of the Yom Kippur War, when Israel was closer to an *endlösung* than ever before or ever since, the government of the German Federal Republic closed German ports to American resupply deliveries urgently needed in Israel. The government of the Federal Republic of Germany regarded the U.S. military assistance for Israel, which passed through German territory, as a violation of its 'political neutrality' in the conflict between Israel and its neighbors. . . . A new catastrophe for the Jews was close at hand, and it would have made the preceding one pale by comparison." Despite the outraged tone and false analysis, Henryk M. Broder made an accurate observation: West Germany's demonstrative push to achieve normality by means of neutrality.

It is correct to state that in October 1973, Israel was in extraordinary danger. It is not correct to claim that, in the midst of the war and Israel's existential crisis, the government of the Federal Republic refused to permit the United States to use German ports to resupply the Jewish State.

To the contrary, *during* the fighting, the West German government deliberately closed its eyes so as to not in any way hinder the flow of U.S. supplies through the country. Only *after* Israel had turned the tide militarily did the Brandt and Scheel government forbid further American transports. At the time, this met with the protests of both the Nixon administration and the Golda Meir government. Years later, however, before his April 1987 visit to Germany, Israel's President Chaim Herzog explicitly acknowledged the assistance thus rendered by the social-liberal coalition.

As a result of its tactics, the Brandt-Scheel government was able to achieve several aims at once: Israel had been helped and the German conscience eased. The outside world was given a graphic illustration of how "normal" German foreign and Middle East policy had become. Both Israel and the United States as the preeminent power in the West had been put in their place. The German government had demonstrated its legal and political sovereignty. Legal niceties and the politics of the day, *tagespolitik*, held sway over *geschichtspolitik*. Last but not least, the government's tactics served to further German interests in the politics of oil and exports by playing to the good will of the Arabs.

The motor of this policy was Foreign Minister Walter Scheel. Chancellor Brandt was less enthusiastic and shortly thereafter found himself on the receiving end of gentle public criticism from the FDP leader. Demonstrated and demonstrative normality was Scheel's specialty; Brandt's was the symbolism of atonement. This was the division of labor in the Brandt-Scheel *geschichtspolitik* in general and toward Israel in particular. To put it another way: Brandt took the high road of history and Scheel the low road of the politics of the day.

■

In substance, the drive to achieve normality continued unaltered under the subsequent social-liberal coalition led by Chancellor Helmut Schmidt (SPD) and Foreign Minister Hans-Dietrich Genscher (FDP), but the new leaders introduced a new style: a policy toward Israel without the symbolism of atonement. Shortly after both German states were seated as members of the UN, this version of normality was demonstrated in the General Assembly. The first representative of a member of the European Community to issue a call for Palestinian self-determination was Bonn's ambassador von Wechmar. Palestinian self-determination was a term known to provoke irascibility in Israel, as it represented, according to the official Israeli position, a propagandistic cover for the demand for a Palestinian state and was thus unacceptable to the Jewish State.

The German Leopard 2 tank became a symbol of the new normality. In 1980 Chancellor Schmidt and Foreign Minister Genscher decided to sell the tank to Saudi Arabia. The prime motive for this decision was to secure both oil imports and commodity exports. In the case of the particular export in question, however, such *tagespolitik* necessarily led to a renewed confrontation with the past. This ought to have been easy to foresee. If we trace the roots of the 1980 Leopard decision back to 1974 (von Wechmar's call for Palestinian self-determination), we find reason to doubt that only routine policy was involved. The real goal seems to have been to establish a new *geschichtspolitik*. The German-Israeli battle of words that followed furnishes further proof.

One reason why this new German policy was easier to sell both at home and abroad was that since 1977 Menachem Begin had been Israel's Prime Minister. In Germany, Begin was neither politically, ideologically, nor personally popular. An Israeli hawk, Begin took an unbending stance toward the Palestinians and did little to avoid confrontations in the course of the peace negotiations with Egypt. For his part, Chancellor Schmidt did little to disguise his political and personal antipathy toward Begin.

Despite all their understandable criticisms of the Israeli Prime Minister, Schmidt and many Germans overlooked the fact that Menachem Begin, unlike all of his predecessors, had been personally and directly affected by the Holocaust. Israel's first premier, Ben-Gurion, as well as his successors Moshe Sharett and Levi Eshkol, had immigrated to Palestine in the early years of the twentieth century. Golda Meir had come from the U.S. in the 1920s and Yitzhak Rabin had been born in Palestine. During the years of the Nazi horror, they had all been far from the scene of the Holocaust. Begin did not share their good fortune. The sensitivity toward other peoples which was expected of an Israeli Prime Minister was all too frequently not granted in Begin's case, although there was every good historical reason why this was so.

■

In October 1980, behind closed doors that were promptly opened to indiscretion, Chancellor Schmidt labeled Begin a "danger to world peace." Shortly thereafter the public learned that Schmidt intended to deliver such peace-promoting equipment as the Leopard 2 to Saudi Arabia. This is the measure of the degree of self-assurance with which the West German Chancellor now thought he could present himself to Israel and the world.

In the wake of the revolution in Iran, packaged as a policy toward Saudi Arabia in the overall interest of the West and as a means of securing both oil imports and industrial exports, this new German policy toward history and toward Israel might well have been bought by the German public, especially in the wake of Begin's political bombshell of May 3, 1981, castigating the former *Wehrmacht* Lieutenant Helmut Schmidt and the entire German people as bearing collective guilt for the crimes committed during the National-Socialist regime.

Begin's broadsides were both polemic and invalid, and Helmut Schmidt enjoyed an unparalleled prestige that included the approval of not just SPD voters but of about three-fourths of all West Germans.

The leaders of the social-liberal coalition, however, failed to sell their policy package to their own SPD and FDP Bundestag factions. In May of 1982 Schmidt and Genscher were forced to abandon their efforts to strike a weapons deal with Saudi Arabia. The coalition's social-liberal parliamentarians were opposed to such a far-reaching liberalization of arms exports in general and against a too forceful policy toward Israel in particular.

Opinions differ as to the wisdom of having prevented the export of modern German weapons to Saudi Arabia. In view of the chain of events since Iraq's invasion of Kuwait in August 1990, and the subsequent Gulf War, the question arises as to whether a greater Saudi defense capability might have served to suppress Saddam Hussein's appetite.

■

The trigger for Begin's explosion on May 3, 1981, is all too often forgotten. Only a few days before Chancellor Schmidt had spoken on German television about the suffering that Hitler-Germany had inflicted on other peoples. Numerous nations were specifically mentioned. The Jewish people was not.

This may explain Begin's conduct, but it cannot excuse his bringing out the old cudgel of collective guilt. As it soon became clear, the core of the problem involved more than German oil imports and industrial exports, more than Saudi Arabia's role in the Middle East, more than general Western worries over the Near East, and more than Israel's purportedly endangered security. In the end, the question had to be faced: Could German foreign policy in the 1980s be "normal"? Helmut Schmidt recognized the problem. During his flight back from Saudi Arabia on April 30, 1981, he had asserted that German foreign policy could and would no longer be overshadowed by Auschwitz. This statement was heard by only a small and unofficial circle, but the decisive ears in both Germany and Israel got the message.

Schmidt had overplayed his hand, and even Begin's blast on May 3 did not help him achieve his goal of normalizing German policy by means of the proposed arms deal with the Saudis. The Chancellor soon realized that he had committed a tactical blunder and a few days later had copies distributed of the speech he had given in November 1978 on the occasion of the fortieth anniversary of the *reichskristallnacht*. In this address Schmidt had acknowledged a direct German responsibility toward the Jewish people and reminded his countrymen that "our friends in Israel" had a voice in German decisions in dealing with the heritage of the past, i.e. in German *geschichtspolitik*. His specific reference was to the debate over the statute of limitations with regard to war crimes committed under National-Socialist rule.

Nevertheless, Schmidt was too late in getting on the historical train that he had originally intended to shunt off onto a sidetrack.

5. Breaking through Thin Ice: The Presence of the Past, 1984–1988

In October 1982 Schmidt's successor, Helmut Kohl of the CDU, began where his predecessor had left off in May: with the plan to sell Leopard 2 tanks to Saudi Arabia.

Kohl's aim was essentially identical to that of the social-liberal coalition, namely to demonstrate normality by employing the same symbolism. Only this time the packaging was even less attractive and the tactics less carefully thought out. During his visit to Jerusalem in January 1984, Kohl's spokesman Peter Boenisch repeated in nearly identical words what Helmut Schmidt had said in April of 1981. There was, however, one fine but decisive distinction: Schmidt had spoken to a small, closed circle and could thus observe the effect of his trial balloon without the need to issue a later denial. Boenisch spoke publicly at a press conference and was thus in no position to issue a denial, even if he had wanted to.

At almost the same time, a historically more sensitive Bonn Foreign Ministry official, Alois Mertes, formulated the Kohl-Boenisch idea in a more gentle manner: Israel ought not to misuse Auschwitz as an argument. In his papers, we find many indications that Mertes, a friend of Israel and the Jews who desired to maintain good German-Jewish-Israeli relations, was therefore disturbed by the political use and misuse of the Holocaust.

Despite the change of governing coalitions, there was an unmistakable continuity in German-Israeli relations. Helmut Kohl's bearing during his January 1984 visit to Israel was anything but gentle. With every word and gesture, the German Chancellor attempted to document the breakthrough to normality. Because of the manner and context of its presentation, even Kohl's now famous formulation of his and all subsequent generations' *Gnade der späten Geburt*—the blessing of having been born later, an indisputable historical fact—gave the impression that the Chancellor was trying, despite all assurances to the contrary, to slip out of his historical responsibility via a back door into day-to-day, politics-as-usual normality, including arms exports to Saudi Arabia.

For both Schmidt and Kohl the desire was father to the thought. And their wish was shared by the great majority of their fellow countrymen, who hoped that history would no longer be used as a political argument or instrument against an unquestionably democratic Germany, which was new both in political and generational terms.

In late 1984, under a radically different ideological banner, a delegation of Bundestag legislators belonging to the West German Green party attempted to introduce new tones and a new approach during their tour of Israel. Without a doubt above any suspicion of lingering anti-Semitism and relying on the good fortune of their being part of a new generation, the Green delegation swept aside considerations of their own national and therefore historical label and freely distributed unsolicited advice on how the Israelis ought to solve their conflict with the Palestinians and the Arab states. The Greens were promptly confronted with their German nationality in a context which they were both unprepared and unable to deal with. Since the opening of the East German archives it has been revealed that at least one member of the Greens' delegation was in the service of the GDR secret police ("Stasi").

That two leaders of the pragmatic *realo* wing of the Greens, Otto Schily and Waltraut Schoppe, proved capable of coping with German history without abandoning basic party positions during their visit to Israel in the autumn of 1987 stirred up a new storm of internal controversy in the party. During the Gulf War in early 1991, the Greens were torn asunder by a battle fought between the two main wings of the party. Not least among the issues at stake were the Gulf War and relations with Israel.

■

We thus recognize that *all* West German parties share a desire to close the books on the past and to begin a new chapter in the history of German-Jewish and German-Israeli relations.

Kohl's trip to Israel differed from the visits by the other chancellors less in substance than in the more open shift from a defensive to an offensive style. But instead of achieving the intended breakthrough to normality, Kohl broke through the thin historical ice separating the new Germany's foreign policy from the depths of the past.

In taking such pains to emphasize historical-political normality to the Israelis and to the world by word and (intended) deed (arms exports), Kohl involuntarily raised doubts about just how normal this normality really was. If normality were so self-evident, it was asked in Israel, in the West and in the East, why did it have to be so pointedly accentuated?

Certainly, the Federal Republic of Germany had, for many years, enjoyed extraordinary sympathy abroad, but Israel and the world in general were apparently not ready to uncritically accept a one-sided declaration of normality. If it was Israel that had raised the ante too high in 1964, West Germany had now overplayed its hand.

Prime Minister Yitzhak Shamir was not content to confine his response to Kohl's policy toward Israel and the proposed export of German arms to mere verbal criticism. He followed up with precisely the actions he had indicated to the Chancellor that he would take.

Since Israel alone was incapable of applying the brakes to Germany's new *geschichtspolitik*, Shamir deemed it time to mobilize American assistance. This was achieved in the following months. The chain of events and aggravations that followed Chancellor Kohl's January 1984 visit to Israel illustrates the maxim that it is not possible to escape from history. Kohl boldly served the political volleyball over the historical net only to find it spiked back into this own court. Despite his well-advertised desires, one politician was visibly absent at the ceremonies commemorating the fortieth anniversary of the Allied D-Day invasion: the German Chancellor. He was not invited. Although this could not be directly traced to Israel or Jewish influence, it did have to do with the burden of German history.

Shortly thereafter, Italy's Foreign Minister Andreotti, like Kohl a Christian Democrat, labeled the German longing for reunification as "Pan-Germanism." As senseless and untenable such an accusation may be, it is clearly derived from and explainable by reference to history. Its lack of validity exposes the instrumental nature of the accusation and underlines the thesis that German politics cannot be divorced from German history.

Another illustration is the accusation of "revanchism" which had repeatedly been hurled at Bonn from the Eastern bloc and was fired with renewed intensity in the summer of 1984. Much sharper and more fundamental was the controversy surrounding President Ronald Reagan's scheduled visit to West Germany. In late 1984 Bonn had included Bitburg—a politically problematic military cemetery, as it contained graves of members of the SS—but none of the former concentration camps in West Germany on the President's itinerary. This was not only questionable, both morally and in terms of domestic politics. It was also a crass misjudgment in the context of both *geschichtspolitik* and foreign policy.

The door was thus opened to a historical-political counteroffensive on the part of Israel and Jewish groups, as well as non-Jewish Americans, including many who considered themselves friends of West Germany but not of its self-proclaimed politics of normality. As already mentioned, this counteroffensive had been announced by Israel's Prime Minister Shamir in January 1984, and any judgment of the Israeli-Jewish reaction must also weigh the previous West German historical-political offensive under Chancellors Schmidt and Kohl.

Expressions of outrage from or directed at either side are certainly inappropriate, as both merely employed the political instruments available to them. Bonn's instrument was the normality of the Leopard 2; Israel and the Jewish groups employed the historical-political instrument of the Holocaust. Whether the use of such instruments can be considered wise, or at least purposeful, is the only appropriate question.

President Reagan's visit and the economic summit organized by Bonn took place in May 1985, forty years after Germany's unconditional capitulation, and were intended as high water marks of the political acceptance that had been achieved by West Germany. The effect was largely spoiled by Prime Minister Shamir's counteroffensive. With the leverage of the American Jewish organizations, Bonn's historical-political express train was derailed. Rather than marking a high tide, the effect was more like a plunge through thin historical-political ice, and it was chiefly President Richard von Weizsäcker's widely admired speech that pulled West German prestige back out of the water.

The level of irritation that had been reached in West Germany was indicated by the controversies provoked in Frankfurt in the summer and fall of 1985 by a new play by Rainer Werner Fassbinder which many Jews and non-Jews considered "anti-Semitic" and by the foolish pronouncements by parliamentarians Count Spree of the CDU and Hermann Fellner of the CSU, who acted as the megaphones for a certain segment of the "people's voice." Their comments about Jews and money, especially concerning Jewish wealth founded on restitution payments, merely repeated broken old records. It must be emphasized that the leadership of both the CDU and CSU were quick to react. Both Spree and Fellner were required to issue retractions and Spree, the political star in a West German provincial town, was forced to relinquish his post.

In any case, the state of German politics could not yet be regarded as "normal." The swirling controversies had made this abundantly clear to everyone, including the Chancellor, who then proceeded to save what he could. In a speech at Bergen-Belsen in April 1985, Chancellor Kohl initiated a cautious change of course. Demonstrative normality was now out; expressions of profound concern were the order of the day. The way had been prepared by President von Weizsäcker's speech of May 8, 1985, impressively portraying the problems and ambivalences of a German polity which must constantly keep its history in mind.

In January 1986 in Berlin, characteristically at the opening of an academic conference on "Jews in Germany, 1933–1939," the German Chancellor set further, almost humble accents. From a profession of historical responsibility, Kohl derived a German obligation toward Israel. His approach in explaining the National-Socialist crimes was more anthropological than national: The horrors of the Holocaust proved not what *the German*, but what *man* in general is capable of.

On the other hand, in a December 1986 speech to the Bundestag and in the presence of Israeli President Chaim Herzog on April 7, 1987, Chancellor Kohl accentuated the unique nature of the National-Social-

ist crimes, thus offering a more national than anthropological interpretation: "We know . . . that this crime of genocide, in its cold, inhu-
man planning and in its deadly effectiveness is singular in the history
of mankind. . . . We do not want to ever forget these crimes. And we
will resist any attempt to repress them or make them seem harmless."

What had happened? Is it possible to discern a sense of direction
after all behind the zigzag course plotted by Germany's political pilot
with regard to Israel and the Jews? The chief pilot was, in fact, no
longer steering the ship of state, as in 1982 and 1985. He was himself
being steered by events. The most decisive of these was the so-called
historikerstreit—which we can most literally translate as the "historians' controversy," but perhaps more true to the tone of the times as the
"battle of historians." The issue at the center of the dispute was the
uniqueness of the Holocaust, as upheld by one group of historians and
intellectuals, including Jürgen Habermas, Eberhard Jäckel and others,
and as disputed by the opposing party, most particularly by Joachim
Fest. Ernst Nolte insisted on recognizing a relationship between the
horrors perpetrated by Stalin and Hitler. To reduce the argument to an
(over)simplified formula, Nolte derived Auschwitz from the Gulag
Archipelago, that is: without Stalin, no Hitler.

Because of its political impact, the *historikerstreit* rapidly exceeded
the dimensions of the standard academic tempest in a teacup and finally grew into a German-Israeli and German-Jewish affair of state. Long
before the outbreak of the controversy, Ernst Nolte had been involved
in a German-Israeli project sponsored by the *Deutsche Forschungsgemeinschaft* (DFG, the German Research Community, a government-
funded research foundation). This was not just another research project. The object was a comprehensive edition of the letters and diaries
of Theodor Herzl (1860–1904). As the founder of Zionism, Herzl is a
symbolic figure and is revered as the spiritual father of the State of
Israel. In early 1987 the Herzl project was up for renewal, normally a
mere formality. Instead, despite numerous official denials, it became a
German-Jewish-Israeli affair of state. Under the circumstances, this
was unavoidable.

As the crisis in German-Israeli relations approached the boiling
point, it became clear that an Israeli gesture to reduce tensions could
not be had for nothing. The storm which had been gathering force dur-

ing for several years, beginning with the proposed arms exports to Saudi Arabia in 1981, followed by the Kohl trip to Israel in 1984, the revival of the Saudi arms deal and the Reagan visit to Bitburg, only partially subsided in the wake of the Weizsäcker speech in 1985 and once again howled after the outbreak of the "battle of the historians" in 1986.

In the meantime, however, both Bonn and Jerusalem had licked their wounds, learned from past mistakes, and were yearning for a de-escalation. The first visit by a presiding President of Israel to the Federal Republic of Germany in the spring of 1987 was designed as a new departure and new high water mark in German-Israeli-Jewish *geschichtspolitik*.

Under the prevailing circumstances however, with the background music provided by the *historikerstreit*, no Israeli politician could justify such a visit domestically. It was thus necessary for both the German President and the Chancellor to take sides in the controversy. To no one's surprise, both came down on the side of the proponents of the unique nature of the National-Socialist crimes and thus against Nolte's thesis. The latter's participation in the DFG Herzl project was terminated in February 1987—an entirely unpolitical move, as it was argued—as it *had to* be argued. The aims of state policy, i.e. German policy toward Israel, German foreign policy in general, and *geschichtspolitik* took precedence over the principle of the separation of politics and academics.

The battle of historians also served to call one of the achievements in the political development of the Federal Republic into serious question, namely the integration of the conservative right into the democratic, parliamentary value system opposed to anti-Semitism. Suddenly, conservatives found themselves being pushed into an anti-Semitic corner where they did not belong (or at least no longer belonged) and where they ran the risk of acquiring false allies, namely true anti-Semites. This was not in the interest of Germany, of Israel, or of Jews in general. A case of good intentions producing some not-so-good results? Or perhaps a case of policy appearing to be so wise at the moment proving not-so-wise over the long term?

■

An interesting political-psychological question remains: Why, in

1986–87, did both political and academic circles find it necessary to subject the questionable theses of an ivory-tower professor (Nolte) to a much more withering criticism than that directed at Chancellor Helmut Schmidt in 1981, when he had listed numerous peoples as having suffered at German hands, but chose to lump the Jewish people into the "etc." group? Did this "etc." not, in the end, call the uniqueness of the Holocaust into question by downplaying the sufferings of the Jewish people in comparison with what Hitler's Germany did to other groups?

This perspective leaves us with a rather pessimistic view of the effect of the battle of the historians on the future course of German-Jewish-Israeli *geschichtspolitik*.

On the optimistic side, the more historical-political than truly historical debate produced by the *historikerstreit* demonstrated how agitated—and sometimes agitating—the debate over the National-Socialist past has been conducted in the West German present. Importantly, this debate took place *voluntarily*. Moreover, absolutely nothing was brushed over lightly or swept under the carpet. It is hard to imagine a more intensive attempt to confront the past. It would appear that, once again after a passage of twenty years, a third cycle of dealing with the past has begun.

6. *Comparative* Geschichtspolitik: *The German Democratic Republic*

Particularly during the early years of the Federal Republic of Germany, the period in which the basic contours of the new, West German *geschichtspolitik* were being formed, the majority of political decision-makers in the Federal Republic of Germany chose not to take the easy way out when it came to dealing with Israel and the Jews. The German Democratic Republic (East Germany) and Austria, the two other German states formed from what had been the territory of Hitler's Great-German Empire (*großdeutsches Reich*) chose to take entirely different approaches in coping with the German past.

"The Government of the German Democratic Republic has done all in its power to eliminate German fascism at the roots and to create conditions that will preclude the possibility of Germany ever again posing any threat to the security and existence of other peoples, including the Jewish people. The victims of fascism living within the territory of the German Democratic Republic have received generous aid and support. The government of the German Democratic Republic has fulfilled all of the requirements of the four allied powers for reparations in order to compensate for the destruction wrought by German fascism."

In December 1955 a representative of the German Democratic Republic handed a note with the above words to his Israeli counterpart. On November 25, 1952, the East German party organ *Neues Deutschland* ("New Germany") had used almost identical language in its first reaction to the agreement concluded between the Federal Republic of Germany and Israel—more than two months after the signing.

Not about to give up so easily, Jerusalem dispatched another note, but East Berlin's second reply of July 9, 1956, was also unsatisfactory to Israel. Jerusalem reacted yet again, but this time only to signal the East Germans that Israel would return to the problem of indemnification for the victims of the Nazi regime "at the first available opportunity."

In fact, Jerusalem long appeared to have permanently filed away its claims for indemnification by the East German regime. But in January 1973 Jerusalem approached West German Chancellor Willy Brandt, an old hand at dealing with the East Germans, with the request that he act as an intermediary. To no avail: East Berlin was not to be budged.

■

We can discern several phases in East Germany's *geschichtspolitik* in dealing with Israel and Jews. From 1949 to 1953 East Berlin rejected any sort of national responsibility for the National-Socialist atrocities. Nevertheless, anti-Semitism in East Germany was remarkably restrained in comparison with events in the Soviet Union and the rest of the eastern block. While the Soviet *Liternaturnaya Gazeta* attacked Israel as an accomplice of U.S. imperialism as early as April of 1950, *Neues Deutschland* did not place Israel "on the side of the American war mongers and imperialists" until March 1, 1951. After the Soviet Union began to deliver arms to Egypt in September 1955, Israel was especially criticized for its actions against the "awakening and progressive" Egyptian people.

Comparison of the official publications of the GDR with those of the Soviet Union reveals that in the period 1953–54 East Berlin abandoned its relative restraint. By 1963–64 the tone emanating from the GDR was fully the equal of the anti-Israel shrillness of the Soviet Union and clearly and consistently surpassed the Soviets after 1967. Apparently, the GDR hoped to thus improve its image in the Third World and on the international stage in general. For motives having to do with the politics of the day, Israel was assigned the role of scapegoat, especially since the conquests of the 1967 Six Day War gave the Jewish State the negative characteristics of an occupier and "colonial power" in the view of many developing countries.

The sometimes rabid anti-Israelism of the GDR press (and therefore the GDR leadership) was moderated a bit by the distinction between the "aggressive aggressor-circles of the government" of Israel (capital: Tel Aviv!) and the Jewish population of the country. This historical-political tactic was intended to free the GDR from its national-historical bind. In the English-language publications originating in the Soviet Union during the same period there is no reference to the "oppressed Jewish population." Was East Germany's particularly shrill anti-Israelism after 1967 supposed to serve as a substitute for its lack of anti-Semitism? Of course, the warnings against the Jewish-Zionist threat so often repeated in Poland and in the Soviet Union in those years would have sounded hollow when one considers that there were fewer than six hundred officially registered Jews in the GDR.

East Germany's policy toward Israel served at the same time to distance the GDR from the Federal Republic. *Neues Deutschland* as well as many other East German publications suggested again and again that the Israeli government was cooperating with the forces of the old Germany. This was the line taken in the wake of the swastika-painting episodes of 1959–60 in West Germany (which, as we now know, were choreographed by East bloc agents), and especially following the Eichmann trial. The GDR media coverage of the proceedings against Adolf Eichmann was less concerned with that trial than with prosecuting Adenauer's close adviser Hans Globke, who as a justice ministry official during the Third Reich had participated in drafting and preparing commentaries on the racist and anti-Semitic Nuremberg laws of 1935.

■

By the mid-1980s, however, the German Democratic Republic appeared to have realized that any improvement in its international standing, especially in its relations with the United States, was inseparable from its historical responsibilities. This was the probable reason for the more gentle line the GDR adopted toward the Jews in its final years.

Whether it wanted to or not, the GDR could not escape the burdens of the past, which, because of West German policies since 1984–85, increasingly aroused emotions in the United States. With regard to German responsibility for the Third Reich, Americans tended to see little difference between the two Germanies. The national inheritance of the Holocaust could not be simply shaken off, not even by a "social revolution."

The East German leadership visibly altered its tactics with regard to the Jewish Diaspora in 1987. For the first time, East Berlin initiated negotiations with representatives of the World Jewish Congress (WJC) regarding the possibility of East German indemnification for Jews of German descent residing in other countries. In January 1988, it was reported that East Germany was, in principle, prepared to make indemnification payments.

East Germany's change of historical-political course in 1987 was signaled not only by its reported willingness to begin restitution negotiations with the Diaspora-Jewish organizations, but also by the introduction of a new Rabbi in East Berlin. The living expenses of the new Rabbi were financed only in small part by the GDR Ministry for Religion; the remainder was assumed by the American Jewish Committee.

7. The End of the German Democratic Republic and the "Jewish Connection," 1988–1990

America was discovered in 1492, the Jews in 1985—at least as far as the German Democratic Republic was concerned. Before, the Jews were considered to be just another group persecuted by the Nazis, like the Communists. Though obviously absurd, this was the official view. And the Jewish State? The latter was viewed as the "spearhead of U.S. imperialism, capitalism and colonialism" in the Middle East, as a "brutal aggressor" and occupier "like the Wehrmacht." Thus it is no wonder that the GDR had refused to even consider moral or financial restitution for the Holocaust.

Why, then, the sudden discovery of the Jews and Israel by the East German leadership in 1985? There were two reasons, one economic, the other political. Since the early 1980s the GDR had been virtually bankrupt. Erich Honecker and his colleagues hoped that Washington would grant them most favored nation status. Secondly, the GDR was seeking to gain additional legitimacy. Honecker wanted to be received officially at the White House, which would have been the climax of his political career. Moreover, 1985 was the year of the Bitburg controversy. For the first time, West Germany seemed to be on the defensive and the East Germans believed they could muster Jewish support for their own ends.

Such is the background of the following drama. The place: the Foreign Ministry of the German Democratic Republic in East Berlin. The date: November 30, 1989, exactly three weeks after the fall of the Berlin Wall. Dramatis personae: an odd couple, Oskar Fischer, who, despite Honecker's fall, continued to serve as Foreign Minister of the GDR, and Dr. Maram Stern, since 1987 the plenipotentiary of the WJC for contacts with East Germany.

A third man joined the confidential discussion between Fischer and Stern: the chief officer of the U.S. desk in the GDR Foreign Ministry, Dr. Herbert Barth. His presence explains nearly everything: The GDR was seeking a dialogue with American Jews as a means of gaining access to the U.S. government. This had been attempted once before, in 1985, but the major American-Jewish organizations had consistently rebuffed the blandishments of the Socialist Unity Party (SED). As Ted Elenoff, president of the American Jewish Committee, put it: "Rabbis, prayer books and shawls and religious support for Jews in the GDR, yes. Political support for the GDR as a state, no." Elenoff had usually dealt with the head of the so-called Office for Church Issues, Klaus Gysi, the father of Gregor Gysi, chairman of the successor organization to the SED, the Party for Democratic Socialism (PDS).

What was it that brought Dr. Maram Stern to East Berlin on November 30, 1989? The World Jewish Congress under the leadership of its president, Edgar Bronfman, was the only American-Jewish organization willing to maintain contacts with the GDR. In the fall of 1988, Honecker had awarded Bronfman the Friendship Star of the

People in Gold, the highest decoration of the German Democratic Republic. As far as the East German leadership was concerned, the honor was well deserved, for on October 17, 1988, Bronfman had made a remarkable statement. According to the Foreign Ministry memorandum of their conversation, Bronfman had told Honecker that "he was aware that the Hitler fascists had subjected the majority of German Communists to the same sufferings as the Jews." Moreover, Bronfman remained loyal to the GDR right down to the very end. Stern, in his meeting on November 30, 1989, with Fischer, "conveyed best regards from President Bronfman as well as General Secretary Singer and expressed their satisfaction at Oskar Fischer's reappointment as Foreign Minister." "The WJC," he added, "is and will remain a friend of the GDR."

Since for years the GDR had rendered not only political but also financial and military support to the PLO, the astonished reader rubs his eyes and reads the passage again, thinking he has misunderstood. But there is no mistake.

Another GDR Foreign Ministry document shows that the infamous terrorist Abu Daud, who supposedly had been shot and killed in Warsaw in July 1981, was not only very much alive, but was also a frequent and welcome guest of the so-called Committee for Solidarity in East Berlin. Abu Daud had been one of the key figures in the massacre of Israeli athletes at the 1972 Munich Olympics. While "residing at the PLO embassy," Daud met with "Comrade Wolfgang Krause." The SED Central Committee and the Foreign Ministry were, of course, aware of these contacts.

In an interview conducted by the Bavarian network TV program "Report" on November 28, 1990, Krause reported that he had met not only with Abu Daud, but also with Georges Habash, Nauf Havatmah, Achmed Jibril (considered responsible for the bombing of the Pan Am flight over Lockerbie in December 1988) and Yasir Arafat. In addition, Krause described his meeting with the executive committee of the PLO in Tunis in November 1989. This meeting, as well as Arafat's visits to the GDR, had all been reported in the press.

To "Report," Maram Stern insisted that Honecker and Fischer had repeatedly assured him that there had been "no contacts for more than eight years" with the PLO and "no training of PLO terrorists." Stern stated that he was "personally very disappointed" to learn that the two East German leaders had lied to him. Had Stern failed to notice that the PLO had maintained an embassy in East Berlin since 1973? Had his missed President Reagan's public statement in 1986 charging the GDR with directing the activities of Libyan terrorists? Anyone who bothered to read *Neues Deutschland* certainly knew of the pro-Palestinian sympathies of the GDR. For years the East German National People's Army had been suspected of being involved in the military training of PLO guerrillas. This was confirmed in 1990 by Minister for Disarmament and Defense Rainer Eppelmann, who finally ordered an end to this policy.

If its publicly proclaimed and practiced policy of "solidarity with Palestine" made the GDR the friend of Israel's enemy, why did the WJC proclaim its friendship with the GDR in November 1989? As Stern explained the position of his organization to Fischer, "the question of [German] unification was not on the agenda. The WJC would do everything in its power to prevent it. The lessons of history still apply. Although it was difficult to take such a position in public, President Bronfman would exert his influence in this direction in the U.S. and elsewhere." "In any case," Stern added, "the WJC will do everything possible to strengthen the GDR politically and economically."

As late as February and March 1990, the new leader of the PDS (i.e., of the transformed SED), Gregor Gysi, was still grasping at this straw. He argued that Jews should have an interest in preserving the two German states and appealed for Jewish financial investments in order to preserve the independence of the GDR. One can hardly accuse Gysi of "anti-Semitism" (if for no other reason than his Jewish background) but his implicit connection between Jews and high finance is more than merely embarrassing. The assumption of this prominent leftist harks back to classical right-wing anti-Semitic rhetoric about the "Jewish Golden International."

The SED/PDS cynically counted on the Jews to have a short memory. East Germany's links to the PLO, its decades-long campaign of denouncing Israel, its refusal to accept any responsibility for the crimes of the Nazi era, all this should be forgotten and forgiven?

"To the contrary," insisted Maram Stern in his interview with "Report." The WJC "wanted at any price an admission of guilt for the

Holocaust on the part of the GDR." This Prime Minister Modrow finally provided in a letter to Edgar Bronfman in early February 1989.

A number of unanswered questions remain. Why, for example, was this admission of guilt addressed to the WJC and not to the Jewish State, with which the GDR had just opened negotiations in Copenhagen? Why this particular friendship? Did the memorandum of the former East Berlin Foreign Ministry distort the content of the conversation between Fischer and Stern?

In his interview with "Report," Stern said that the memorandum of conversation contained statements that had been made and others that had not, but he did not dispute the basic accuracy of the document.

The East German Foreign Ministry document appears to be credible in substance. That is not at all surprising, as such memoranda were intended for internal use only and the decisionmakers of the Foreign Ministry would hardly have wished to deceive themselves. Besides, in October 1988, Stern's superior, Bronfman, had already expressed his full satisfaction with the new East German approach, stating that it was reassuring that the GDR had "assumed responsibility for the past" and had "done everything to help the survivors of the Holocaust living within its territory."

State Security Police records indicate that from January 1 to the fall of the Berlin Wall on November 9, 1989, approximately 360 anti-Semitic incidents were registered—but not reported—in the GDR. The implicit assumption was that such activities were imported from the "neo-fascist Federal Republic." As the Central Committee of the SED had proclaimed to the world in June 1988: "the Jewish citizens had found their true home" in the GDR.

Invited to comment on the conversation between Bronfman and Honecker, the World Jewish Congress categorically denied that Bronfman had equated the National-Socialist genocide of the Jews with the persecution of the Communists. Such an equation, we were told, was "absurd." It is absurd, and the response of the WJC is encouraging.

Apart from the equation of the Holocaust and the persecution of the Communists, however, Bronfman's unpublished declarations differed little from his published comments. In the October 31, 1988, issue of

Newsweek Bronfman is quoted as stating that "from a Jewish point of view there is no reason" to deny the GDR most favored nation status or to object to a visit by Honecker to the United States. Possibly he was confusing Jewish with private interests. During his visit to East Berlin, Bronfman had also discussed business relations between the GDR and his own Seagram company with Minister for Foreign Trade Beil.

What else did Fischer and Stern discuss? The memorandum continues: "Oskar Fischer described current developments in the GDR. He assumed that the GDR would remain a socialist state, that there would be no reunification and that the process of reform would be irreversible." "The GDR," said Fischer, "is interested in gaining support. . . . The trust-building contacts between the GDR and the WJC are of fundamental importance. . . . At the same time, the GDR recognizes its moral obligation to continue its talks with the Jewish Claims Conference."

It was precisely this "moral obligation" with regard to restitution which the GDR had continually and in principle disputed from 1949 up until 1988. Even the verbal assurances of 1988 had not led to any action.

After the fall of the Berlin Wall, Fischer seemed inconsolable: "Unfortunately," he remarked, the negotiations had not resulted in progress and "now the GDR has no money." Of course, the East German leaders could have faced the issue just a bit earlier. The claims of Israel and the Jewish Claims Conference had been on the table since January 1951. Stern, however, was sympathetic and replied that "neither Bronfman nor Singer expect monetary payment at present. This would in fact be damaging, as it could encourage anti-Semitism in the GDR." Over and over again, the good Germans of the SED/PDS had lectured the world that there was no such thing as anti-Semitism in the German Democratic Republic. If we accept Fischer's argument, we might just as well take it a step further: According to this logic, Israel and the Claims Conference ought never to have asked for restitution in the first place.

By what route did the GDR arrive at general German responsibility for the Holocaust? For Stern and Bronfman it appears to have been the high road: It was "not for legal but for moral reasons," Bronfman told Honecker on October 17, 1988, that the GDR should provide "symbol-

ic help for underprivileged former Jewish victims of the Nazi regime."
In his *Newsweek* interview, Bronfman also spoke in terms of the "symbolic responsibility" of the GDR, apparently ready to accept a bowl of soup as a symbolic substitute for restitution.

The United States government seemed to be unable to follow the twists in this yellow brick road. On November 30, 1989, Stern told Fischer that Washington regrettably "did not understand, and insisted on the fulfillment of the Jewish claims." Stern reportedly informed Israel of the WJC's interest in establishing relations between the GDR and the Jewish State. Fisher gave Stern "full powers" to communicate his good intentions to the Israeli side. "Even a meeting," he pointed out, would represent "a fact of considerable weight."

Stern recommended continuing the contacts between the GDR and Israel via its ambassador in Bucharest and to go through the Israeli ambassador to Belgium rather than through the ambassador to France. Having offered so many valuable tips, it is not surprising that WJC representative Stern also expressed a wish of his own at the November 30 meeting. He asked his interlocutor to refrain from doing anything that might contribute to a situation in which Heinz Galinski, the leading representative of the Jewish community in West Germany, could "again achieve a monopoly on the representation of the Jewish citizens of both states."

As early as April 19, 1988, Saul Kagan of the Jewish Claims Conference (JCC) had stated in the presence of Fischer, WJC representatives, and other GDR Foreign Ministry officials that "Heinz Galinski is not empowered to speak in the name of the JCC" with regard to restitution. According to the GDR Foreign Ministry memorandum, Kagan further stated that he "well understood" the "irritations" of the East Germans. Obviously it was especially irritating that Galinski had kept insisting on solid financial and not just "symbolic" measures.

In a conversation on August 15, 1988, with the chief U.S. desk officer in the GDR Foreign Ministry, Stern expressed his disapproval of Galinski's "all-German" activities. As one of his reasons for criticizing Galinski, Stern stated that the WJC was interested in maintaining "earnestness." Peter Kirchner, the chairman of the Jewish community in East Berlin, was also present. Even in late 1990, Kirchner still found words of praise for Erich Honecker. According to the Israeli daily

Maariv of November 16, 1990, Kirchner claimed that Honecker had been made a "scapegoat." The deposed East German leader, Kirchner argued, had brought "improvements" to the Jewish community in East Berlin, "in complete contrast to his predecessor Walter Ulbricht, who allowed for no compromises. . . . Now the Jewish community in East Germany is faced with another problem: Heinz Galinski, who has led the community in West Berlin with a strong hand, is now grasping for control of the East Berlin community."

■

After the opening of the Berlin Wall on November 9, 1989, the disintegration of the GDR proceeded at an ever accelerating pace and the supposedly all-powerful World Jewish Congress looked on helplessly. By the time of their conference in Berlin in May 1990, Bronfman and the WJC had accepted German unification and the "all-German" activities of Heinz Galinski, who was among the sponsors of the spring 1990 conference.

That the SED/PDS leadership under Gysi and Modrow thought that they could slow down or even prevent reunification with the help of the WJC was both grotesque and cynical. Like many other politicians, the East German leaders had succumbed to the widespread misconception that the World Jewish Congress represented the Jews of the world—a legend that the representatives of the WJC energetically and enthusiastically promoted. "The World [Jewish] Congress possesses considerable world-wide political and economic influence and has a voice in all political decision-making in the USA." This incredible statement was supposedly made by Stern to Fischer on April 19, 1988. At least that is what we read in a memorandum dated one day later, prepared by Norbert Reemer, an official of the U.S. desk in the East German Foreign Ministry. The document was classified "personal" and "confidential."

In reality, only a number of the smaller Jewish organizations in the United States belong to the WJC and the Jewish State obviously does not need outside representation. Except for the WJC itself, only an odd coalition of the well- and the ill-intentioned believe in its power. The well-intentioned do not realize that the WJC is not a representative organization and remember only the man who was its president for many years, the impressive Nahum Goldmann. The ill-intentioned see in the activities of the WJC clear proof for the validity of the *Protocols of the Elders of Zion*, the argument that Jews secretly rule the world. The SED/PDS politicians Modrow and Gysi appear to have succumbed to this old superstition of the extreme right.

But the secret power of the WJC was not sufficient to prolong, much less preserve, the existence of the German Democratic Republic. This failure, of course, will not prevent the new anti-Semites of the right and left from continuing to embellish the legend of Jewish conspiratorial omnipotence.

Does criticism of the leadership of the WJC further the cause of the anti-Semites? I prefer to answer the question with a counter-question: Can criticism of a policy harmful to Jewish and Israeli interests be considered anti-Semitic? As the Israeli newspaper *Yediot Acharonot* pointed out on October 20, 1988, immediately following Bronfman's visit with Honecker: "Bronfman represented neither the State of Israel nor the survivors of the Holocaust in the GDR."

A double moral standard remains a double standard, no matter who practices it, whether Jew or non-Jew, German or non-German. Morality is not divisible by national heritage or history.

8. Soviet Jews to Germany or Israel? 1990–91

In the summer of 1990, as the two Germanies were heading full steam toward unification, thousands of Soviet Jews suddenly began knocking at the door. The result was a tangled German-Jewish-Israeli problem.

The "good Germans" repeatedly expressed their indignation over their "bad" countrymen who would not open the doors of the country more than a crack to the Jews of Russia. But were the "good Germans" not, in fact, saying: "Jews, yes. Israel, no"? At best, the "good Germans" displayed little sensitivity toward Israel and thus lost a good deal of their credibility as friends of the Jews.

The cast was familiar: Among the "good Germans" were the supporters of the Greens, the PDS, and some Social Democrats. The role of the "bad German" was played by members of the government, the supporters of the Free Democrats, and the Christian Democrats.

Since they did not qualify for entry either as ethnic Germans or as political asylum seekers, the Russian Jews were denied permission to remain in the country. The "good Germans" were incensed that, of all people, Jews should become the "victims" of the government's newer, stricter policy concerning foreign residents.

As the successor to the communist SED, the PDS continued a tested tradition. In June 1988 the Central Committee of the SED had proclaimed that "the Jewish citizens have found their true homeland in the German Democratic Republic." Both before and after this pronouncement, the National People's Army had trained PLO terrorists. Nevertheless, on October 25, 1990, PDS member of the Bundestag Bittner told her fellow legislators: "Whatever happens to the Jews happens to us." This was pure chutzpah.

A member of the governing "red-green" coalition (SPD and Greens) in Frankfurt am Main perceived a connection between the new-German present and the National-Socialist past: "It is our particular responsibility to ensure that the injustice of that time is not allowed to continue." In an official Day of German Unity commemoration in the Frankfurt St. Pauls Church, the mayor of Frankfurt, Volker Hauff (SPD), called for the admission of all Russian Jews seeking permission to immigrate "without any quotas and limits." Hauff stated his belief that "nothing good can develop in the future if we forget the past." Similar comments were made by Johannes Rau, Minister-President of the state of North Rhine Westphalia and his Interior Minister Schnoor.

Even the highly esteemed White Rose Foundation (dedicated to the memory and tradition of the White Rose, the anti-Nazi resistance movement among German students, most prominently Hans and Sophie Scholl, who were executed by the Nazis) felt prompted to state that "one cannot imagine a more unfortunate new beginning to German history than a ban on Jewish immigration."

The clear implication was that those favoring a restrictive immigration policy were trying to forget the Holocaust or even resurrect the Nazi past. Dietrich Wetzel, a member of the Bundestag from the Greens, put it most drastically: "Once again, the Germans want their state to be *judenrein*" ("clean of Jews," a Nazi catchword).

What was taking place was, in effect, a new round in the "as though" resistance game: As though the legal system of the Federal Republic of Germany were somehow comparable or even equivalent to the National-Socialist terror state. As though Helmut Kohl were another Adolf Hitler. As though anyone whose opinion on this issue differed from that of the Greens, Social Democrats, or even the PDS were a "bad" German, or even some kind of Nazi. As though every critic of the government's policy qualified as a resistance hero.

The references to the past, often reinforced by the mention of Auschwitz, are intended to force a bad conscience upon one's political opponents. Günter Grass and Walter Jens are the great masters at this game. At the same time, it provides the opportunity to highlight one's own words and deeds as a "good" German in contrast to the supposed neo-Nazis. The "good" German needs the Jews in order to enhance his image.

Even the Christian Democrat Michel Friedmann of the Frankfurt Jewish community found the actions of the Christian-Democratic-dominated government "outrageous." And despite the broad spectrum of support voiced throughout the country, Micha Guttmann, General Secretary of the Central Council of Jews in Germany, claimed "no one" had put in "a good word for the Soviet Jews." Guttmann's boss, Heinz Galinski, added that the decision on Soviet Jewish immigration would demonstrate whether or not the new Germany had learned the lessons of the past. It is a bit surprising that Galinski desired to bring his co-religionists into a Germany in which, as he steadily claimed, "not a day has passed since unification without attacks against Jews."

By equating the anti-Semitic rabble-rousing antics of fringe groups with the systematic murder of the Jews conducted by the National-Socialist state, Galinski placed today's democratic Germany on the same plane as Hitler's Third Reich. The accusation not only was devoid of reality, but also undermined Galinski's credibility. What is more, when the state of Baden-Wurtemberg suggested raising the immigration quota for Soviet Jews from 1,000 to 2,500, Galinski described the proposal as "selection" and drew a comparison with Auschwitz.

In the October 11, 1990, issue of the *taz*, a daily whose readers (chiefly from the Green and "alternative" scenes) can be counted among the best of the "good" Germans, a law professor from Darm-stadt recalled that "about 750,000 Jews" had lived in Germany in 1933 (the actual number was about 550,000 but we don't want to nitpick) and suggested that in order to reach this number again Germany ought to permit the immigration of 5,000 Soviet Jews per month over a period of ten years. "That is 60,000 per year and 600,000 in ten years." Just "as though" the Holocaust had not taken place. Lea Rosh, one of the country's most well-known journalists, juggled with a different figure but a similar thought: "A hundred thousand Jews from the Soviet Union in Germany? I cannot deny that I would greet that with joy."

■

Oddly, the Jewish State displayed no enthusiasm at this prospect. The explanation for this reaction is really quite simple: The Jewish State is struggling to survive. For years, Jewish immigration to Israel had been dropping, emigration from Israel rising, and the demographic balance between Jews and Palestinians shifting in favor of the latter. In addition, the Jewish population of Israel is becoming more "oriental," and that means, despite enormous efforts in the education sector, less modern and less educated. Israel's technological advantage over the Arab world is in danger of shrinking. From the military perspective, this represents a mortal threat to the Jewish State.

Since the fall of 1989 a stream of Soviet Jews has poured into Israel. Of these, 44 percent have completed occupational training, 22 percent are university graduates, 13 percent engineers, 4 percent technicians, and 5 percent highly skilled workers. For Israel, the Russian-Jewish refugees are a source of life. The country has virtually no other source of Jewish immigration.

The "invitation" by the Greens "to all Soviet Jews" (all two million?) to come to Germany is "not an unfriendly act" toward Israel, stated Green legislator Dietrich Wetzel before the Bundestag on October 25, 1990. Not unfriendly, true, but life-threatening nevertheless.

On October 31, even the usually circumspect SPD Bundestag member Willfried Penner argued that "Israel's immigration policy has nothing to do with Germany's willingness to permit immigration." The only legislators to even mention Israel's interests during the Bundestag debate over the immigration issue were Burkhard Hirsch of the FPD and Johannes Gerster of the CDU. But, of course, as members of the coalition parties, they are not to be counted among the "good" Germans.

■

There is no doubt that the Russian Jews are in dire need of help. The country's traditional anti-Semitism has resurfaced and already achieved a fearsome militancy. The Russian Jews leaving their homeland are not immigrants seeking economic betterment; they are refugees fleeing for their lives.

Before the fall of 1989 about 90 percent of Russian Jewish refugees fled to the United States, where they were sure of political asylum. They were aided by American Jewish organizations, despite the protests of the Israeli government. Like the SPD's Penner, the American Jews were "guided by consideration for the right of the Soviet Jews to self-determination."

Today, many Russian Jews want to immigrate to America, but cannot; they can go to Israel, but do not want to. Therefore, some go to Germany. In 1989–90 they were about three thousand in all. Most arrived during the final phase of the GDR in the spring and summer of 1990. In September the Interior Ministry imposed what amounted to a ban on further immigration. At least 40,000 applications for immigration remained in the German consulates in the successor states of the former Soviet Union. Unofficial estimates range as high as 100,000. It is impossible to even guess how many it would have been if Germany had been prepared to accept all applicants.

What needs to be resolved in the debate over the immigration of Russian Jews to Germany is not the issue of the past, but rather a dilemma of the present: the individual right of self-determination versus the collective security of the Jewish State.

The Israeli position is that the Jewish State was founded in order to provide asylum to Jews in need of a safe haven. Israel therefore feels it has the right to expect that the refugees at least give the Jewish State a chance. If they don't like it in Israel, they are then free to immigrate. It is a free country, after all.

■

The arguments and actions of the German Jews bore no small

resemblance to the reaction of American Jews toward the immigration issue. Their motivation was even more understandable, as the Jewish community in Germany was so tiny (less than 30,000 mostly elderly members) that it was in desperate need of new blood to survive.

Galinski, Guttmann (and the "good Germans") are right: Germany should not and must not become *judenrein*. In this they find themselves in agreement with such supposedly "bad" Germans as Johannes Gerster of the CDU and Burkhard Hirsch of the FDP, who argued that such a complicated issue required that "earnest and serious" discussions with the Central Council of Jews in Germany and the State of Israel be conducted in an atmosphere of mutual confidence. Hirsch was also right in pointing out that those who wield Auschwitz like a political cudgel dishonor the memory of the victims.

■

On January 9, 1991, just a few days before the outbreak of the Gulf War, the chief ministers of the sixteen German states faced the decision on immigration quotas. Since they had no desire to burn their fingers on a German-Jewish hot potato, it is not surprising that the German minister-presidents unanimously decided not to impose an annual quota on the immigration of Soviet Jews. Who could blame them for desiring to be to be counted among the "good" Germans? Together with Interior Minister Wolfgang Schäuble (CDU) the chief ministers tried to have it both ways. They declared that there would be no specific limit imposed on Jewish immigration from the states of the former Soviet Union, while Schäuble asserted that, out of consideration for the interests of Israel, unlimited immigration would not be permitted. Imposition of a non-quota as a form of restriction—a miracle of political geometry.

By firing off his accusation of "selection," Galinski offended a large number of Germans whose intentions with regard to German-Jewish reconciliation are serious, including the minister-presidents of the German states and Wolfgang Schäuble. What were they to do? It would be naive to expect them to have dared a political counteroffensive in the face of a certain bludgeoning with the Auschwitz cudgel. Naive, but a necessary expectation nevertheless. The chief executives of the German states need not and should not submit to such pressure tactics. Precisely because the Federal Republic of Germany is not and cannot be compared with the Third Reich, an objective discussion of the accusation should have taken place. Both the political and moral conditions were favorable, as not only Israel but also many Diaspora Jewish organizations were critical of Galinski's position and tactics.

The opportunity for an orderly, reasonable, and objective discussion of how Germany can best fulfill its responsibilities toward the Jews living within its borders and in the Jewish State was unfortunately lost. Auschwitz must not be misused as a political instrument.

What was the effect of the entire debate on German public opinion? When asked in an EMNID poll taken in December 1991 whether potential Jewish immigrants to Germany should be treated differently from other asylum-seekers, 91 percent of the respondents said "no."

9. The Rubble of the Gulf War: 1991

Can we compare the effect of the Gulf War on German-Israeli relations to the rubble viewed by German Foreign Minister Hans Dietrich Genscher in Ramat-Gan after a hit by an Iraqi SCUD rocket?

Despite the understandable arousal of emotions, the answer is clearly no. What was reduced to rubble was the facade of German-Israeli historical-political rhetoric, which had hitherto served as a convenient screen to hide behind. It became obvious that empty phrases could no longer be substituted for concrete policy.

The strategic dimension of German-Israeli and Jewish-Christian relations was once again not only visible but also palpable. The sensation was both new and historical. Before the process of secularization reduced the role of religion, Europeans and Germans, as Christians, could not be indifferent toward Jews. Because they were persecuted by the Christians and did not recognize Jesus as the Messiah, the Jews also could not be indifferent toward Christians. It is obvious that in the aftermath of the murder of millions of Jews during the Holocaust, Germans could not remain indifferent toward Jews or Israel.

Now and then, however, this fact is overlooked, particularly when the policy of "European political cooperation" is involved. Since 1971, the Federal Republic of Germany has occasionally and conveniently taken cover behind the European Community's efforts at achieving a coordinated Near East policy.

The Jewish Dimension of German Identity

The strategic dimension of German-Israeli and German-Jewish relations is the catastrophe of the Holocaust.

As the French Jewish philosopher André Glucksman correctly observed in connection with the debate over the historical legitimacy of German reunification, "Only fools view the German as a perpetual Nazi." No doubt, the younger generations of Germans were not born with eternal guilt. They bear none for the crimes of the National-Socialists of the earlier generation, but, as Germans, they must assume a certain liability. The issue of historical (not criminal, and not individual) responsibility is at the center of German identity. It is more than a question directed at Germans by the outside world; it is a question Germans must confront individually and collectively. Since the Holocaust, German existence has a permanent Jewish dimension.

Conversely, the trauma of persecution and the ur-trauma of the Catastrophe is central to the contemporary Israeli and Diaspora-Jewish identity. Therefore, without the Jewish there can be no German, without the German no Jewish identity. Germans and Jews remain bound to one another, more than ever since the Holocaust.

Public Opinion

In contrast to the formalized and often empty rituals of recollection, the Iraqi SCUD rockets and the threat of poison gas served as drastic reminders of the strategic dimension of German-Jewish-Israeli relations. Before the outbreak of the Gulf War, the German public appeared to have largely forgotten or repressed this central issue, and opinion polls in Israel had also indicated a greater relaxation in attitudes toward Germany.

Israel had, in fact, become very unpopular in Germany. By late 1990, the People's Republic of China ranked well above Israel in the estimation of the German public, as indicated by the results of an Infratest poll published by the Munich *Süddeutsche Zeitung* on January 4, 1991. Data gathered by other opinion research organizations also

document a decline in Israel's popularity in Germany since the outbreak of the intifada.

So it appeared until, on January 18, 1991, the first SCUD rocket hit
Israel. The danger loomed that Saddam Hussein might use chemical
weapons developed with German assistance against the Jewish State.
The EMNID Institute, which—apart from cyclical shifts—had registered a nearly steady decline Israel's popularity among the West German public since the late 1970s, measured a dramatic increase in sympathy for Israel in early February 1991.

This was more than mere sympathy for one of Saddam Hussein's
exchangeable victims. Once again it became clear that the strategic
dimension of German-Israeli relations could not be ignored or avoided. Saddam Hussein forced Bonn's hand. Although the vast majority
of the German public had come to regard the export of German
weapons technology with increasing outrage well before the outbreak
of the Gulf War, the German public responded with instant approval to
Bonn's decision in late January to supply weapons to the threatened
Jewish State. This reversal of opinion on an explosive political issue
would have been unthinkable had there not been more involved than
merely transient political considerations.

Since the early 1970s, Israelis had (again, apart from cyclical shifts)
come to view Germany in an increasing favorable light. Even with
regard to the issue of German unification, public opinion in Israel proved
much more open and positive than published opinion or the politicians
of the Jewish State. (For more data see my *Who's Afraid of Germany?*)

As in Germany, Saddam's rockets also produced a reversal of the
trend of public opinion in Israel, where the image of Germany turned
toward the negative. A poll conducted by the Israeli Dahaf Institute in
early February 1991, while Iraq was still attacking Israel with SCUDs,
revealed that Israelis were outraged over the inaction of the German
authorities with regard to the involvement of German firms in Saddam
Hussein's weapons production. At the same time Israel was increasingly popular among Germans, Israeli respondents ranked Germany
as the least popular country. It is, however, too early to draw long-term
conclusions from this disparity, as similar cyclical shifts have taken
place before.

Nearly half of the Israelis polled (49 percent) replied that their "negative image of Germany" had been confirmed. On the other hand, 32 percent agreed with the statement that "on the whole the Germans today are a good people." In a March 1991 PORI poll, 56 percent of the Israeli respondents said they believed in a new, good Germany, as compared to 62 percent a year before. This was the first drop since PORI first posed the question in 1982. The short-term trend is clear enough. It remains to be seen if the damage will prove permanent. In any case, despite their anger, two-thirds of the Israelis polled were in favor of maintaining proper relations with Germany.

The message would appear to be that Israelis were angry about German export policies, but did not view German intentions as deliberately murderous. The results are more indicative of basically rational rather than purely emotional attitudes. This remarkable message was all but lost in the political fracas.

The "Continuity" of German Gas, Or: Kohl, Another Hitler?

When discussing the issue of German unity, "good" German moralists repeatedly used the historical term *anschluss*, thus equating the results of the peaceful, democratic revolution in the German Democratic Republic with Hitler's annexation of Austria. Those German intellectuals, like the prominent author and cultural functionary Walter Jens, who constantly referred to Auschwitz and the Holocaust in connection with German unification, could ill afford to remain silent over Saddam Hussein's very real *anschluss* of Kuwait. Their silence was especially disturbing when one considers that Jens encouraged and sheltered American deserters in January 1991 at the same time the U.S. Air Force was attempting to knock out the Iraqi rocket-launchers that were attacking the Jewish State.

Authors and intellectuals, like Günter Grass, who seldom pass up the opportunity to shed rhetorical tears over the Jewish victims of Auschwitz, largely ignored the reports of the threat to Israel posed by the development (with German assistance) of Iraqi chemical weapons. By 1987 at the latest this was knowledge available to any informed newspaper reader.

If indeed "attack is the best defense," perhaps this was the reason why Grass, three weeks after the outbreak of the Gulf War, preferred to attack the German government for having permitted, for the second time in this century, Jewish lives to be threatened by German gas. Would it not have been proper to recall that Hitler had ordered the genocide of the Jews whereas the Kohl government was embarrassed and betrayed by the criminal activities of companies and private individuals? Grass should at least have been able to distinguish between active and passive involvement. Or did he deliberately intend to suggest that Kohl had the same murderous intentions as Hitler?

The institution exhibited little more moral mettle than its most prominent members. During the Gulf War the German Authors' Union published weak-kneed appeals for an end to the shooting.

The "noble souls" of the German peace movement (as Saddam Hussein described them) waxed indignant over the previous policy of supplying arms to Iraq and other countries of the region and roundly criticized the attempts on the part of the United States and the United Nations to contain and reverse the Iraqi aggression. Perhaps unwittingly, they thus only enhanced the Baghdad dictator's moral and political position, while undermining their own.

The high (or low) point was reached during the visit of a delegation of Greens to Israel. The spokesman for the executive committee of the Greens, Wolfgang Ströbele, informed his Israeli hosts that they had only themselves to blame for the Iraqi rocket attacks. Not only did Ströbele dig his own political grave, but also the entire German peace movement managed to disqualify itself morally and politically from the realm of German-Israeli and German-Jewish relations for the indefinite future.

The same is true for elements of the Evangelical Church in Germany and also for the German Roman Catholic Church, which echoed, albeit in somewhat more subdued tones, the criticisms of American policy voiced by Pope John Paul II without finding a similarly clear voice to condemn the original aggression by Saddam Hussein.

The Reeducation of the German Hun

The process of reeducation, at first imposed by the Allies, was continued by the Germans under their own volition in consequence of the horrifying experiences of the Second World War and the impact of the

Holocaust. The result was both a new Germany and new Germans. The image of the drum-thumping, saber-rattling, aggressive and murderous Hun has turned into that of a softy. These new Germans displayed little inclination toward military involvement in the Gulf crisis.

Among West Germany's teachers in the reeducation process after 1945 were not only Uncle Sam and his Western colleagues, but also Israel and the Jewish Diaspora. The East Germans were subjected to an "antifascist" brainwashing. The reeducation of the Germans achieved its goal, but suddenly the former teachers are no longer pleased with their pupil. Virtually overnight they have now come to expect a re-reeducation of the seemingly badly educated reeducated Germans. What we have here is a clear case of historical dis-synchrony, with the former "teachers" and "pupils" drawing contrary conclusions from the "lessons" of the past.

Ritual and Protest

Every new year in Germany presents occasions for the remembrance of the events of the Holocaust. This is quite properly so. In November 1988, for example, numerous commemorations recalled the *reichskristallnacht* of fifty years before. But despite all the ritual, or perhaps because of it, Jews as well as non-Jews, Germans as well as Israelis, have failed to recognize the links between the past and the present. In the spring and summer of 1988, for example, Saddam Hussein used poison gas against the Kurds and the Iranians. Any informed reader knew with whose assistance that gas had been produced. Demonstrations and protests? Only individual voices were raised, barely heard, and in any case unheeded. And in the spring of 1991, where were the massive protests and demonstrations against Saddam Hussein's renewed genocide of the Kurds? Those who had protested so loudly against the Americans in January and February were unmasked by their silence in March and April.

Not only Germany but also most of the rest of the world paid little attention to the mass-murder of the Kurds. In Israel, this indifference is read as a clear message: Little confidence can be placed in the expressions of solidarity and the good advice offered from outside, even by Israel's friends. Israel's hawks interpret this as a confirmation of their uncompromising policy toward the Palestinians. This is sure to lead to further irritations among politicians, publicists, and the public at large in Germany. The German-Israeli gap is all but certain to grow wider.

10. Political Biologism, Political Mechanics, and Anti-Germanism

Whether the political hue is black, red, green, or blue-and-yellow, German parties and their leaders articulate with greater or lesser skill and tact what, according to the polls, the majority of the public thinks, namely that the generations born after 1945 bear no guilt and cannot be held responsible for the National-Socialist crimes. (Some of the results of public opinion surveys are discussed in chapter 6.)

On May 8, 1985, German President Richard von Weizsäcker convincingly explained why guilt cannot be collective but only individual in nature. He is theoretically correct, and the distinction between collective and individual guilt is not only convincing but also honorable and desirable. This theory, however, remains purely academic in nature. Practically, and therefore politically, in the realm of foreign policy it is the state which acts as a collective, not the individual citizen, whether old or young, guilty or not-guilty.

Germany's Nazi past has long ceased to be a matter of history. It now represents a political instrument wielded, whenever it is deemed necessary, by non-Germans, Jews as well as non-Jews. The nature of this instrument has, in the meantime, become entirely divorced from the real Germany and real Germans, but for this very reason it remains so effective. And who is willing to voluntarily forswear the use of a proven, successful political instrument?

The instrument of *anti-Germanism* is as effective as anti-Judaism, which is also divorced from its object. Anti-Judaism, too, has little or nothing to do with real Jews and Judaism. Anti-Germanism draws upon, distorts, and exaggerates the Germany of today just as, in earlier times, the Jew was portrayed only as a caricature. For thousands of years, Jews have had to live with anti-Judaism. For better or worse, Germans will also have to learn to live with the omnipresence of anti-Germanism, and it will continue to generate difficulties, not just in the sphere of German policy toward Israel and the Middle East.

To overstate the case somewhat, we can draw an analogy between the history of the Jews and the future of the Germans in order to illustrate the *political mechanics* involved. For about two thousand years, the Jews were branded as the murderers of Christ. For centuries, the Germans will be unable to detach themselves from the stigma of the Holocaust. In neither case did the contemporaries bear collective guilt. In both cases, the following generations bore no guilt whatsoever, neither individual nor collective. Yet the stigma was and is passed on as an instrument and argument against past, present, and future generations. The world reacted in a manner akin to Pavlov's dogs: In the case of the Jews the conditioned reflex was: "Christ-killers"; in the case of the Germans it is, and will long remain: "Auschwitz." Collective historical memory apparently cannot do without distorting generalizations and collective guilt.

We call this passing on of historical memories from one generation to the next *political mechanics*. We have briefly sketched the political mechanics of anti-Semitism and anti-Germanism. It is understandable that Germans, particularly those born after 1945, react to the political mechanics of collective national guilt with increasing irritation, and can be expected to find even more cause for irritation in the future. It is understandable, because these Germans do not bear any individual guilt for the past. It is also understandable because serious and honest efforts have been and continue to be undertaken to build and maintain an anti-fascist Germany. Moreover, it is understandable that, in view of the biological change of generations, anti-Germanism, like anti-Semitism, in the final analysis creates a sort of political biology.

This "political biology" categorizes people—for all time—according to their national and religious heritage rather than their individual qualities and behavior. What is worse, there are only two basic categories: the forces of light and of darkness. This represents a radical violation of the traditions of the enlightenment, which sought to free individuals from the shackles of their birth.

From 1933 to 1945, Nazi Germany enshrined political biology as part of its sacred ideology. Now, the instrument is deployed against the new, democratic Germany—another irony of history. It is as outrageous to automatically assign Germans born after 1945 to the forces of evil as it is to do so with their Jewish, Israeli, or other contemporaries.

If, on the one hand, Israel, Jews, and others view the Germans from the perspective of the German past, and, on the other hand, the Germans view themselves from the perspective of the present and the future, then we can speak of dis-synchronism. In other words: both sides live in the contemporary world, but think in differing time-frames. The collective identity of the Germans born since 1945 is oriented to the here-and-now, whereas the collective orientation of contemporary Jews is toward the past. One may criticize this, but whoever wants to see changes made in the future ought to be cognizant of the facts of the present situation.

This theoretical description of dis-synchronistic perspectives has potentially explosive political implications. With each new generation, the dissonance between Germany and Israel, Germany and the Jews, Germany and the outside world, is likely to grow in intensity. On the political-historical plane, the subsequent generations of Germans and non-Germans, Germans and Jews are moving ever farther apart.

The political mechanics and political biology of anti-Germanism will make Germany's future historical-political relations with the outside world, and with Israel and the Diaspora Jews in particular, more rather than less difficult.

The image of Germans, including the new generations, is negatively influenced by the Holocaust. Jewish identity, and to a lesser extent, Israeli identity is decisively shaped by the Holocaust, even, and especially, among Jews belonging to the subsequent generations. In a largely a-religious world, Judaism as a religion no longer serves as the wellspring of identity for the majority of Jews. History, the story of the sufferings of the Jewish people, particularly the Holocaust, is now the chief determinant of Jewish identity. An identity de-Judaized from the religious point of view is re-Judaized by recourse to history, thus binding Jewish identity to the Holocaust. This, in turn, requires a Germany stigmatized by the Holocaust. Even if we ignore both the political biology and political mechanics of anti-Germanism, we see that the Jews are as bound to Germany as Germany is to the Jews. In the chapters on the function of the Holocaust in Israel and on Germany's Jews we will examine this phenomenon in the context of the Israeli and Diaspora-Jewish perspectives.

Some on the one side, mainly latter-generation Germans, want to break out of these unavoidable links. The other, Jewish side cannot allow the Germans to escape this historical bind without endangering their own Jewish identity. The process of making the Holocaust the dominant, or even the exclusive symbol of Jewish identity, warns German historian Christian Meier, is threatening to open up another gap, namely between the descendants of the perpetrators and the descendants of the victims.

11. *Comparative* Geschichtspolitik: *The Austrian Connection*

For many years, Austria was apparently in a position to practice the art of *geschichtspolitik* under skies unclouded by the National-Socialist past. However, in 1986 this era ended with the election of Kurt Waldheim as Austria's president. In contrast to the West Germans, Austrians seemed to be far less encumbered by the political burden of the Nazi era. The Austrian position was made considerably easier by the moral support rendered by the Allies during the Second World War. In the Moscow Declaration of November 1, 1943, the Soviet Union, the United States, and Great Britain stated that the *anschluss*, Austria's annexation by Nazi Germany in March 1938, had been forced upon the country and was thus "null and void." Austria was declared to be the "first free nation" that had fallen "victim" to Nazi aggression.

In September 1952, Israel made it even easier for the Austrians by giving a similar interpretation to Austria's Great-German past. In the political climate of the Cold War, East and West also became rivals in ignoring the historical blemishes in the pristine image of the alpine republic, and successive Austrian governments saw no particular need to wake a sleeping beast.

When it came to the politics of history, the conservative Austrian People's Party (ÖVP) and the Socialists (SPÖ) formed a permanent, if informal, grand coalition. Both steadfastly resisted any and all pressures to make concessions to Israel or the Diaspora Jewish organizations. The ÖVP turned a deaf ear to the insistent whisperings of its West German counterpart, the CDU, and the SPÖ was equally unheeding of the promptings of the French socialists and the British Labour Party. In 1954, Erich Ollenhauer, chairman of the West German SPD, tried to convince Austrian SPÖ leader Bruno Kreisky to come out in favor of indemnification for the Jews. For a time it appeared that Kreisky intended to do so, but the way was soon blocked by an SPÖ declaration that, should indemnification be granted to Jews for the crimes perpetrated against them by the National-Socialist regime, the Socialists would demand equal treatment, as they, too, represented a group that had been systematically persecuted during the Nazi period on the basis of their political affiliation.

The well-publicized accusations of "anti-Semitic" behavior emanating from Israel in the 1970s because of the Kreisky government's Middle East policy were not the first. We shall not concern ourselves here with the validity of the use of the term "anti-Semitic." In any case, the charge was repeatedly leveled against the Austrian Socialists in the early 1950s by Israeli politicians and diplomats. As early as February 1954, Kreisky, who was of Jewish extraction himself, demanded of an Israeli diplomat what sense there was in applying the label of "anti-Semitism" to the SPÖ, a party in which Austrian Jews held numerous leadership positions far in excess of the proportion of Jewish SPÖ voters. Kreisky's criticism of Israel had its own tradition and was based on conviction, not—as was loudly claimed in the 1970s—on the flow of Arab money to Austria.

In West Germany, the term *wiedergutmachung* (literally: "to make good again," a term implying a moral obligation and usually translated as "restitution" or "indemnification") was applied to the payments made under and subsequent to the Luxembourg Agreement. By contrast, Austria applied the term *entschädigung* (compensation for damages) to the fund established in September of 1955 to aid victims of Nazism residing outside of Austria. The sum provided for this fund, 550 million Austrian schillings, amounted to about 2 percent of the amount provided by West Germany and represented far less than the Austrian proportion of the population in Hitler's "Great-German Reich." In addition to this fund, Vienna also provided five million schillings in compensation for damages to synagogues and for lost religious objects.

To put it in a simple formula: the Austrian government chose to tackle the problem from a legalistic standpoint, whereas the West German approach was guided by moral, political, and educational considerations.

The perspective of the Vienna government can best be seen in the guidelines laid down in 1953 for all of the ministries involved in the indemnification issue. The document states that, for Austria, *wiedergutmachung* or "restitution" was out of the question: "Only the German Reich, i.e., its legal successor, bears the responsibility for restitution, as it ordered the persecution of the Jews. Austria was at this time occupied and incapable of action in the sense of international law."

The guidelines state further: "The payment of any sort of restitution (*wiedergutmachung*) is out of the question because Austria did not harm anyone and is thus not obliged to make restitution. . . . If Austrian citizens took part in inflicting such damage [characteristically there is no mention of murder, M. W.], they did so not as Austrian citizens but rather either on their own or on behalf of those then in power."

Vienna categorically rejected all moral and historical-political arguments and even attempted to turn the tables. In a meeting with representatives of Jewish organizations in June 1953, an official of the Austrian Finance Ministry emphasized that the National-Socialists did not persecute just the Jews alone, as "a certain propaganda would have us believe."

In a report on that meeting, Finance Minister Kamitz, who was not a member of, but nevertheless closely affiliated with the ÖVP, argued that the Austrian constitution precluded the enactment of any law for individual groups. Jews, the Finance Minister claimed, should be treated like all other victims of the war. In other words: If not *only* the Jews, but *also* Jews were victims of Nazi terror, their fate therefore having been no different from that of other victims, it was not possible, for the sake of the Jews alone, to enact compensatory legislation different from that applicable to the other victims.

Vienna soon broadened its counteroffensive, criticizing the Jewish organizations for becoming a "monopoly" in representing the victims of Nazism. Similar criticism by the Catholic church was also cited. In addition, it was claimed, the numbers put forth by the Jewish representatives included "double counting." In plain language: the Jews were attempting to enrich themselves by dishonest means.

Austria also reinforced its moral defenses against possible charges by non-Jews in other countries. In early 1938, "trusting in its membership in the League of Nations," Austria had called upon the great powers to extend their "protection and assistance." Not only had this appeal passed "unheard," but the diplomatic representatives of the other powers had promptly and formally withdrawn following the German occupation.

By the mid-1980s, Austria appeared to have become overconfident in its belief that the Austrian past as part of the "Great-German Reich" no longer bothered or interested anyone in the present. That proved to be a political miscalculation of the first order. In contrast to East Germany, Austrians failed to realize that, in the face of the controversies raging in the West-German–American–Israeli–Jewish *geschichtspolitik* of the mid-1980s, their nonchalance with regard to their nation's past was tantamount to rattling the skeletons in the national closet. With the election of Kurt Waldheim to the Austrian presidency in 1986, the alpine republic broke through the historical-political ice that had, until then, proven amazingly solid.

3

GERMAN-ISRAELI

GESCHICHTSPOLITIK

The Political Function of the Holocaust

The observation that history is a powerful force with political functions in the present does not in any way detract from the monstrous character of the Holocaust, which in Israel is called the *Shoa*, the Catastrophe. The object of dealing with the political function of the Holocaust here is not to ritually reemphasize its self-evident catastrophic nature, but rather to analyze its meaning in and effect on the present.

1. The Holocaust as Filter

The Jewish-Israeli fixation on the Holocaust is by no means limited to Germany and German-Jewish or German-Israeli relations. It is also linked with the history of Jewish sufferings through the whole of Jewish history. The contemporary fixation on the Holocaust is not focused solely on the crimes of the Nazis. The view also encompasses those who did little or nothing to prevent the sufferings. It includes Great Britain, which shut the doors of Palestine against refugees fleeing the National-Socialist regime. It also includes the Allies of the Second World War who, despite numerous appeals from the Jewish Agency, consistently refused to take measures such as bombing the approaches to Auschwitz, even though they were aware of what was taking place there.

The Holocaust fixation, however, serves not only as a filter applied to Jewish historical experience but also as a *political argument*. Many Israelis and many Jews compare the PLO, for example, with the Nazis. In 1956, and again in 1967, it was argued that Nasser was aiming to perpetrate a new Holocaust. The power of the past to influence the present thus derives additional force from the impact of current events.

What is more, the *sabras* (i.e., the Israelis born in Israel) and the sons and daughters of those who experienced the Holocaust, were forced, first in Palestine, then later in the State of Israel, to learn what it means to fight for one's very existence. In 1929, Jews were massacred in various parts of Palestine, particularly in Hebron. The Arab Revolt of 1936–39 cost numerous Jewish lives. The struggle from 1944 to 1947 against the British mandate exacted a further price in blood. In the 1948–49 War of Independence the new State of Israel lost one percent of its population. There then followed the sacrifices of the Sinai Campaign of 1956, the Six Day War of 1967, the 1969–70 War of Attrition across the Suez Canal as well as the frequent skirmishes with Palestinian guerrillas, the Yom Kippur War of 1973, the 1982 War in Lebanon against the PLO, and the rocket attacks on Israel in the 1991 Gulf War. Although we cannot describe these events as Holocausts— and the issue of responsibility is debatable—they all served to reinforce the ages-old Jewish-Israeli perception that Jews continue to be persecuted by other peoples simply because they are Jews.

Political circumstances and political symbols heighten the Holocaust fixation. Outside observers sometimes find this impossible to understand. When, for example, PLO leader Arafat spoke before the UN General Assembly on November 13, 1974, and when on November 10, 1975 (on the anniversary of the Nazi *reichskristallnacht* of November 9–10, 1938) that same assembly passed a resolution equating Zionism with racism, painful political and symbolic memories were stirred in Israel, and were employed as political arguments.

Of course, the more often the Holocaust is used as an argument, the less its validity. Inflationary use leads to a loss in value. In September of 1991 the Bush administration put the Israeli government under considerable political pressure. In an attempt to slip out from under this pressure, Prime Minister Shamir argued that a continuation of the American policies would subject Israel to another "Holocaust." As the prominent Israeli journalist Dan Margalit put it in the September 17, 1991, issue of *Haaretz*, Shamir "used the Holocaust" like a "political atomic bomb."

The Holocaust has also been used thoughtlessly and heedlessly, even and particularly against Israel and Jews. At the height of the Israeli campaign against the PLO in Lebanon in 1982 at least one German newspaper trumpeted that Israel's behavior toward the Palestinians was comparable with the Holocaust. The actions of the Israeli military in the occupied territories have frequently been described as "fascist" or "worse than the National-Socialist atrocities." This was also the interpretation expounded by Egyptian newspapers following the outbreak of the intifada in December of 1987.

A derivative of the Holocaust fixation is the perception of isolation, which is also a result of Israel's geopolitical situation. Until the conclusion of the Israeli-Egyptian peace treaty (March 26, 1979), Israel's neighbors were, without exception, Israel's enemies. Its friends were few and far away. On the eve of the Six Day War in 1967, the Israeli public felt a sense of isolation akin to the period of the Holocaust, when no one in the outside world came to their help, even though the plight of the Jews was obvious to all who would see. Although the United Nations and the United States had given guarantees of free navigation in the Straits of Tiran following the 1956 Sinai Campaign, Nasser blockaded this vital waterway to Israeli shipping in 1967 and nothing happened. Arab armies mobilized on Israel's borders and nothing happened. Whether one approves of Israel's preventive strike in 1967 or not, Israel's Holocaust fixation and its sense of isolation provided significant, if not the decisive, political-psychological motives.

The November 6, 1973, declaration of the EC foreign ministers on the Middle East, issued just after the end of the Yom Kippur War, also brought out similar feelings in Israel. As long as the Arab states had not made use of their oil weapon, the European Community was virtually invisible as an active force in the Middle East. The initially successful surprise Arab attack had renewed Holocaust fears in the Jewish State. The EC declaration only added to Israel's sense of political isolation and rejection.

During the Gulf War, Israel lived under the potential threat of Iraqi use of chemical weapons. As early as 1984, Israelis were aware that German companies were helping Iraq to produce such weapons. Not only Israelis and Jews, but also many Germans (for example the author Günter Grass) saw a connection between the poison gas of the Holocaust and the threat against Israel in the Gulf War. Although the negligence of the German authorities was inexplicable and inexcusable, the Kohl government cannot be justly accused of planning or abetting the murder of Jews.

One indication of Israeli perceptions and reactions is to be found in the lyrics of a song that stayed at the top of the Israeli hit parade for an unusually long time in 1969: "The whole world is against us. But that is no matter, we will make it, for it has always been this way, and our forefathers also sang this song." The Holocaust and the sense of isolation have given rise to a feeling in Israel that the historically rooted social isolation of the Jews, their ghetto existence within various national political systems, is comparable to the present-day political isolation of the Jewish State in the international system: Israel as a modern-day ghetto of the contemporary international community.

It is, once again, not our aim here to test the objective validity of this perception. What we cannot ignore, however, is the significance and effect of this subjective, collective, historically conditioned filter on Jewish and Israeli perceptions. The belief that a continuity of the Jewish situation persists from the past to the present is a factor which must be taken into consideration, independent of whether or not it is valid objectively.

2. The Holocaust as Secular Religion and Focus of Jewish Identity

Every state has its symbols, rituals, myths, and articles of secular faith. These serve to legitimize the prevailing political, social, economic, and cultural order and can be described as secular state religion. The focal points of state religion serve as secular shrines. Like all religions, state religion relies not only on the forces of reason, but also draws on emotions, not least of all through its shrines.

The most important secular shrine in Israel is the Yad Vashem Memorial in Jerusalem. Its status did not, however, prevent its very existence from being called into question in 1987–88 when its funding threatened to evaporate in the face of massive budget cuts. The sacred character of this memorial and documentation center is second only to that of the so-called "Wailing Wall" in the old city of Jerusalem. It ought to be noted that the secular-religious significance of this section of the wall of the Second Temple stands in contradiction to traditional Jewish religious understanding, which does not recognize any shrine other than the Holiest of Holies of the former temple. This, too, is an indication of the religious emptying of Judaism as a result of its historization.

Whether in Israel, the United States, or elsewhere, Holocaust memorials are really highly un-Jewish. The creation of such images is a violation of the prohibition in the first commandment. Put even more sharply, Holocaust memorials are an indication of the de-Judafication of the Jewish people.

In Israel, the symbolic-sacred character of the Holocaust becomes most dramatically evident on the annual Day of the *Shoa*, which is commemorated exactly one week before Independence Day. Holocaust and independence, destruction and secular resurrection are brought into close connection. The most impressive ceremonial of this day involves the sounding of sirens for two minutes throughout the land, during which time all traffic comes to a stop and Israelis everywhere in the country rise to stand in silence. This otherwise loud country falls into a profound silence in commemoration of the victims of the Holocaust.

The Holocaust summarizes and symbolizes the entirety of the sufferings of the long and often sorrowful history of the Jewish people. It has become the abbreviation for Jewish history. In the process, a development took place which can been regarded as typical of all groups that have dissolved the bonds with their religious traditions in the course of an increasing secularization. Suffering, which was perceived as divinely ordained in an era dominated by religion, has come to be viewed as the product of secular history, as the work of man rather than of God.

The certainly anything but harmless persecution of the children of Israel under the pharaohs of Egypt in Biblical times was, for millenniums, understood as a divinely inflicted period of suffering, which was followed by the revelation in the Sinai and the conquest of the "Land of the Fathers," all of which was also regarded as God's will. The temporary victories of the Philistines, Ammonites, Amalekites, Edomites, and Moabites were interpreted as "divine retribution" for the "sins of Israel." So, too, the conquest of the kingdom of Israel by the Assyrians in 721 B.C., the destruction of the First Temple by the Babylonians (586 B.C.) and of the Second Temple by the Romans (70 A.D.) as well as the later persecutions in the Diaspora were all viewed as God's retribution.

This tradition was broken as a result of the secularization of the Jews, and, in further consequence of this process, by the rise of secular Zionism. According to the new, Zionist worldview, the persecution of Jews was the work of the non-Jewish environment and could be prevented only by Jewish political activism in the here and now, for example by the creation of a Jewish state.

Zionists, Israel, and the secularized majority of Diaspora Jews do not, of course, interpret the Holocaust as a manifestation of God's wrath, but as Hitler's work. A tiny Orthodox-Jewish minority, however, apparently took the opposite view. According to reliable sources, a Hungarian rabbi regarded his imminent death in the gas chambers of Auschwitz as divine retribution for his having failed to combat the blasphemy of Zionism more energetically, a logically coherent interpretation within its religious context, even though it is barely comprehensible today.

In the last several years Rabbi Schach (who has served as the spiritual force behind several Orthodox political parties in Israel) has offered a number of variations on the theme of the Holocaust as God's punishment for the godlessness of the Jews. An essay by Dina Portah in the April 12, 1991 issue of *Haaretz* offers revealing insights into these phenomena.

As Judaism both inside and outside Israel became progressively

devoid of religious content and the basis of Jewish identity simultane-
ously shifted from the Jewish religion to Jewish history and the Jewish
State, Israelis and Diaspora Jews began to concern themselves more
with the survival of the Jews than with the survival of Judaism. The
Holocaust fixation serves as an indicator for the religious de-Judifica-
tion of Judaism and the Jews, and the particular Holocaust fixation on
Germany represents a break with the religious traditions of Judaism.
The emphasis on the unique character of the Holocaust, which was
mentioned in the first chapter, breaks the continuous chain of sufferings of the generations and demolishes the religiously determined
Jewish view of history, in which the sufferings of one generation have
no more and no less weight than the sufferings of other, earlier generations.

The de-Judafication of Judaism is a result of the loss of religious
content. The historization of Jewish suffering means that Jewish history and Israel, that is the present-day Jewish situation rather than the
Jewish religion, form the focus and definition of Jewish identity. Israel
and Jews require the Holocaust as a general and Germany as a special
symbol. They are bound to Germany for the purpose of preserving a
Jewish identity that is no longer defined by positive self-determination
and reflection but by a negative determination from outside, by anti-
Semitism. Anti-Germanism is regarded as a necessary instrument, as
well as, at least periodically, Holocaust trials such as those of Adolf
Eichmann and John Demjanuk. But what will happen once all the
greater and lesser executioners and their assistants are dead? Perhaps
then there will be no other choice but to return to the positive, Jewish
contents that Israel and Jewish culture offer in abundance? Hopefully
this will be the case. This will be more difficult, but also more reward-
ing. Or it will end in total assimilation and de-Judafication.

Israel's founding father, David Ben-Gurion, had a solid grasp of the
real and the possible. He often warned of the dangers and attempted to
provide a counter-example. Ben-Gurion propagated a non-orthodox,
but nevertheless fundamentally Jewish, prophetical sense of history.
He envisioned a Jewish identity that would be self- rather than Holo-
caust-determined. This approach was clearly and positively manifested
in his policy toward Germany. But the realistic as well as visionary Ben-
Gurion was followed by party functionaries, careerists, and ideologues.

For many Germans, the anti-German political mechanics just described represent a painful aggravation; for Jews and Israelis they are a danger. The exclusive preoccupation with Jewish history can lead to a blindness toward the rest of Judaism, which is not solely determined by the current situation of the Jews but also, and above all, by the Jewish religion. This unpleasant truth can and ought not to burden Jews and Israel, nor can or should it unburden Germans. The object here is to analyze the present Jewish-Israeli understanding of history in its historical context, to recognize the break in traditions, and to point out possible consequences.

Identification with the Holocaust, as polls of adults and youth in Israel have repeatedly shown, strengthens the sense of Jewish identity. To be more precise, the Holocaust, more than any other factor, determines the Jewish sense of community among Israelis, most especially among the young. Nearly two-thirds of the Israeli high-school students interviewed in a 1968 survey agreed with the statement that every Jew is or ought to feel that he is a survivor of the Holocaust. The formulation was similar to what, in the Jewish religious tradition, was reserved exclusively for the identification with the trials of the children of Israel in Egypt and their subsequent exodus. Through the annual reading of the Passover Haggadah, the religious Jew associates himself with this traditional story of suffering and salvation. Today, however, the Holocaust carries this function of identification, which it achieves with greater effectiveness, even and particularly among the more religious in Israel. In the last several decades, the thinking of religious Jews, who were firmly anti-nationalist in the early days of Zionism, has undergone a radical about-face. Many of these same Jews are now to be found among the more extreme proponents of Israeli nationalism. In the last ten years this development has driven many religious traditionalists in Israel into the arms of the religiously extreme but nationalistically moderate parties. Nonreligious Israelis have turned to the Orthodox because they view religious renewal as the only legitimation for their return to the Promised Land and as the only hope for a general Jewish renewal. A return to the old on the way to the new?

The so-called "ethnic" division between Israelis of Euro-American and Afro-Asian heritage has blurred. This was demonstrated by numerous public opinion samplings between 1968 and 1983. In 1983, in fact, Afro-Asian Israelis were somewhat more likely to identify with the Holocaust than their Euro-American contemporaries. The tendency to identify with the Holocaust is least pronounced among the *sabras*. Recent polls have confirmed these earlier findings. Apparently there is a gap between the rituals of the politicians and the feelings of Israeli youth.

■

On the whole, the Holocaust has proven to be an effective political-educational instrument. This certainly played a role in the decision to introduce an expanded program on the Holocaust in the history curriculum for Israel's schoolchildren in 1982. No other historical-political-ideological theme is covered as extensively as the *Shoa*, as a survey of Israeli students showed in early 1987. Not even the history of Zionism receives as much attention in Israel's schools, not to mention such themes as "democracy" or Israeli-Jewish-Arab relations. Students in the state religious schools learn even more about the Holocaust than their colleagues in the nonreligious institutions.

This trend is not to be seen as evidence contradicting the theory that the process of its historization is rendering Judaism devoid of content. To the contrary, like the National Religious Party, Israel's religious school system emphasizes nationalism as much as it does religion. Over the long term, this is driving religious but non-nationalistic Israelis into the extreme Orthodox camp.

The theory that historization is working to the detriment of religious content is also supported by the results of a survey conducted in the autumn of 1986. The aim was to assess the importance Israeli high-school students attached to various school subjects. The results showed that 92 percent considered "Israeli history" to be "extremely important," 89 percent mentioned "Jewish history," 84 percent the "natural sciences," 82 percent "world history," 61 percent "English literature," and only 51 percent mentioned instruction in the most important collection of Jewish religious precepts and commentaries, the Talmud. Apparently, Israeli students consider the study of English literature more important than the Talmud. The issue is certainly one that could be hotly debated, but the poll results offer a clear indication of how far the fixation on Jewish and Israeli history has contributed to the de-Judafication of Judaism.

A further result is that Israel, and the Jews of the Diaspora, are increasingly becoming a "people" just like any other, with their unique identity based on the peculiarities of their history rather than on Jewish tradition. Again, the necessity or desirability of this development can be debated, but not the fact that this convergence between Jews and non-Jews stands in contradiction to traditional Jewish consciousness. The "chosen people," the "people of the book" were not called to be just like others, but instead to proclaim a vision and to act as a beacon to other peoples.

If the Jews and Israel become a people just like any other, then two developments will necessarily follow: First, the Jewish Diaspora will lose its Jewish substance and assimilate into its surroundings. Second, Israel will lose its power to attract Diaspora Jews. If, as is to be fervently hoped, the persecution and murder of Jews definitely becomes a thing of the past, the Jewish State will no longer offer the attraction of the safe haven. In view of the country's long-term economic difficulties and their effect on material living standards, the military dangers so dramatically illustrated by the Iraqi missile attacks during the Gulf War and the loss of traditional Jewish substance, Israel will no longer represent a goal for immigration from the Jewish Diaspora.

What is more, Israel's attraction for Jews from Europe or America has considerably diminished, not only because of the social process of "orientalization," the increasing influence of Israelis of Afro-Asian backgrounds, but also, and especially, because Jewish substance in Israel is to be found only among the extreme Orthodox. Since there is hardly a middle ground to chose from in Israel, Euro-American Jews remain in the Diaspora.

Israelism, a form of nationalism devoid of Jewish-religious content and based exclusively on the achievements of the state of Israel, does not provide a way out of the dilemma. Israelism is a continuation of Zionism in the secularized era of the nation-state which substitutes for God the idols of the nation and nation-state. With a historically very understandable longing for salvation intensified by the sufferings of the Holocaust, a large part of secularized Jewry, "accompanied by messianic overtones" chose the "utopian retreat to Zion" (Gershom Sholem). The messianic overtones of Zionism show that Israeli nationalism could not and cannot be a nationalism like any other, for that would amount to a form of self-demolition.

Yet Israelism is much like the nationalism of other states and thus makes Israel a country "just like the others." This would not present a problem to a secularly oriented state, but Israel must offer its inhabitants and potential immigrants more because it demands more of them just to secure its survival. If the State of Israel becomes a consumer society just like any other, if Israel imposes heavy sacrifices but offers no special rewards, the willingness of Diaspora Jews to immigrate will decline even further—and the desire of Israeli Jews to emigrate will rise. Only idealists—and those who have no other choice—choose to stay on and continue to shoulder the burden of special sacrifices and risks.

In Europe and in the United States, Israelis can readily find consumer societies where life is both easier and less dangerous. With the help of their countrymen who have gone before they generally find it easy to assimilate. The number of ex-Israelis with their permanent residence in the United States is estimated to be between 300,000 and 500,000. These numbers represent one of the unavoidable results of the processes of historization and secularization. The alternative would seem to be a sort of religious fundamentalism, which we find not only among Muslims in Iran and elsewhere, but also among the Orthodox in Israel. For those in positions of leadership in Israel and the Diaspora, this is akin to a choice between the devil and the deep blue sea.

The historization of Judaism entails a further far-reaching consequence: It ultimately undermines the legitimacy of the Jewish State. To the extent that "the people of the book" no longer cleave to the Bible, they also lose their claim to the land of the Bible. The Jewish claim is rendered historical and, like all things historical, it becomes relative rather than absolute. This is one reason for the increasing criticism of the Jewish State by many Israelis demanding more Jewish substance rather than more Jewish land. But they, too, have been unable to arrive at an acceptable middle ground between fundamentalist orthodoxy and total secularization. In any case, the people of Israel cannot be accused of making it easy for themselves.

3. The Holocaust as Legitimization

That most Jews allowed themselves to be led off like the proverbial lamb to the slaughter of the Holocaust was frequently cited in the 1950s as an admonitory example by opinion- and decision-makers in Israel. In the proud, young state just learning to flex its muscles, the historical example considered worthy of emulation was that of the Zealot rebellion against the yoke of imperial Rome. The image of the Jewish defender, not the defenseless Jew, provided an object of identification and at the same time a justification for a Zionist state capable of defending itself.

In the period leading up to the Six Day War of 1967 the apathy and inaction of the rest of the world convinced many Israelis that, like the Diaspora Jews of a generation before, the Jewish State was being abandoned by the world. A somber nation interpreted this experience as a continuation of Jewish history. Anti-Semitism, or what appeared as such, legitimized a refocusing of attention onto the Jewish collective, which, to all appearances, had only itself and its state to rely upon. Such were the conclusions drawn in Israel. No Zionism without anti-Semitism—a familiar pattern in the history of the Jewish national movement.

The role of the Holocaust as a source of legitimation for Zionism was documented by a poll conducted in 1979. After having viewed the *Holocaust* series on television, 68 percent of the younger Israelis and 55 percent of the adults interviewed agreed that the series made "the meaning of Zionism and the State of Israel clearer than before." Later polls produced similar results.

Mostly it was Oriental Israelis, but also the young and the less educated, who agreed that they had understood the stated connections better as a result of viewing the television series. Once again, we recognize the instrumental and argumentative value of the Holocaust. We of course also observe that Israelis of Oriental background exhibit less of a Holocaust fixation than their Euro-American countrymen. This is historically understandable, as the Holocaust took place in Europe. But it is also often overlooked or forgotten that the German Wehrmacht was present in North Africa from February 1941 to November 1942. The extermination camps were also intended for the Oriental

Jews. What is more, Amin el-Husseini and the Palestinian National Movement had offered the Germans their assistance in carrying out an *endlösung* in the Middle East. UN war crimes documents released in 1991 furnished further proof of this connection.

4. The Holocaust as an Integrator

There is yet another dimension to the Holocaust. In Israel it also serves as an instrument for the social integration of groups otherwise not directly affected, namely the underprivileged Oriental Israelis. Although they formed a demographic majority (at least until the arrival of about half a million Russian Jews since late 1989), in terms of social, political, and economic power, and also with regard to the formation of the norms and values of the Jewish State, the Israelis of Afro-Asian descent still remain a fringe group.

The intense treatment of the Holocaust in school and society serves to inculcate the norms of the fathers and grandfathers among the following generations, the *sabras*. The Holocaust thus serves as a means of integrating both social fringe groups and generations. In addition, a Holocaust of Oriental Jews was not only planned but actually on the verge of being put into operation at the time the Wehrmacht was defeated in North Africa, which forms a historical bridge between Euro-American and Afro-Asian Jews.

5. The Economic Benefit of the Holocaust as a Boomerang

"When cash rings in German registers, the Israelis and the Jews are quickly on the scene." Such statements can still be heard in Germany, and, every now and then, there are even parliamentarians who misunderstand their representative function and serve as mouthpieces for such opinions. With their aggressive prejudices, they are all too ready to overlook a basic fact, namely that the acceptance of German money was—and remains—anything but uncontroversial, both among Diaspora Jews and in Israel. Before it was even possible to begin negotiations with the Germans, the Israeli government had to overcome vehement domestic resistance. The acceptance of restitution payments from Germany represented the first hesitant signal of reconciliation across the historical abyss. Measured against the horrors that had gone before, this hesitant signal was like a bright torch. The man who lit it was Israel's first prime minister, David Ben-Gurion.

Neither Israel nor the Diaspora ever disputed the economic benefit of the German restitution payments (a total of roughly 110 billion German marks or about 70 billion dollars by late 1991) in building up the Jewish State or in providing individual survivors of the Holocaust with a decent level of material existence. Nevertheless, in the turbulent Knesset debate in early 1952 over whether or not to negotiate with Germany, Menachem Begin was not alone in describing material restitution from West Germany as "blood money," which should not be permitted to stain the hands of the Jewish people. To accept such blood money, as many Israelis and Diaspora Jews argued and still argue, is to profane the victims of the Holocaust, trade their blood for silver, and render the millions of murdered Jews into an object of political horse-trading.

Even if we do not agree with these objections, it must be conceded that a number of these apprehensions proved accurate. The 1952 negotiations between Israel and Germany displayed many of the attributes of a financial and political haggle over human wares. A source of particular embarrassment was the accounting basis for Israel's claims, which were for the costs incurred by the Jewish State in absorbing the refugees from the Nazi-ruled areas of Europe. The entire Bonn delegation, including such well-disposed representatives as delegation chief Franz Böhm and his deputy, Otto Küster, agreed that the Israeli numbers were too high. An expert from the West German ministry responsible for the integration of refugees was called in. He compared the reported costs in Israel with those incurred by West Germany in absorbing the expellees from that nation's former eastern territories and found that Jewish refugees were more expensive than German refugees. The Bonn reaction was to put a significantly lower counter-offer on the negotiating table. There were numerous other examples of how human sufferings were turned into the object of financial calculation in the process of carrying out restitution.

The willingness to negotiate with the Federal Republic of Germany on a subject that was really non-negotiable considerably restricted the political maneuverability of Israel and the Diaspora-Jewish organizations involved. As soon as negotiations were entered upon and certain results achieved, one became subject to pressures, as any misstep could jeopardize what had already been achieved.

In addition there was the danger of losing ideological credibility. What should apply to Germany? *Tagespolitik*, i.e. the political requirements of the day? Or *geschichtspolitik*, fundamental principles and credibility? In terms of *geschichtspolitik*, the economic benefit of the Holocaust proved to be a boomerang.

6. The "Land of the Murderers" in the Mirror of Public Opinion

In the 1970s and 1980s a number of polls were carried out in Israel on the topic "Germany and the Holocaust," several of which were repeated several years later with identical questions. In interpreting the results of these surveys, we need to make a distinction between fundamental issues (issues having to do with *geschichtspolitik*) and opinions with regard to day-to-day politics (*tagespolitik*).

"Are all Germans living today guilty of the Holocaust?" was the inquiry put to a representative sampling of Israeli Jews by PORI, the Public Opinion Research Institute of Israel, in March 1982. Among the respondents, 41 percent answered no, only 9 percent yes, and the rest were undecided. However, 43 percent of the respondents believed that the Germans born before 1928 (who had to obtain a visa for entry into Israel) bore guilt for the Holocaust. It is possible to speak of a modified collective guilt theory held by a large block of Israeli public opinion, a theory which differentiated between but not within generations of Germans.

A second fundamental question was put both in July 1972 and in June 1981: "Is a revival of Nazism or something similar likely in Germany?" In the early years of the Social-Liberal coalition, 39 percent of the Israelis polled saw such a possibility, nearly as many did not, and 21 percent expressed no opinion. Near the end of the Social-Liberal coalition, in June 1981, 55 percent saw a chance for the revival of Nazism, 29 percent did not and 10 percent refrained from expressing an opinion. This particular poll was conducted just one month after

Menachem Begin's verbal assault on Helmut Schmidt and the German people. It is to be presumed that the responses were strongly influenced by the attending public controversy. It would have been strange indeed if this short-term aggravation, which on the German side sparked a long-term and fundamental shift in public opinion, had been entirely without consequences in Israel.

The extent to which Israeli feelings had been aroused in June of 1981, not only against Chancellor Schmidt but against West Germans in general, was demonstrated by the responses to a question directly concerning Begin's attack on the German Chancellor and his countrymen. Exactly 50 percent of the Jewish Israelis polled regarded their prime minister's accusations as justified; only 32 percent did not.

The answers given to a third fundamental question—"Is the present Federal Republic of Germany a different Germany than Nazi Germany?"—further document the extent to which opinion is influenced by current events. In June 1981, 43 percent answered that they believed in a "different Germany" as compared to 64 percent in March 1982; 28 percent of the respondents in 1981, but only 13 percent in 1982, did not see a "different Germany." The undecided responses dropped from 29 percent to 22 percent.

The results of the June 1981 poll thus cannot be described as particularly dramatic. Despite the emotionally charged atmosphere of the time, 72 percent of the respondents did not deny that Germany had changed.

In the chapter dealing with Israeli tourism we recognize that German-Israeli tensions did not reduce West Germany's attraction for Israeli tourists. Practical, everyday behavior was not significantly affected by the public controversies. There was an obvious gap between Israeli public opinion and actual behavior—a welcome sign of relaxation in a cramped relationship.

A fourth fundamental question was posed in October 1979: "Do you think that now, 35 years after the end of the Second World War, indemnification payments ought to cease, or should further claims continue to be dealt with as before?" An overwhelming majority of 71 percent spoke out in favor of continuing to treat further claims as before, only 17 percent were for ending indemnification, and 12 percent expressed no opinion. In other words: the process of indemnification should not be disturbed. Was this result directly related to the interests of individuals actually receiving payments from Germany? If so, the proportion in favor of continuing indemnification ought to have been much higher among the population group benefiting most directly. By this logic, Euro-American Israelis should have been more strongly for continuing indemnification than their Afro-Asian countrymen. In fact, 72 percent of the Euro-American and 69 percent of the Afro-Asian respondents were for an unaltered indemnification process. The difference is not significant enough to interpret the overall results in terms of personal involvement and advantage.

This interpretation is supported by the following facts: An almost identical proportion of *sabras* and Israelis who immigrated before 1947 were in favor of continuing the established practice. The early immigrants, those who directly and personally benefited, were 70 percent in favor, as compared to 69 percent of the *sabras*, who enjoyed no direct advantages. Age differences also did not result in significant differences in opinion: Among the youngest age cohort (18–29), 70 percent were in favor of continuing as before, as compared to 73 percent of the oldest age group (60 and above).

More than four-fifths of all Israelis (84 percent) agreed that restitution represented "a moral obligation to the victims of the Nazi regime on the part of the Federal Republic of Germany." Only 6 percent did not consider the payments a moral obligation, and 10 percent were undecided. At the same time, 71 percent claimed to recognize the instrumental character of West German restitution, namely that it was Germany's willingness to make financial atonement that had formed the precondition to once again becoming a "partner in world politics and economics." Only 12 percent considered the German financial efforts as having been "not important" in this respect, and 17 percent did not express an opinion.

It would hardly be surprising if the presence of German military triggered emotional reactions in Israel. In September 1974 PORI put the following question to its interviewees: "Israel and West Germany plan to name military attaches to their embassies in Bonn and Tel Aviv. Would it disturb you if an officer in German uniform were stationed in Tel Aviv?" Surprisingly, 57 percent responded that it would "not disturb" them, 31 percent said they would take exception, and 9 percent offered no opinion. Even the explicit mention of a German uniform no longer upset a majority of Israelis in the autumn of 1974, an extraordinary sign of a relaxation in underlying tensions. The Jewish people, in possession of armed forces of their own for the first time in nearly two thousand years, are apparently prepared to make such distinctions. To Israelis, a West German officer in uniform obviously no longer represented a personification of the caricature of the brutal Hun.

Let us now turn to a number of questions involving current affairs but with fundamental character. In May 1972 PORI asked: "Are you for or against relations with Germany?" The poll was conducted before the massacre of Israeli athletes at the Munich Olympics, but at a time in which there were clearly audible dissonances between the two governments. The German government's displeasure at Israel's continuing occupation of the territories taken in the 1967 war was being articulated ever more openly. In May 1971 Bonn had agreed to a declaration of the EC foreign ministers that was withheld from publication but nevertheless leaked to the press. Among other things, the draft EC declaration called on Israel to return the occupied territories, proposed that Jerusalem be internationalized, and in diplomatically guarded language supported the right of the Palestinians to self-determination.

Despite all of this, in May 1972, 56 percent of the Israelis polled said they were in favor of relations with Germany, 18 percent were opposed, another 18 percent desired only "necessary relations," and 8 percent expressed no opinion.

Almost exactly one year later, in late May 1973, a few days before Willy Brandt's arrival as the first West German Chancellor to visit Israel while in office, two-thirds of the Israelis polled said they favored not only "relations" but "good relations" with the Federal Republic of Germany. Although only slightly, the percentage of those opposed increased from 18 percent to 20 percent. Only 3 percent were opposed to any relations whatsoever, and 11 percent chose not to respond. On the whole, this survey also indicates a greater openness toward Germany, as not only the proportion of those in favor of relations, but especially the proportion desiring good relations, rose in the second survey.

"What are you most afraid of in the Federal Republic of Germany?" was a question included in a March 1982 PORI survey, in which a list of themes was also offered. By far the largest number of Israelis were afraid of "anti-Semitism" (32 percent). The other fears followed at a considerable distance: "indifference toward the State of Israel" (13 percent) and "sympathy for Arabs, for example the PLO" (12 percent). Other responses ranged below "don't know": "a return to fascism because of an economic crisis and unemployment" (7 percent), "xenophobia" (6 percent), weapons deliveries such as the Leopard tank to the Arabs (6 percent), "nationalism" (4 percent), "extremism on the left," "pacifism," and "extremism on the right" (3 percent each), "all others" (2 percent) and "militarism" (1 percent).

The worries related to current affairs clearly predominated, as the theme of "anti-Semitism" must be seen as a historically conditioned response to current events. "Indifference toward Israel" and "sympathy for Arabs" are clearly fears related to the present. Anxieties rooted in German-Jewish history ("a return to fascism," etc.) ranked well toward the bottom of the list.

The Israeli Public and German Unification

As measured by the polls, the reaction of Israeli public opinion to the gentle October Revolution in East Germany was significantly more relaxed than the reactions of published opinion in Israel. The public did not reflect the initial hysteria of the politicians. In the final analysis it was not the supposed governors and manipulators of public opinion, the politicians and the media, but the supposedly governed and manipulated, the public, who led the way.

In a U.S. television interview in November 1989 Prime Minister Shamir conjured up a German devil, alleging that a reunited Germany could once again murder millions of Jews. By April 1990 the tone had changed dramatically: "The Jewish people has memories, doubts and questions. It is therefore difficult to say that we are pleased by the thought of German unity. Nevertheless, we understand that the time for German unity has arrived."

Just a few days before, an Israeli poll had revealed sensational results: In March 1990 two-thirds of the Jewish Israelis interviewed had raised no objections to the unification of Germany. In fact, 26 percent were expressly in favor, 41 percent were undecided, and only 33 percent were actually opposed. What is even more significant for long-term German-Israeli relations, younger Israelis were least opposed to German unification. For obvious geographical and historical reasons, the responses among Oriental Israelis were by far more relaxed (only 24 percent opposed) than among Euro-American Israelis, 42 percent of whom were against German reunification.

Whereas the question in March was "Are you for or against the union of the two German states?," in May 1990 the inquiry was rephrased: "Must Israel be for or against German unification?" The individual was thus asked to respond as a representative of the state, and thus more in accord with general expectations. But anyone expecting a more negative response to German unification was certainly disappointed. The proportion of those opposed dropped from 33 percent to 21 percent, whereas 27 percent were in favor and 41 percent expressed no opinion.

Another question in the May 1990 poll was: "In your opinion, does German unification pose a danger for Jews?" Nearly half of the respondents, 49 percent, said "no," while 34 percent said "yes," and 17 percent "don't know." A puzzling gap: only 21 percent were opposed to German unification, but 34 percent recognized a danger for Jews.

The well-known Israeli opinion researcher Mina Zemach wanted to know more and conduced a poll in June 1990 for the large Israeli daily *Yediot Acharonot*. In her poll, Zemach found both more Israelis (36 percent) in favor and more opposed to German unification (28 percent), with 35 percent giving no opinion.

The shower of commentary poured out in the Israeli media turned out to be something of a cold shower for the would-be opinion makers and shakers. In May 1990 63 percent of the Israelis polled considered relations with Germany "normal." No wonder that only 10 percent agreed to the statement: "All Germans living today bear guilt for the Holocaust." This was the same proportion as in 1982. In May 1990 64 percent agreed that a "new Germany" exists, again the same proportion as in March 1982, as opposed to only 41 percent in June 1981 in the overheated atmosphere in the wake of Menachem Begin's verbal assault.

In late summer 1991 a wave of xenophobic incidents began to sweep through Germany. One name stands out among many others: Hoyerswerda in the former East Germany. By the end of the year the violence subsided, only to return with shocking unexpected force in Rostock in August 1992. By the end of the year, seventeen people had been murdered by rightist extremists in Germany. The small northwest German town of Mölln, where three Turkish women died as a result of the fire-bombing of their home, became the symbol of this shameful development, which included the desecration of numerous Jewish cemeteries as well as the Jewish concentration camp memorials in Sachsenhausen, Ravensbrück, and Überlingen.

As could be expected, the reaction of the Israeli public was intense. It remains to be seen whether this reaction will mark a cyclical or a longer-term change. That depends in no small degree on the future actions and reactions of the German society and body politic in the face of the renewed wave of violence.

In December 1991 (before the incidents at Hoyerswerda) a Gallup poll found that nearly half of the Israelis polled (48 percent) held a "good" or "very good" opinion of Germany while 40 percent held a "bad" or "very bad" opinion. In contrast, only 36 percent felt "sure" or "fairly sure" that Germany would remain democratic; 58 percent were "fairly" or "very unsure," and 79 percent saw German democracy in "danger." In addition, 42 percent were in favor of "reconciliation" with Germany and, on a scale from plus to minus five, 47 percent of the Israelis polled ranked German reunification on the positive side, while 36 percent ranked it as negative. There was little change in comparison with data gathered in 1990 except that the proportion of undecided had diminished.

In December 1992, according to IIASR data published in *Yediot Acharonot,* 75 percent of the Israeli respondents said they feared an even stronger revival of neo-Nazism in Germany.

The Diaspora and German Unification

The attitude of the Jewish Diaspora toward Germany appears much more ambivalent. At least the majority of U.S. Jews displayed more mixed emotions toward German reunification. In response to a March

1990 poll, 42 percent of the American Jews found the idea that the two German states should become one nation again to be "very disturbing," another 32 percent as "disturbing," and only 24 percent as "not very disturbing." This represents virtually a reversal of the opinion expressed in Israel. Why?

It is difficult to arrive at a definite answer. One suspects that, despite all the problems involved, the Israeli-Jewish identity is more secure than that of the Diaspora, which, as discussed previously, has in a sense lost both the legs it stood on for three millenniums: both the Jewish religion and Jewish history. The process of secularization "amputated" the religious "leg" for a majority of Jews. The other, historical "leg" has been foreshortened into the most terrible years of Jewish history, the Holocaust. Israel has proven unsatisfactory as a prosthesis, as the Jewish State stands as the antithesis of the Diaspora, which, according to Zionist theory, was to disappear as a consequence of Jewish immigration to Israel. That did not happen, as the Jews of the Diaspora preferred donations to immigration. Although the Diaspora failed to stand on and further develop its own traditions, unqualified identification with the Jewish State has been made much more difficult in the last decade as a result of Israel's policy toward the Palestinians. What remains is the catastrophe of the Holocaust, Germany as the crystallization point of Jewish identity. Not, of course, the real, the new, but the old Germany of the murderers.

■

In summary, we recognize that the cares of the present have begun to displace the burdens of history. We recall the following findings:

- The Holocaust represents a past that directly influences the present in Israel. This applies to domestic as well as foreign policy, and especially to what we call *geschichtspolitik*. Despite all the declarations on the part of the politicians, the effects of Israeli *geschichtspolitik* are much less evident in public opinion and everyday behavior than in the political-ideological arena of published opinion.
- The Holocaust fixation, the indelible link to Germany, the historization of Jewish suffering and pseudo-messianic Israelism

bring with them the danger of hollowing out the Jewish content of Judaism. The nearly exclusive preoccupation with the survival of the Jews endangers Judaism itself.

- With the passing of generations, the distance to the Holocaust will increase not only in terms of time, but also emotionally. This is inevitable, even though the official *geschichtspolitik* is aimed at preventing this very development and has, as we have seen, achieved some successes.

- The distance to the Holocaust also mirrors domestic Israeli social polarizations, both the polarization between Israelis of Euro-American and Afro-Asian heritage, as well as that between Orthodox and non-Orthodox Israelis.

- For Zionism, Israel, and the Diaspora, the Holocaust functions as a source of both identity and legitimization.

- Domestically—both within Israel and among the Jews of the world—and in the realm of international relations, the Holocaust is used as a political argument and instrument.

- The Holocaust is an important filter in determining how Israelis perceive their non-Jewish environment.

4

GERMAN-ISRAELI ROLE REVERSAL

Or, the Legend of the Hair-Shirt

"Democracy in Germany? Is it possible?" These questions appeared as the headline of an article in the Israeli daily *Haaretz* in 1952. It is indicative of Israel's understanding of its role with regard to Germany, at least in the early phase of mutual relations. At that time Israel's role as schoolmaster on the subject of political morals was beyond dispute. Germany was the pupil and humbly accepted its lessons, and if the acceptance was sometimes with a grumble, it was at most only a barely audible one.

Nowadays, voices of protest are clearly audible in Germany, and some of the protests are, to say the least, vociferous. Forty years are enough, they shout. One even hears politicians demanding that the country step out from under the "shadow of the past," cast off the "penitent's hair-shirt," and learn to "walk upright" again. The endless repetition of such demands does not, however, prove the false assumption upon which they are based, namely that the Federal Republic of Germany is forced to stand before other nations with a bowed head. This has not been true for a long time.

There is no better proof for just how wrong this image of the German republic as penitent in hair-shirt is than the dramatic reversal of roles in Germany's relations with the state casting the longest shadow from the past, namely Israel. Furthermore, the history of the two nations' evolving roles documents the fundamental shift in the Germans' perception of their own role as well as the Federal Republic's growing influence in world affairs.

Regardless of political stripe, many Germans of the postwar generation have not only increasingly freed themselves from the constraints of the assigned—but rarely freely accepted—role of penitent pupil. They have also began to administer—generally unsolicited—advice on Israel's current problems, particularly in matters concerning territorial boundaries and peace. Germans also advance proposals for a resolution of the Israeli-Palestinian conflict and deliver—totally unsolicited—sermons on political morals. The frequency of the schoolmasterly advice directed at Israel has increased parallel to the series of West German successes in bettering relations with its Eastern European neighbors, beginning in 1969–70.

The lectures were not well received in Jerusalem and generally met with more defiance than willingness to listen. In December of 1987 Israel's ambassador to Bonn, Yitzhak Ben-Ari, described the effect of the teacher-pupil role in relations between the two states: "Schoolmasterly advice from Germany only produces the opposite effect in Israel. It strengthens the radicals and not the forces working towards a solution of the problems."

There is certainly room to debate the wisdom of the behavior of the other side, but there can be no doubt that a reversal of roles took place about midpoint in the first forty years of German-Israeli relations. This turnabout was, in part, made possible when, in 1967, Israel took on a role that has always and everywhere been ugly in nature, namely that of occupier.

The ideological, political, and generational changes in West German society furthered the reversal in roles. The rise of a "we-are-somebody-again" mentality, the maturation of new generations, particularly the "1968" and the "eco" generations, which appear to have specializedin moral sermonizing directed at Israel, Bonn's increasing participation in world affairs and, as already mentioned, Germany's heightened international prestige as a result of its successful policy in Eastern Europe all contributed to the German-Israeli role reversal.

The "political class" in Israel, as well as large segments of Israeli society, have failed to fully recognize the fact, much less the consequences, of this role reversal, and they certainly don't approve of it. The reason is readily apparent: With regard to fundamental issues, Israelis view Germany from the perspective of the past, whereas Germans prefer to view Israel, the world, and themselves from the perspective of the present and future. We can apply the term "dis-synchronism" to this divergence in historical-chronological perspectives. In Germany, this phenomenon as displayed on the Israeli side is somewhat polemically labeled *gegenwartsschäche*—a weakened sense of the present—or as *realitätsschwäche*—a weakened sense of reality. In Israel, the manifestations on the German side are frequently described as an "inability to mourn" or as "historical irresponsibility."

The weakened awareness of contemporary Germany among Israelis is as understandable as the heightened German consciousness of the present. The role of the humble penitent was, from the early days of the Federal Republic on, more a perceived than an actual role. In any case, it is one which the German side no longer plays. Germany holds its head high, both on the German-Israeli as well as on the wider international political stage. What is more, in the postwar period the Western countries made it easy for the West Germans to again stand tall.

The actual or perceived role of *mediator* on the world stage has also undergone a fundamental reversal between Israel and Germany. That Jerusalem could or should have served as a mediator between Bonn and Washington is a legend repeatedly heard in connection with the German-Israeli Restitution Agreement. In this context, it is often claimed that Adenauer concluded the treaty with Israel in order to improve the atmosphere between Bonn and Washington.

The legend sounds convincing. It has just one blemish: As was pointed out in chapter 2, delineating the stages of German-Israeli relations, the legend is based on a false assessment of the actual state of German-American relations at the time.

Israel has never desired, nor has it ever actually attempted to warm the atmosphere between Bonn and Washington. Particularly in connection with the restitution issue, it has become clear that, in the early 1950s, West Germany was much more important than Israel in the eyes of the U.S. government. In order to improve its standing in Washington, the Federal Republic of Germany was not in need of Israel's services, and the Bonn decision to conclude a restitution agreement with Israel was made less in response to American wishes than despite Washington's trepidations that it could increase the burdens on the American taxpayer.

While there is no lack of would-be negotiators in all political camps in West Germany, the country has played no role at all in mediating the Arab-Israeli conflict. The reason for this is that the Federal Republic has little or no political leverage among any of the parties to the conflict.

On the other hand, Germany has rendered valuable services to the Western Alliance in establishing communications and contacts behind the scenes. It has been able to maintain channels of communication with Israel and the Arab world as well as with other regions. Because of "traditional German-Arab friendship" Germany has more connections in the Middle East than France, Great Britain, or Italy. This "traditional German-Arab friendship" exhibits certain nostalgic traits for the Arab side, but is free of the burdens of the colonial past that cloud British and French relations with the Arab world. From the German perspective, however, a certain brown tinge from the past darkens the otherwise bright picture of Arab-German friendship.

Bonn's good connections with Moscow have proven of help to Israel. For one example, Germany provided channels of communication in connection with the freeing of the Russian-Jewish dissident Anatoly Sharansky in 1985.

It may be that the ability to render such assistance has, here and there, led to the temptation to open one's mouth too wide. One example is the declaration issued by the European Community heads of state in Venice in June of 1980, in which West Germany played a leading role. The tone is not that of the penitent in hair-shirt, but rather that of the censorious schoolmaster.

In assuming such a role, however, the EC demonstrated little sensitivity to political and military realities, especially since the EC, and with it the government of the Federal Republic, indirectly issued military guarantees for what it considered to be a solution to the Arab-Israeli conflict.

The value of the actual or perceived solution, or lack thereof, is not of central interest here. The fact is that the states of the European Community, all of which face serious difficulties in motivating and mobilizing their own populations for the eventuality of defending their own territories, are incapable of doing so with regard to foreign territories. No Western European in the 1930s was willing to die for Danzig, and it does not appear to be the case today with regard to Israel, which, in contrast to Danzig of the 1930s, is quite capable of defending itself.

In 1982–83 France and Italy undertook, and failed, their trial-by-fire in Lebanon. When the situation got hot, both chose to withdraw. The Italians pulled out completely in 1984; the French withdrew to an apparently less dangerous role within the framework of the United Nations forces in Lebanon (UNIFIL). The multinational force deployed in the Sinai in 1982 to oversee the Egyptian-Israeli peace functions with European participation, but, except for the weather, this front is anything but hot. In both cases, the Federal Republic of Germany is conspicuous by its absence.

There are good reasons for this absence, among them the German constitution, which makes it difficult to deploy German armed forces outside the NATO area, but which, contrary to popular political legend, does not actually forbid such deployments. This structural taming of the German armed forces is, of course, closely related to the historic circumstances surrounding West German rearmament. In this respect, German politicians enjoy the unexpected convenience of Germany's historical burdens and do not hesitate to make reference to history.

The parties to the conflicts of the Middle East are, of course, fully aware that the Europeans are paper tigers. For this reason they also put no faith in a European role in the resolution of the Arab-Israeli conflict.

With European help, a number of Arab states have attempted to bring about a change of course on the part of the United States. The European, and thus the German role is indirect at best, but has not exactly proven a balm in the less-than-calm state of European-American relations. With regard to potential solutions in the Middle East, Europeans frequently exhibit differing perceptions than Americans. Bonn has attempted—usually without success—to influence the Middle East policy of the United States not by putting on its penitent's hair-shirt, but by emphasizing the fundamental identity of German and American interests.

On the level of day-to-day policy—but not on the deeper historical-psychological plane—another role reversal has taken place, illustrating a more or less harmless form of dis-synchronism, namely between the roles of the courter and the courted.

Up until 1955 West Germany sought to court the favor of the Jewish State, which, for its part, reacted defensively. In May 1955 the Federal Republic of Germany achieved sovereignty and it became important to pay close attention to current events, particularly as they potentially affected policy with regard to the two German states.

Out of a fear that the Arab states might restrict their trade with the Federal Republic or upgrade their relations with the East German regime, the West German government rebuffed what, from 1956–57 on, was an increasingly evident desire on the part of Israel for the establishment of diplomatic relations.

Nevertheless, Bonn wanted to be accommodating toward Israel. Beginning in 1957, West Germany procured weapons from and later supplied weapons to Israel. This took place under a heavy blanket of secrecy, as what was being attempted was another squaring of the circle. Bonn wanted good, but not diplomatic relations with Israel. Jerusalem wanted both with Germany, but was continually put off until 1965. When Bonn finally more or less skidded into establishing full diplomatic relations in 1965, it was in no position to continue the weapons deliveries, which in the meantime had been, at least partially, disclosed.

Despite its attempts at "normalization," the West German government continued to be courted by Israel, especially in the realm of economics and regarding relations with the European Community. Israel was no longer able to afford the luxury of basing policy on history alone. This, too, is indicative of the change in time and in roles.

Since 1955, little has changed in the basic division of roles: Israel has remained in the role of applicant, and, in highly critical situations, has wielded the extreme political instrument: the Holocaust. In May 1981, Prime Minister Begin demonstrated the use of this instrument. The devastating results are well known. We will examine them further in connection with public opinion data in chapter 6.

The roles of courter and courted form one extreme, those of (potential) punisher and punished the other. Immediately after the Second World War it was anything but precluded that numerous non-Jews as well as Jews might choose to boycott German wares. But soon, "made in Germany" came to be regarded as a mark of quality rather than shame.

In the immediate postwar years Germany was the outcast on the international stage. In the meantime, Israel has increasingly come to be seen as the outcast. The point here is not to debate whether or not this is properly so. The fact as such is documented most dramatically by the resolutions of the United Nations, which have on more than one occasion called for sanctions against Israel.

Since Israel took on the role of occupier, especially during the 1982–83 war in Lebanon, calls for economic sanctions against Israel have not infrequently been heard in the debate on the Middle East in Germany. Politicians from both the governing coalition and the opposition have called for a cut-off of the low-interest 140-million mark loan extended annually to Israel since 1966. (Before then it had been 130 million marks.)

The payments were continued. What is revealing and of fundamental importance in this context is the role reversal between subject and object of proposed sanctions. It demonstrates how dramatically the political winds have shifted.

The role of occupier has already been mentioned. This is a very new role for the Israeli, for the Jewish people, and stands in sharp contrast to the traditional image. The role is more suited to the picture of the ugly German of the years 1939 to 1945. However one chooses to judge Jerusalem's policy in the occupied territories, Israel's functional role as occupier is undeniable.

Israel's unaccustomed and unusual role as occupier points to a further German-Israeli role reversal, namely in attitudes toward the use of force. The traditional German image abroad was, more often than not, the product of imperial Germany's pursuit of power and in keeping with a popular motto of the militant Wilhelminian era: *Viel Feind, viel Ehr*—many enemies, much honor. Since the Second World War this image has undergone a fundamental transformation in West Germany. Not just the men and women at the helm of state, the whole of West German society unequivocally renounced the resort to violence as a means of international policy. Cologne political scientist Hans-Peter Schwarz found a brilliant and convincing formulation to characterize the abstinence from power politics in the policy of the new German republic: Germany, Schwarz wrote, has switched from *Machtbesessenheit* to *Machtvergessenheit*, from the aberration to the abjuration of power.

It is quite a different case with Israel. The image and the attitude of the gentle, defenseless Jew has been transformed. One of the central goals of Zionism was to create the "new Jewish man." This goal has been achieved.

The role reversal between the onetime brutal German and the formerly gentle Jew is related to the lessons which both sides have drawn from their history. The Germans have recognized that resorting to violence can lead to catastrophe, for themselves as well as for others. This remains true for the vast majority of Germans even though the escalating violence on the part of a tiny neo-Nazi minority since 1990 has led to a revival of the image of the barbarian Hun. The experience of the Jews and the Israelis is that nonviolence and defenselessness can mean death. We will ponder this phenomenon further in the next chapter.

Only time will tell if, in another role reversal, the Israeli and Jewish world will once again regain its former position of moral superiority. Without question the events of 1992 mark a significant break in the previous trend of developments. "Business as usual" was rendered impossible.

We must, however, keep in mind that even at the high point of xenophobic incidents reached in late 1992, the overwhelming majority of Germany vehemently rejected such anti-foreign acts. A poll conducted by the Mannheim opinion research institute Forschungsgruppe Wahlen among West Germans in December 1992 showed that fully 94 percent declared that they had "no sympathy at all for violence against foreigners," and only 5 percent said they "understood" such violence.

In another poll, 91 percent of the West and 89 percent of the East Germans agreed that it was "good" that Germany granted asylum to the politically persecuted.

In November and December 1992 millions of Germans demonstrated against xenophobia and anti-Semitism. Most impressive was the first "chain of light" demonstration in Munich on December 6, which brought out between 300,000 and 400,000 people—nearly a third of the city's population—in an entirely peaceful demonstration with lighted candles and church bells; it was soon imitated in cities and towns throughout the country.

In a Europe-wide survey of attitudes toward foreign residents conducted by Eurobarometer, the Germans came out relatively well. In France, Spain, Ireland, the Netherlands, Portugal, and in the European Community average, higher percentages of the respondents were unwilling to tolerate a foreigner as their neighbor. Only the Greeks, Belgians, Italians, and Danes were more tolerant. All in all, Europe presented a rather unpleasant picture, but one that does not justify a particular emphasis on Germany. It must also be recalled that, since 1990, Germany has taken in more than one million refugees and asylum-seekers, and must therefore face far greater problems in this regard than other European countries. In 1992 alone Germany admitted nearly half a million such persons; Great Britain welcomed 21,000.

5

GERMAN-ISRAELI

LANGUAGE PROBLEMS

Different Meanings for the Same Terms

Israelis and Germans, especially those born since the Second World War, often conduct a strange dialogue. They use the same terms but fill them with differing contents—the results of differing historical experiences. Israelis—and Jews in general—extract their historical lessons from the experience of the victims; Germans from that of the perpetrators. The later generations on both sides are motivated by the desire to avoid the mistakes of their parents and grandparents.

The terms "force," "self-determination," "resistance" and "Holocaust" are particularly well suited to illustrate the confusion in language.

In the clear case of defense against an attack in which the roles of aggressor and defender are unambiguous, where good and evil are indubitably distinguishable, majorities on both sides approve of the use of force. The use of preemptory force to thwart an impending attack is much more problematic. Israel has repeatedly demonstrated the use of preventive strikes, to the increasing disapproval of large segments of the German public and politicians, including many friends of Israel.

At the root of the resulting German-Israeli irritations is the fact that both sides speak of "defense." Both employ the same term, but imply quite different meanings. The content of the term "defense" depends on the general system of values, prevailing attitudes toward violence and the willingness to employ force. It therefore cannot be defined objectively. Above all, it is determined by the historical experience of a people, and the historical experiences of Germans and Jews are of a contrary nature.

After the unfathomable sufferings of their parents' generation, younger Israelis are likely to resort to force sooner rather than later. After the aberrations of their fathers, young Germans tend to abjure the use of force. Young Israelis believe in the dogma of the effectiveness of military deterrence; many young Germans regard it as a potential cause for war.

The use of force against civilians is condemned without qualification in Germany. It is also rejected in Israel, but with one exception: the pursuit of Palestinian guerrillas. Apart from the value judgment involved in labeling these people "freedom fighters" or "terrorists," the basic fact remains that the PLO employs guerrilla tactics, which are generally resorted to only by those in a militarily weak position. Such tactics include the use of the civilian population, among which the guerrilla seeks to move about. In fact, the civilian population is often held hostage. In southern Lebanon, for example, rocket attacks against Israeli territory were launched from dwellings and schools, the presumption being that the Israelis would hesitate to bomb civilian targets.

Those who combat guerrillas, Israelis in this case, find themselves in a horrible dilemma. On the one hand, they are convinced of the necessity to strike back. On the other hand, they realize that innocent civilians will suffer.

The Israeli decision regarding this dilemma is well known: Israel hits back. The reaction in Germany, as well as everywhere else in Western Europe—and more recently in the United States as well—is outrage over Israeli violence and brutality.

As long as the Israeli-Palestinian conflict is carried out by force of arms, the militarily weaker Palestinians will resort to guerrilla tactics and the Israelis, although they have no desire to harm civilians, will risk the possibility of civilian casualties in their retaliations.

Germans and Israelis disagree not only on the actual or perceived justification for the use of force, but also on the issue of what constitutes violence. In Germany, as in Western Europe in general, the use of violence in responding to violence is condemned, even if the preceding action included the use of innocent civilians as hostages as part of the overall plan. Both views are understandable, but they remain irreconcilable.

The German-Israeli language problems concerning the use of force will persist. One reason is widespread ignorance in Germany and Western Europe of the fundamental dilemma of guerrilla and anti-guerrilla tactics. The more fundamental reason is that the two sides have necessarily derived differing lessons from history. "Never again the victim" is the determination of young Jews and Israelis. "Never again the aggressor" is the motto of young Germans—with the exception of a tiny but murderously violent group of skinhead extremists in 1991–92. Both the young German and the young Israeli are right, and if they cannot understand each other, it is because the past decisively influences their attitudes in the present.

Confusion also obtains with regard to the issue of the self-determination of peoples. For more than forty years, numerous Germans clung to the hope that respect for the principle of self-determination would some day result in the peaceful reunification of their divided country. These hopes were finally fulfilled in 1989–90. Those longing to achieve self-determination for their own nation are naturally predisposed to advocate the principle elsewhere as well, especially since it reflects the liberal-democratic tradition of Western Europe.

Many Israelis fear that the application of the principle of self-determination would lead to the establishment of a Palestinian state and the destruction of the Jewish state. Israelis recognize the ideological contradiction involved in having demanded the right of self-determination for their own community and yet denying that same right to the Palestinians. This position is justified with the argument that the Palestinians rejected the opportunities presented by the British Peel Plan in

1937 and the UN resolution of 1947, both of which would have led to a Palestinian state, and subsequently directed their efforts to the destruction of the Jewish state, thus forfeiting their right to self-determination. The argument is so oversimplified that it cannot hold water, but it serves to salve a bad conscience. Recently, the cracks behind the facade have become all too apparent, but the historical construction still stands. Our purpose here is not to debate the issue of whether the creation of a Palestinian state would actually lead to Israel's destruction. Our concern is a problem that appears rooted in language but in realty is a question of contents. The pre-programmed result is irritations whenever Germans and Israelis take up the subject of self-determination.

The inflated use of terms blurs contours and blunts contents. Examples are "fascism," "Holocaust," "resistance." Let us take a brief look at the deflation and redefinition of such terms.

In Israel and in the Jewish Diaspora the term "resistance" is generally associated with actions directed against dictatorial regimes that oppress their own and sometimes other peoples. The goal of resistance is the forceful overthrow of a violent regime and includes the risk of death. Critical Israelis also employ the term in this sense to the Palestinian resistance against the Israeli occupation.

The inflationary German usage of the term often produces a mild—and usually friendly—smile of disbelief among Israelis and Diaspora Jews. Ex post facto the Germans, at least verbally, have styled themselves into a people of resistance fighters. The sort of everyday contradictions and controversies common to all democratic systems and the necessary activities of the parliamentary opposition—which hardly involve physical danger—are blown up into acts of resistance.

Apart from the original Greek word, the term "Holocaust" referred from 1945 on to the mass-murder of Jews as a part of the National-Socialist regime's *endlösung* (final solution). In recent years the term has come to be applied to other genocidal actions, and even more recently to almost any instance of brutal treatment of another people. In this manner the Holocaust has come to be divorced from its original German context and has become universalized, thereby making it possible to describe Israel's battle against the Palestinians as "genocide" and as a "Holocaust" without regard to the historical circumstances.

In 1982, the public debate in Germany over Israel's "Holocaust" of the Palestinians in Lebanon documented this linguistic development. Many thoughtful Germans cautioned against such thoughtless use of language. The mark of Cain cannot be so simply transferred to Abel and murder does not make a Holocaust. The debate also demonstrated that it was possible to sharply criticize Israel's tactics in the Lebanon war without having to apply the label "Holocaust." The avoidance of the term was by no means equivalent to a justification of Israel's treatment of the Palestinians.

Here and there Jewish and Israeli critics interpreted the widespread but by no means general use of the term "Holocaust" as a deliberate historical malevolence. In most cases, the use of the term was more the result of thoughtlessness than willful malice. One indication is that since the 1982 debate very few voices in Germany have accused Israel of carrying out a Holocaust against the Palestinians.

Devaluation through inflationary use is apparently generic to the political process of dealing with the past. It is a phenomenon that knows no national borders. One example from Israel: Ben-Gurion repeatedly felt impelled to explain to his countrymen that Konrad Adenauer and Ludwig Erhard were not "another Hitler."

6

PUBLIC OPINION

A Mirror of Generational Change

U ntil the Six Day War of 1967, public opinion in the Federal Republic of Germany was characterized by restrained and distant sympathy for Israel. From 1967 to 1981, until Prime Minister Menachem Begin's verbal attacks on Helmut Schmidt and the German people, about half of the West German population articulated far more sympathy for Israel than for the Arabs.

During this period, the levels of sympathy for the Arab states remained well below 10 percent. After mid-1981, Israel's lead over the Arabs shrank. The clear majority of West Germans no longer expressed particular sympathy for either side in the Arab-Israeli conflict.

This development is consistent with the pattern throughout Western Europe, although the trend set in somewhat later in Germany. The shift began among Germany's neighbors as early as 1967 and accelerated in the early 1970s. Arabs, especially Palestinians, were "in" much earlier in the rest of Western Europe, where they appeared enveloped in the aura of the popular Third World, for which one's conscience bled and which one supported mainly by word and demonstration, but rarely in the form of concrete action.

As citizens of former colonial powers, the peoples of Western Europe had a bad conscience toward the Third World, and the Palestinians profited from this. While Germany had not been a colonial power since the end of the First World War, it obviously had a bad conscience toward Israel since the end of the Second World War. The Six Day War of 1967 brought forth a great wave of sympathy for Israel in Germany. Thus the chronologically based shift in the curves of public sympathy for Israel in West Germany versus the rest of Western Europe.

The age factor deserves special attention. Until the mid-1960s it was possible to generalize: the younger the age group, the more pro-Israeli. The "1968" generation reversed that trend. Since then, the younger the age group, the more pro-Arab it tends to be, although the differences between the age groups have become less pronounced. The "eco-generation" also articulates distinct reservations toward Israel. On the other hand, the 1968 and the "eco" generations evidence far fewer inhibitions toward Jews than elder Germans, a clear sign that the anti-Israelism, or, if you will, anti-Zionism of these generally more left-leaning generations does not represent a rise in anti-Semitism but is instead indicative of a less cramped and inhibited set of attitudes.

In order to avoid misunderstandings: when speaking of political generations we mean the clear majority of a particular age group. This is not to contend that all members of any age group think and feel alike. Differences within as well as between political generations can also be highly significant. The data with regard to the 1968 and eco generations are, however, so clear-cut that the generalizations stated above are both permissible and necessary.

There are no fundamental differences in attitudes toward Israel among the supporters of the "traditional" parties in Germany. This does not, however, apply to the followers of such right-wing parties as the National Democratic Party (NPD), nor to the Greens. Although these groups occupy opposite ends of the political spectrum, they do have one thing in common: pro-Arab leanings. There is still a decisive difference: in contrast to the followers of the NPD, the polls show that the Greens have remained immune to the virus of anti-Semitism.

With regard to education it was possible to generalize until the early 1970s: the higher the level of education, the more sympathy for Israel. This, too, changed fundamentally with the advent of the 1968 generation, which developed its political attitudes at the West German universities. While the majority kept its distance from Israel, much more sympathy arose for the Palestinians and Arabs. Since then the pattern has been the more educated the interviewee, the more likely a pro-Arab or pro-Palestinian attitude: more cautiously restated, the less likely pro-Israeli. It must be kept in mind that we are speaking here of tendencies but not of majorities.

The difference in attitudes expressed by urban and rural respondents has also shifted. The pattern in the early 1970s was the more urban the population, the more pro-Israeli. Now we find more pro-Arab sympathies among the residents of the largest cities and in the rural villages than elsewhere. The fact that higher than average levels of sympathy for the Arabs was registered in West Berlin, Hamburg, and Bremen indicates the influence of the 1968 generation on their surroundings, as the students of these university cities were in the forefront of the student unrest of that period.

A comparison of the Middle East policy pursued by the Bonn government with the trends in public opinion presents the following picture: Until the early 1980s, the policy of every government in Bonn was at crosscurrents with public opinion. This is particularly apparent with regard to the 1952 Restitution Agreement, which was opposed by 50 percent of the West German public, with only 25 percent in favor, including those with strong reservations. From 1967 to 1981, the official position of neutrality assumed by the West German government did not reflect the attitude of the West German people, who sympathized with Israel by an overwhelming majority.

Since 1981–82 German public opinion and government policy with regard to the Middle East have converged. While neutrality and distance are the preferred course, Israel still commands greater public sympathy.

The Middle East is of relatively little significance in German eyes.

This is unsurprising, as East-West relations have always been the object of intense scrutiny and most directly affected the citizens of the Federal Republic. West Germans directly felt the effects of developments in the Middle East during the 1973–74 oil crisis. Middle East policy and relations with the Arab states promptly increased in significance in the estimation of public opinion. Parallel to their increased importance, the Arabs also gained in public sympathy. Once the energy supply became less worrisome and oil prices declined dramatically beginning in 1983, the West German public no longer regarded good relations with the Arab states as quite so vital. With the decline in oil prices, the German public's sympathy for the Arabs also dropped, and the level of sympathy for Israel rose.

We have seen that the large reservoir of sympathy for Israel which obtained in West Germany from 1967 to 1981 and which was largely independent of individual events is no longer to be found. In the rest of Western Europe it had vanished at a much earlier date. Since 1981, sympathy for Israel in West German public opinion has risen and fallen in response to the concrete policies pursued by the Jewish State. This is illustrated by the poll data for 1981 (Begin's lambasting of Chancellor Schmidt and Germans in general), 1982 (the war in Lebanon against the PLO), as well as for the period following Begin's resignation in 1984, after which Israel succeeded in projecting a more gentle image. Jerusalem's iron-fisted policy since the beginning of the intifada in the occupied territories in late 1987 again reversed the trend and led to a more negative image for Israel in West Germany.

The EMNID Institute, which —apart from cyclical shifts—had registered a nearly steady decline in Israel's popularity among the West German public since the late 1970s, measured a dramatic increase in sympathy for Israel in early February 1991. By December 1991 Israel was (once again) "a state like any other" in the eyes of 76 percent of the German respondents.

The suffering of the fathers and grandfathers no longer automatically precludes criticism of the suffering inflicted on others by the sons and grandsons. The present is overshadowing the past.

German public opinion with regard to the Arabs reflects bald-faced opportunism, since, with the exception of the 1968 and the eco generations, the Arabs have never enjoyed any deepfelt sympathies. They prof-it either from Israel's temporary negative image or from rising oil prices.

The picture of Germans as reflected in public opinion surveys in Israel needs only to be summarized in brief, as we have already examined and interpreted specific data in chapter 3.

In their responses to all of the questions posed, the younger age groups in Israel were consistently more well-disposed toward Germany and Germans than their older countrymen. In 1981–82 about 50 percent in the 18 to 29 age bracket said they believed in a "new Germany," as opposed to around 40 percent in the older age cohorts, but even this represents a surprising degree of open-mindedness overall. By 1990, 64 percent of all Israelis agreed that a "new Germany" existed.

One of the results of the Gulf War was a new generational pattern in the way Israelis viewed Germany. A March 1991 survey conducted by the PORI Institute showed that the opinion of the younger generation had hardly changed—51 percent of the respondents in the 18–29 age bracket believed in a new Germany; but much higher percentages in the older age cohorts agreed that Germany had changed for the better—as many as 67 percent in the 50–59 age group. It remains to be seen whether this shift in opinion will prove to be lasting.

Immigrants, very many of whom came to Israel to escape persecution or discrimination, tend to display a more reserved attitude toward Germany than *sabras*. These results demonstrate the limited effects of the massive efforts at *geschichtspolitik* in Israel, i.e. the attempt to employ history as a basis for and instrument of political policy.

We are confronted by what may appear to be a contradiction: In chapter 3 we showed that the Holocaust is the single most important factor in establishing Jewish identity both in Israel and the Diaspora, but here we indicate that younger Israelis have a more positive picture of Germany. Apparently, younger Israelis are especially inclined to differentiate between the old Germany of the Holocaust and the new one. While the official approach has been to attempt to inextricably link Germany and the Holocaust, the two have in fact become separated in Israeli society. The image of the present and real Germany has been projected over that of Holocaust Germany. The growing temporal and generational distance has also generated a divergence in contents. The less Israelis and their families were directly affected by the Holocaust, the less likely they are to equate the two images of Germany.

This is proven by a comparison of the responses of Israelis of Afro-Asian backgrounds with those of their countrymen of Euro-American heritage. In all of the surveys, the responses of the former have been less prejudicial and more open, although the gap has narrowed considerably. In a 1991 PORI poll the difference was only 1 percent (57 percent of the Afro-Asian vs. 56 percent of the Euro-American Jews believed in a "new Germany"). A Gallup poll on attitudes in Israel toward German reunification produced similar results. At least in this area the official *geschichtspolitik* has apparently achieved its goal of assimilation between Oriental and Euro-American Jews.

Does the level of education influence Israelis' image of Germany? The polls do not permit a definitive answer. They do indicate that the opinions of Israelis with higher education are less volatile than those of their lesser-educated countrymen. The academically educated tend to be more skeptical with regard to Germany but less inclined to react to cyclical trends and individual events, i.e. they are influenced less by the passing irritations and jubilations of the day. To put it in a friendly way: their view of the world is more firmly established. To put it in a less friendly way: they are more stubborn.

7

PUBLIC BEHAVIOR

Tourism as an Indicator?

"Israel is more than a vacation" is the slogan of Israel's state tourism office to the German tourist. The advertising slogan is politically accurate, as the stream of German tourists to Israel has proven anything but nonpolitical, and the numerous Israeli visitors to the Federal Republic of Germany can, indeed must, be interpreted politically.

The development of German-Israeli tourism is a mirror of the two nations' relations. Because it reflects actual behavior and not just an unbinding verbal expression of attitude, it is perhaps even more revealing than the shifting picture of mutual opinion traced in the last chapter.

The German still does not tend to visit Israel "just for fun," in order to bask under guaranteed blue skies. For that, the historical-political climate in Israel is still too hot. On the other hand, many Israelis do appear to travel to Germany for pleasure—an unexpected phenomenon that demonstrates the gap between basic Israeli attitudes and actual behavior with regard to Germany. The behavior of these Israelis is a much stronger indicator of normality and a relaxation of tensions than is the case with the German tourists. This contention is supported by the actual numbers as well as by the images deliberately created and projected in the advertising campaigns of both the German and the Israeli tourist industry.

In the year 1950, only 180 travelers from the Federal Republic of Germany visited Israel and 172 of these were Jews. In 1987, 180,000 West Germans visited the Jewish State. These numbers do not mean much at first glance, as it is necessary to interpret them in relation to the steadily rising tide of German tourism abroad since the 1950s. At that time, nearly every fourth West German went on a holiday trip, but only a quarter of these wanted or could afford to travel abroad. Until the early 1960s, not more than 30,000 Germans had ventured to Israel, whereas more than 3,000,000 had traveled elsewhere.

Since the early 1960s the annual number of German visitors to Israel has risen more rapidly. By 1965 it surpassed 10,000, but dropped briefly as a result of the 1967 Six Day War. By 1971 the number had risen to 35,000 and reached 42,000 in 1972. This increase must be viewed in the context of the generally improved financial situation of the West Germans and their growing desire to travel to other countries. About 12 million West Germans did so in 1972.

The statistics for 1973 and 1974 indicate that travel to Israel remained both rare and subject to political considerations, as the number of German visitors remained at the 1972 level. Because of events in the Middle East, Germans apparently had less desire to visit Israel in the wake of the Yom Kippur War, which broke out in October 1973, with clashes between Israel and Syria continuing until May 1974, and with an increased frequency of PLO attacks against installations and the civilian population in Israel thereafter.

Nevertheless, the number of German tourists in 1973 and 1974 was considerably higher than in the 1960s, and this indicates that at least a part of the German public had a more relaxed attitude toward Israel. This contention is strongly supported by the disproportionately large increase in German tourism to Israel in the period between 1975 and 1977 in comparison with overall German travel abroad. The number of

Germans visiting the Holy Land more than doubled, rising from 50,000 in 1975 to 110,000 in 1977. Even the negative image of Menachem Begin, who took office as Prime Minister in 1977, did not alter Israel's attractiveness for German tourists. In 1980 the number reached 158,000.

Then came the political turnabout. In May 1981, Prime Minister Begin unleashed his verbal barrage against Chancellor Helmut Schmidt and the German people as a whole for complicity in the crimes of the Nazi era. Then, in 1982, Israel fought a bitter war against the PLO in Lebanon. The result: the numbers of German visitors to Israel fell dramatically from 155,000 in 1981 to 107,000 in 1982. It was not until 1987, when 182,000 Germans visited Israel, that the number of German tourists exceeded the level of 1981.

The precipitous drop in German tourism to Israel in 1982 considerably exceeded the decrease in the numbers of visitors from other Western countries. In other words: the decline in Israel's attractiveness for German tourists was more a function of irritations in German-Israeli bilateral relations than a result of Israeli-Palestinian tensions. German travelers in the 1980s apparently felt self-confident enough to deliberately give the cold shoulder to a country where the leadership (including at that time the opposition Israeli Labor Party) hurled insults at them. Only in the mid-1980s were the Germans willing to forgive Israel. It is hard to imagine any other explanation for the concrete numbers, and officials and experts in Israel and Germany did not offer any other interpretation at the time.

The outbreak of the intifada in December 1987 marked a sharp drop in German tourism to Israel. The number of German visitors fell to less than 155,000 in 1988 and plummeted again (to less than 120,000) in 1990. The Kuwait crisis and the Gulf War caused a further reduction in 1990, when the number of German visitors to Israel fell below 98,000—the lowest level since the mid-1970s. For 1992, however, Israel's expectations were that German tourists will have returned in near-record numbers.

For German travelers, Israel's image is apparently not only that presented in the official travel brochures: "first a little course in history in Jerusalem" and then "a little course in scuba-diving in the Red Sea."

German visitors to Israel find themselves diving not only into the Red Sea, but also frequently enough into the brown sea of the German past, the depths of which they have no desire to explore.

The trends in German tourism to Israel throw light on certain aspects of overall German-Israeli relations. What we observe fits into the general pattern of German-Jewish-Israeli approaches in dealing with the past: Since the early 1980s, both the German public and the Bonn government have acted contrary to the expectations of Israeli-Jewish *geschichtspolitik*. The Germans' desire to free themselves from the chains of history have led them to take to the offensive.

With regard to the Jewish State, German opinion, as articulated in the polls, and actual German behavior, as expressed in terms of tourism, have proven consistent. We can thus regard the trends in German travel to Israel as an indicator of the fundamental shift in German-Israeli relations. At first, German sensibilities were defensive in nature. Germans did not venture to travel to Israel, even when they once again could afford to do so. Since the early 1980s, German sensibilities have taken the offensive: Germans were no longer willing to take everything Israel dished out. In the future, Israelis responsible for policy toward Germany and the Jewish world as a whole will have to learn to deal with this increased German self-confidence.

While Germans remained sensitive to Israel, Israelis increasingly and quite clearly were casting off their inhibitions with regard to Germany. For Israeli tourists, Germany is anything but taboo.

As late as 1976 only 49,000 Israelis visited the Federal Republic of Germany. In 1977, Begin's Likud came to power and, at the expense of the public treasury, initiated a consumer-oriented economic policy that also gave considerable impetus to Israeli tourism. In 1983, the last year in which Begin, who was certainly no friend of Germany, held office, some 131,000 Israelis visited the country their Prime Minister had labeled the "land of the murderers." The numbers for 1981 and 1982 are especially revealing: In 1981, 86,000 Israelis traveled to West Germany. That was double the number of the year before. In 1982 the number rose to 100,000, in 1983 to 131,000, and in 1984 to 152,000. In the years 1983 and 1984, more visitors from little Israel (with a population then of less than 3 million) traveled to West Germany (with a population of more than 60 million) than Germans to Israel—even though for Israelis, with their generally lower levels of income, foreign travel involved a considerably greater financial sacrifice.

As a result of the belt-tightening policies of the government that took office in 1984, travel abroad became virtually unaffordable for Israelis. Nevertheless, in 1985 nearly 122,000 Israelis visited the Federal Republic of Germany. In 1986, 139,000 and, in 1987, a still impressive 135,000 were willing to pay the exorbitant price of a trip to Germany. From 1988 to 1990 the number of Israeli visitors to Germany remained nearly stable at just above or below 125,000 annually. Only in 1991 did the number drop again to 113,000—a result of Israel's continuing economic difficulties or the Gulf War? In any case, the total still remained impressive.

The behavior of the Israelis thus stands in contradiction to public opinion as expressed in the polls. With their responses to the questions in the surveys, Israelis thus articulated their official national identity, with its internalized image of the ugly German. On the plane of personal behavior, as tourists, they paid little or no attention to this historical super-ego. This is a remarkable contradiction and it indicates a fundamental change on the Israeli side. With regard to Germany, the actual behavior of the Israeli public is relaxed, but the language is tense. Israelis coolly distinguish between word and deed.

Advertisers involved in the German tourist industry in Israel have drawn their own conclusions from all of this. In contrast to the image presented in all other areas, Germany is portrayed in old, rather than new, terms: dreamy vineyards and forests, romantic vistas and, of course, a punctual airline. Romanticism pervades, although it has so often been contended that it was precisely the romantic streak in German history that helped to prepare the way for the rise of National-Socialism. But in terms of travel marketing this is all forgotten, and the Israeli consumers react as intended: they buy the romantic product. History apparently causes no anxiety pangs. This is a further sign of relaxation in German-Israeli tensions.

It is historically grotesque that nothing less than the old, romantic Germany is in such demand in the Jewish State. But even today's little David prefers to concentrate on present pleasures rather than the past sufferings of his parents and ancestors.

8

PERSONALITIES

The history of German-Israeli relations of the last forty years is in no small part the work of two men: Konrad Adenauer and David Ben-Gurion.

1. Konrad Adenauer

In the historical interview published by the leading German-Jewish weekly newspaper in November 1949, Konrad Adenauer expressed his government's readiness to render Israel financial support in its struggle to built a Jewish society. In September 1951, he made a public statement before the German Bundestag and two months later a financial commitment to Nahum Goldmann. Adenauer did so without regard to the possible financial consequences of his decision. The opposition within Adenauer's cabinet, led by Finance Minister Fritz

Schäffer, could not or would not recognize the Chancellor's historical farsightedness and wisdom. In the opinion of the opposition within the government, the financial commitments Adenauer was so heedlessly ready to assume would prove unfulfillable.

Adenauer chose not to enter into a bare-knuckles struggle against Schäffer, but instead proceeded with cautious tactics, skillfully playing the bureaucracy of the Finance Ministry against its chief and employing tactical tricks in order to neutralize Schäffer's potential power to block legislation. For his part, Schäffer acted fairly and even the foreign press (including the *New York Times*) confirmed his integrity and expressed understanding for his financial worries. In addition to Schäffer, Adenauer was faced with the problem of persuading a large proportion of the CSU parliamentarians, including the powerful Bavarian politician Franz Josef Strauss, to at least abstain during the Bundestag vote on the Luxembourg Restitution Agreement. Vice Chancellor Blücher and Justice Minister Dehler (both Free Democrats), the ministers of the German Party, Hellwege and Seebohm, as well as two members of the cabinet from the left wing of Adenauer's own CDU, Storch and Kaiser, also joined in articulating reservations. Hermann Josef Abs, Germany's representative at the London Debt Conference, contributed financial arguments against the Chancellor's restitution proposals.

In short, Adenauer was forced to navigate around obstacles to his left and right within his own coalition, and parliamentary approval of the restitution treaty with Israel was ultimately due in no small part to the support of the opposition Social Democrats. Nevertheless, Adenauer himself made all the key decisions. The archival record documents this beyond a doubt.

There can also be no doubt as to the seriousness and integrity of Adenauer's intentions with regard to restitution, his lack of attention to the issue of the financing, and his deliberate neglect of the desires of right-wing supporters and members of his own party. Finance Minister Schäffer was particularly worried that these voters might well choose to punish the party at the next national elections, due in the fall of 1953. His worries were not without foundation, as the restitution agreement was received with serious reservations by the German populace. The polls show that this continued to be the case until rather recently.

It is also clear that Adenauer, though he was certainly never bitten by the bug of anti-Semitism, did conjure up "the great economic power of the Jews in the world" (cabinet meeting of July 11, 1952), especially the resulting political weight of the Jews in the United States. The German Chancellor either actually misread the attitude of the Truman administration, or he was deliberately overstating the case in order to overcome the opposition within his cabinet. As demonstrated by his memoirs, Hermann Josef Abs persisted in misinterpreting the U.S. approach as late as 1991.

If we compare Adenauer's repeated references to American pressure with the actual behavior of both the Truman and Eisenhower administrations, then we recognize an American interest, but little that could be described as pressure, much less as intervention.

Adenauer also refused to bow to the mixture of Arab cajoling and threats which culminated in the visit of a delegation from the Arab League to Bonn in the autumn of 1952. The Arab delegation sought to persuade the Chancellor's right-hand man on the restitution issue, Deputy Foreign Minister Hallstein, not to seek ratification of the already concluded Luxembourg Agreement. The Arabs indicated their belief that Bonn had negotiated only under pressure from the Western powers. The delegation argued that, as the losing parties of the second world war, Germans and Arabs ought to work together. Much to the chagrin of leading figures in West German industry, Hallstein firmly rejected the insinuations and suggestions put forth by the Arab League delegation.

Adenauer strongly opposed any proposal not to fulfill the provisions of the treaty with Israel. As he confided in a letter to Heinrich von Brentano, then chairman of the CDU/CSU faction in the Bundestag, in December 1952: "With certainty, any such treaty violation would do more damage to our position in the world than temporary tensions in German-Arab relations."

In substance and style, Adenauer's treatment of the restitution issue was significant both historically and in terms of *geschichtspolitik*. Despite the legends to the contrary, Adenauer did not conduct policy with a bowed head or clad in the penitent's hair-shirt. It is well known that, in his declaration to the Bundestag on September 27, 1951, Adenauer rejected the theory of collective guilt on the part of all Germans.

We have seen that he was prepared to conclude a restitution agreement, but by no means ready to grant any and every wish advanced by the Israeli side. His remarks on the lack of credibility of the calculations presented "by the Jews" show that he knew how to make pragmatic distinctions between historical obligations and political negotiations.

No, Konrad Adenauer did not in any way allow himself to be pushed around by the other side in the restitution negotiations. The Chancellor refused to grant the Israeli side any sort of historically derived moral monopoly with regard to Germany's past or the German people.

Certainly, Adenauer bowed to the pressures of current events, financial considerations, and Germany's difficult international position. Under his chancellorship, Germany did not take up diplomatic relations with Israel. All the same, he never swerved when it came to vital aspects of German-Israeli relations, and remained especially steadfast in his efforts to secure Israel's ability to survive.

In 1956–57, when the United States was seeking to increase the pressure on Israel to withdraw from the Sinai and had cut off American aid to the Jewish State, Adenauer refused to even consider a suspension of restitution payments. In 1957 he approved the purchase of weapons from and the sale of arms to Israel. He lent a personal hand in the establishment of relations between Israeli and German scientists and academic institutions. But he never submitted to historically motivated political pressures aimed at influencing current issues, neither during the restitution negotiations nor during the controversy over the activities of German rocket engineers in Egypt; and, although he wanted to see Eichmann convicted, he dared to publicly criticize Eichmann's kidnapping in an Israeli intelligence operation.

With the dignity and steadfastness of his sincere desire for atonement and reconciliation, Konrad Adenauer personified the new Germany. This may be one of the reasons why (anti-Semitic?) extremists desecrated his grave in October 1991.

It was rare historical good fortune that Adenauer found in David Ben-Gurion a partner who shared similar feelings and, moreover, was prepared to act accordingly.

2. David Ben-Gurion

In December 1986, a parliamentarian from the German provinces undertook a rhetorical excursion into the realm of world politics with a number of pithy observations: "For more than forty years it has been the policy of foreign powers to inculcate guilt-complexes among the German youth, to plunge an entire people into a dilemma of conscience in order to extract foreign policy and even financial advantages from Germany, and in order to perpetuate moral blackmail against the Germans. Whoever makes one-sided assignments of guilt or nurtures feelings of guilt as a central aim of policy must not expect to see the concept of reconciliation taken seriously. In the meantime it ought to have become clear that German restitution payments have not accelerated the desired process of reconciliation, but rather the contrary."

Which state could this people's tribune have meant with his references to a foreign power and restitution payments? Although we all know that Israel is the only state to have received the form of payments specifically mentioned, the parliamentarian from the provinces replied to his critics: "I did not even mention the State of Israel in this context."

Enough of such dreary political theater! There is no doubt that an unbridgeable chasm separates such provincial dwarfs from the giant Ben-Gurion, the Israeli architect of the Luxembourg Agreement. David Ben-Gurion not only sought to extract money *from* Germany; he also aimed at reconciliation *with* Germany. The comments by the German provincial parliamentarian are but one indication that, to this day, German-Israeli reconciliation has by no means been universally accepted, much less achieved. That Ben-Gurion took up the challenge of reconciliation in the early 1950s, only a few years after the Holocaust, the very fact that he could bring himself to do so, is certainly to be counted among the greatest personal and political achievements of this statesman. The process of initiating reconciliation with Germany marked both the high tide and the end of Ben-Gurion's political career.

As in many other areas, Ben-Gurion's policy toward Germany is remarkable for its pragmatic, nonideological approach. There is no question that Ben-Gurion had an initially negative relationship to Germany as a result of the Holocaust. He at first considered Germany politically untouchable, as taboo. But his thinking soon adapted to the realities of the day, even when the developments at first caused him considerable personal discomfort. In contrast to most of Israel's other politicians, David Ben-Gurion recognized early on, at the latest with the outbreak of the Korean War in June 1950, that the Federal Republic of Germany would no longer require Israeli and Jewish approbation before it would once again be welcomed on the international stage. The West needed a re-armed West Germany. At the same time, the new State of Israel that Ben-Gurion had founded and led was struggling for its bare survival, not just in military but most especially in economic terms.

Within three years, from 1948 to 1951, the population of Israel had doubled. Whereas some 600,000 Jews had lived in Israel at the time its independence was proclaimed, a country which had no economic or financial resources to call its own was faced with the task of providing for 1.2 million people by 1951. Outside assistance was essential, but who would provide it? For a number of reasons, the United States was unwilling. The Truman administration was under pressure from Congress to decrease spending while at the same time it had to finance the war effort in Korea. Israel could not expect more than the level of loans that had already been provided, and this was by no means sufficient. England was economically exhausted and, after having virtually been bombed out of Palestine by the Zionists, was in any case not very well-disposed toward Israel. Nor could any economic assistance be expected from France, which was itself in dire financial straits.

Ben-Gurion and his inner circle of advisers soon recognized that only Germany was left. Hardly anyone in 1950–51 could have foreseen the advent of the German economic miracle, but at least the country was morally obligated to Israel. Ben-Gurion was convinced that Germany, which was responsible for the death of millions of Jews in the immediate past, could not and would not allow the very existence of the Jewish State to be imperiled. He decided to demand restitution from Germany, which could thereby aid Israel financially and improve its moral, as well as its military standing.

As we have seen, the restitution payments to which the West German government committed itself in the 1952 Luxembourg treaty were never very popular—in fact, were largely rejected by the West German population. Konrad Adenauer—with the aid of Kurt Schumacher, the leader of the opposition Social Democrats (and, after Schumacher's death, his successor, Erich Ollenhauer)—steered the negotiation and ratification process around internal opposition and against the current of public opinion.

The decisions to demand restitution and then to negotiate and accept payments from Germany were extraordinarily controversial in Israel. Ben-Gurion's opponents—and they were numerous—labeled such payments "blood money" and accused Ben-Gurion of forcing his personal will in this matter not only against the will of the rest of his government and party as well as of the other parties both left and right, but also against the will of the Israeli people. This was apparently ignored by the German opponents of restitution, who also failed to notice that Ben-Gurion was, however cautiously, extending his hand in reconciliation. When viewed from this perspective, the German-Israeli restitution agreement represented a greater burden on Israel than on Germany.

"There is no German who did not murder our parents. Every German is a Nazi. Every German is a murderer. Adenauer is a murderer." These were the words of David Ben-Gurion's most vociferous opponent, Menachem Begin, before an agitated crowd in Jerusalem on January 7, 1952. Begin went so far as to threaten civil war in order to prevent negotiations with or the acceptance of money from Germany.

Ben-Gurion did not hesitate to use Israel's armed forces in order to nip the threat of civil disorder in the bud. In a radio address to the nation on January 8, 1952, Ben-Gurion warned that the state possessed sufficient means to defend Israel's sovereignty and freedom "against rowdies, political assassins, or terrorists." He also used the term "fascist" to describe the ideology of the left- and right-wing opponents of negotiations with Germany. For their part, the other side did not hesitate to raise the threat of violent extraparliamentary opposition.

We ought to pause here for a moment of reflection: A bare seven years after the Holocaust, the Prime Minister of the Jewish State labels the opponents of his policy toward the formerly fascist Germany as Jewish "fascists." What is more, he states that he is prepared to use force against them. Not the state of the former murderers, but his own Jewish countrymen, the survivors of German fascism, are labeled "fascists." Who was taking on the greater burden here, the Germans or the

Israelis? For the new West Germany, the restitution agreement represented not an unbearable burden, but a stroke of good fortune. The victims were offering the legal successor of the state of the murderers a possibility to overcome the past together.

The economic cure Ben-Gurion prescribed for Israel was at the same time a drastic treatment for the psyche and emotions of his countrymen. Even Ben-Gurion himself did not find the cure a pleasant one: "I don't hate the Germans any less than the others, but I must look out for the state" he confided to a friend (Cited in Michael Bar-Zohar, *Ben-Gurion* [Hebrew] [Tel-Aviv: Am-Oved, 1977] 3: 920). This is called statesmanship, but at what emotional price both for Ben-Gurion and his people!

German restitution payments soon constituted one of the chief pillars of the Israeli economy. As a result of the Sinai Campaign of 1956, the basis of this economic foundation was seriously threatened. Having considered German rearmament a higher priority than restitution to Israel at the time of the German-Israeli negotiations in the early 1950s, the United States roundly condemned the joint British-French-Israeli actions against Egypt during the Suez crisis in late 1956 and the Eisenhower-Dulles administration sought to mobilize all possible direct and indirect pressure on Ben-Gurion and his government to promptly withdraw from the Sinai peninsula. This included an automatic cut-off of American aid, and it is clear that Washington would have welcomed a Bonn decision to suspend its much more vital restitution payments until such time as Israel began its withdrawal.

On October 31, 1956, two days after the outbreak of the fighting, government spokesman von Eckhard indicated that Bonn might possibly freeze its transfer payments to Israel. One day later, Prime Minister Ben-Gurion wrote to Chancellor Adenauer, appealing to him not to take any such step. Ben-Gurion emphasized: "I cannot imagine that such a far-reaching proposal [. . .] would meet with your approval." He expressly praised Adenauer's "noble role" in the "historic development" represented by the Restitution Agreement. This role, he assured, would "never" be forgotten. Eleven years after the end of the Second World War the Prime Minister of the Jewish State thus appealed for help to the Chancellor of Germany. And Ben-Gurion's appeal was not in vain. German restitution payments continued without interruption.

This decision on Adenauer's part represents the true turning-point in German-Israeli relations. From that point on, Ben-Gurion pressed not just for restitution, but above all for cooperation, for diplomatic relations—which he had sought to avoid before—and not least of all for military cooperation. Military relations began immediately, in 1957, and to this end Ben-Gurion was willing to endure two government crises, in 1957 and again in 1959. This policy proved highly controversial in Israel, and Ben-Gurion's opponents were far more numerous than his supporters. It was only by the strength of his personal authority that the Prime Minister was able to turn a majority of opinion against him into a parliamentary majority in support of his government.

Thus began a military relationship that was briefly interrupted in 1965, but then resumed under the German social-liberal coalition and has continued ever since. The shock of Iraqi SCUD missiles launched against Israel strengthened this relationship and made it more visible. Among the minority of those supporting military relations back in 1957 were three of Ben-Gurion's young protégés, whose political influence in Israel has grown greatly since then: Asher Ben-Nathan, Shimon Peres, and Chaim Herzog.

In the eyes of a majority of his countrymen and numerous Diaspora Jews, Ben-Gurion's policy of reconciliation with Germany constituted an insult to the dead. Ben-Gurion's reply to this accusation is remarkable: "Of course one can be against restitution from Germany; of course one can be against weapons from Germany; of course one can be against weapons for Germany. But no one may speak in the name of the victims of the Holocaust! The Holocaust must not become a political propaganda article to be used by one party or another."

Ben-Gurion was, in other words, warning his countrymen and the Jews of the Diaspora not to use the Holocaust as a political argument or as a political instrument. This is a warning that continues to be frequently ignored by Jews as well as non-Jews. Morally, Ben-Gurion was right, as constant reminders of the horrors of the Holocaust lead to a dulling of the senses. Politically, Ben-Gurion was also right, as every over-used argument eventually loses its power to convince.

That Ben-Gurion can in no case be counted among those who would achieve reconciliation by forgetting was demonstrated not only by his move toward greater cooperation with Germany beginning in 1957, but also by his decision to capture Adolf Eichmann and place him on trial in Israel. Contrary to the fears of many Germans, the purpose of this trial had less to do with policy toward Germany than with domestic Israeli and Zionist goals, namely to demonstrate to the younger generation of Israelis and Jews both the security provided by the Jewish State as well as the insecurity of the Jewish Diaspora. As Ben-Gurion explained: "Our chief concern was to demonstrate to our youth [. . .] the horrible tragedy that happened to a dispersed people dependent upon the mercy of strangers."

When asked about the political dimension of the trial with regard to Germany, Ben-Gurion added: "My opinion of today's Germany has not changed. Nazi Germany no longer exists. Our religion teaches us: 'The fathers should not die for the sins of their children, nor the children for the sins of their fathers, but everyone shall die for their own sins.'" Ben-Gurion was referring to Deuteronomy 24:16 and Ezekiel 18:20. These words also represented an indirect appeal to his countrymen and to the Jews of the Diaspora to overcome their inhibitions and to recognize the new Germany without forgetting the old. Ben-Gurion was attempting to cure the German-Israeli dis-synchronism.

These comments by Ben-Gurion are also significant in another context: He was also warning against the use of political biologism, the political doctrine of heredity (see chapter 2.10). Ben-Gurion knew that such interpretations were widespread among his co-religionists and underlined his warning against the use of such arguments with the aid of a biblical quotation. Here, and in many other ways as well, Ben-Gurion's legacy is a charge to posterity, to both Jew and non-Jew.

Ben-Gurion's legacy and charge remain valid in evaluating the weight of the past, present, and future in German-Israeli relations and with regard to the ability of both sides to conduct policy despite the past. "Israel's national interest requires intact relations with Germany," Ben-Gurion stated before the Knesset in December 1957, and added: "Today we are dealing not with the world of yesterday, but with the world of tomorrow, not with recollections from the past but with the necessities of the future, [...] not with past realities but with existing realities which are shifting and changing."

Ben-Gurion's fall from political power was due in no small degree to the fact that this message was heard, and either not followed or actively combatted. In June 1963, David Ben-Gurion resigned the office of Prime Minister. Certainly, his stepping down was not solely a result of his controversial policy toward Germany. Numerous other domestic and internal party developments also played a role, while the luster of even the most impressive personality eventually wears thin when charisma becomes routine. Ben-Gurion's policy toward Germany was not the root cause, but certainly the trigger for his resignation.

When it became generally known by the summer of 1962 that Egypt was working on a rocket program with the help of West German scientists there was a great deal of disquiet in Israeli political and military circles. According to rumor and intelligence information, these rockets were to be equipped with chemical, bacterial, and even nuclear warheads.

Ben-Gurion wanted to play down the affair so as not to endanger his good relations with Germany. His chief of intelligence, however, attempted to turn the issue into a state scandal. This gave Ben-Gurion's opponents within his own party an opportunity to revolt against the "old man." Their motivation was given further impetus by Ben-Gurion's attempts to favor his young protégés such as Peres and Dayan over the older party veterans and thus strip the party apparatus of its power. The anger at the "old man," who, with the help of his young supporters, held fast to his policy toward Germany despite the activities of the German rocket scientists in Egypt, broke out in a political storm. Ben-Gurion was accused of not putting sufficient pressure on Bonn to see to it that the rocket experts were removed and thus of endangering the existence of the state with a much too lax policy toward Germany. For the first time, the aging Ben-Gurion's reaction proved weak and lacking in political skill. Finally, he resigned his office. In the end, Ben-Gurion stumbled over his policy toward Germany, but it remains the legacy and the charge for his posterity, both in Israel and in Germany.

3. Those Who Followed

Neither the German nor the Israeli leaders who followed Adenauer and Ben-Gurion wanted or were able to make any basic changes in the course these two leaders had set. It will therefore suffice to take a brief look at some of the later shapers of policy.

The achievements of Adenauer's successor, Ludwig Erhard, in the sphere of German-Israeli relations are often underestimated. In the face of great difficulties, pressure from the Arab states, and over the objections of his Foreign Minister Gerhard Schröder, Erhard mustered the courage to establish formal diplomatic relations with Israel. He assisted in the highly discreet but effective buyout of the German rocket scientists in Egypt, who were quietly offered lucrative jobs back in Germany. Erhard also spoke out in favor of extending the statute of limitations for National-Socialist crimes. Because he was a generally weak chancellor, Erhard is often not given due credit in the area of German-Israeli relations.

Under Chancellors Kiesinger (CDU) and Brandt (SPD) the West German government embarked on its "normalization" course. One of many Israeli worries during the era of Willy Brandt was that West Germany might sacrifice its Middle East and Israel policy on the altars of detente and *ostpolitik* (the policy of reconciliation with Eastern Europe), especially under the strong influence of Foreign Minister Walter Scheel (FDP). Chancellor Helmut Schmidt (SPD) sought to accelerate the pace of the economically motivated gallop toward a supposed normalization of relations. His successor, Helmut Kohl (CDU), mounted what he hoped would be an even faster horse, but fell off in 1985. Since then the pace has slowed to a trot or a walk.

The rhetorical storm over German unification and the involvement of German firms in Iraqi dictator Saddam Hussein's chemical and nuclear weapons programs proved once again that German-Israeli relations had not yet achieved "normality."

Ben-Gurion's successor, Levi Eshkol, sometimes adopted an almost rude tone of voice toward Germany. In an apparent attempt to free himself of the political super-ego of his predecessor, Eshkol seldom spoke of the new Germany, but often of the old. His attempt to establish a personal profile placed no small burden on relations with Germany.

Golda Meir also could not be counted among Germany's friends in Israel, but she was a pragmatic enough practitioner of *realpolitik* to recognize the advantages of a functioning relationship with West Germany. Under her watch as Prime Minister the first visits of an Israeli foreign minister to West Germany (Abba Eban in 1970) and of a German foreign minister to Israel (Walter Scheel in 1971) took place. Golda Meir received Willy Brandt in 1973 as the first German chancellor to visit the Jewish State while in office. This did not prevent her from categorically rejecting both Willy Brandt's efforts at "normalization" and the German Nobel Peace Prizewinner's advice on how to make peace with the Arabs.

Her successor, Yitzhak Rabin, the first Israeli Prime Minister to have been born in Israel, perhaps aided by the good fortune of his birth, took a quieter, more sober approach toward Germany. Rabin was the first Israeli Prime Minister to visit the Federal Republic (in 1975).

With his verbal blasts against Helmut Schmidt and the German people, Rabin's successor, Menachem Begin, nearly succeeded in uprooting the delicate growth of German-Israeli relations. In the end, however, the roots of the relationship initiated by Ben-Gurion and Adenauer proved strong and deep enough to survive.

Prime Minister Shimon Peres, the student and imitator of Ben-Gurion, sought to continue the tradition of the great master, including relations with Germany.

Prime Minister Shamir played neither the role of planter nor that of uprooter, but he did mount a campaign to put a stop to the Kohl government's plans to sell weapons to Saudi Arabia. In doing so he reached for the political instrument of the Holocaust in order to frustrate the German plans by means of a hail of criticism from the United States. He once again wielded the Holocaust cudgel in the debate over German unification. Less than a year later, Shamir used the Holocaust argument against the Bush administration. In the meantime, in connection with the Gulf War, Israel had received more than half a billion dollars in German military aid.

In 1992 Yitzhak Rabin became Israel's Prime Minister once again. His first trip outside the country took him to Egypt, the second to the United States, and the third to Germany, where his visit fell in a difficult time. Just a few weeks before,a mob had burned down the center for asylum-seekers in Rostock. Rabin nevertheless attempted to return to the tradition of Ben-Gurion and, in the face of the historical-political crises, to acknowledge that a new, democratic Germany still existed. His gesture was warmly welcomed by the majority of Germans, but the incorrigibles thanked Rabin in their own way: Only a few days after Rabin's words of reconciliation in the Sachsenhausen concentration camp memorial, the "Jewish barracks," which had been preserved on the site, were burned down by arsonists. The symbolic, historical-political damage was massive, even if this act, as the great majority of the other incidents throughout the country, was the deed of the young, often enough under-aged skinheads and so-called "neo-Nazi" extremists, usually acting as individuals rather than as part of an organized group. The point is that they interpreted the political climate as favorable enough for violence.

After the deaths of the three Turkish women in Mölln, the until then silent majority of democratic and tolerant Germans took to the offensive. Nevertheless, Rabin and Foreign Minister Shimon Peres were hard pressed to fend off calls for a Jewish boycott of Germany, the initiative for which came from both the rightist Likud Party as well as the left-liberal Meretz bloc, including Rabin's Education Minister, Shulamit Aloni.

And Nahum Goldmann? Israeli Ambassador Meroz once tartly reported back to Jerusalem: "Whether they know better or not, his interlocutors in Germany overlook the fact that he does not represent Israeli, but rather non-Israeli interests. He—and some of his listeners—derive pleasure from sneering at Israel's desires and expectations and to brand its political leaders as naive, provincial or chauvinistic. To someone who lives in comfort in New York, Paris and Switzerland and honors Jerusalem only with the occasional whirlwind visit the worries and anxieties of the citizens of Israel mean little indeed." This characterization is bitter and exaggerated, and, at least with regard to Goldmann's role in the restitution negotiations, false. In 1951 and 1952 Nahum Goldmann was Israel's honest and best mediator. All available information and archive materials—and not just those collected by the admittedly vain Goldmann himself—document his key role.

It is, however, correct to state that on later occasions, Goldmann sometimes asserted his personal influence and the weight of Diaspora Jewish organizations at the expense of Israel. In the eyes of many Israelis, Goldmann personified the typical Diaspora Jew claiming to be building bridges to Israel but in fact being, and allowing himself to be used as an alibi-Jew. Like many other Diaspora Jews, Goldmann lost his balance in this high wire act. Israel's resentment sits so deep that in 1987 the city council of Tel Aviv refused to name a street after him.

One of Goldmann's successors, Edgar Bronfman, was also active in the field of German-Jewish-Israeli relations, but in a totally different manner and context. We have already narrated that story in connection with the end of the East German regime.

In March 1992 Chancellor Kohl met with Austrian President Kurt Waldheim in Munich, just before the latter's term of office expired. As could be expected, Kohl's decision met with protest both at home and abroad, and Bronfman also attacked the Chancellor sharply. But Kohl no longer considered Bronfman a moral authority and called public attention to his efforts on behalf of the GDR to hinder the Germans' right to national self-determination.

9

INSTITUTIONS AND ORGANIZATIONS

U p to this point we have examined and interpreted mainly the conditions and consequences of political decisions, but not the course of the decision-making process. We thus concentrated on governments, mentioning parties and institutions only peripherally. Many organizations have undertaken respectable and successful efforts toward the betterment of German-Israeli relations. We can take but a brief look at a few selected examples here. Among the activities certainly worth examining more closely is the history of partnerships between German and Israeli cities, the German-Israeli youth exchange programs, the exemplary work of the German party-sponsored foundations in Israel, the German-Israeli Society, the Federal Center for Political Education, and the cooperation between German and Israeli universities, but we must confine ourselves here to those institutions that have stood in the political limelight.

1. Political Parties

With the exception of the various Communist parties and the ultra-right-wing NPD, no West German party has taken a consistently pro- or contra-Israel line. The smaller parties of the right and left have tried to keep Israel at arm's length. Where the Communists employed vehement rhetoric, the so-called "national democrats" treaded cautiously, so as to avoid coming into conflict with the Federal Constitutional Court over illegal anti-Semitic utterances.

The early anti-Israelism of the Greens had to do with their romanticized view of the Third World, which led them to prefer the Palestinians to "westernized" Israel. In the meantime, however, more differentiated statements have been made by various Green politicians. In any case, with its more youthful following, this party of the "1968" and "eco" generations has taken a more uninhibited approach to Israel and Jews.

Within the Christian-Democratic Union parties, CDU and CSU, the German-Jewish-Israeli spectrum has always been extremely broad. Adenauer's policy toward Israel met with anything but universal approval in his own party and the CSU was generally opposed. Both Finance Minister Schäffer and his ally, Bavarian Minister-President Ehard, opposed Adenauer's restitution policy. Later, as Justice Minister, Schäffer involved himself in a public controversy with Franz Böhm (CDU) over uses and abuses of the restitution system. Böhm, one of Israel's staunchest friends in the Union, went so far as to accuse Schäffer of anti-Semitism. A party tribunal was convened and Böhm was forced to issue an apology.

The attitudes expressed by CSU leader Franz Josef Strauss toward restitution were anything but consistent. In October 1952 he supported the Luxembourg Agreement. In January 1953 he spoke out against it and he abstained in the Bundestag vote on the treaty in March 1953. By 1957 at the latest, then Defense Minister Strauss had come to view Israel as a bastion of the West against Soviet advances in the Middle East. With conviction and great energy he thus initiated the era of German-Israeli military cooperation. In contrast to Foreign Minister Schröder (CDU), Strauss supported the assumption of diplomatic relations in 1965. From the early 1970s until his death in 1988, however, the Bavarian politician's economic and export interests, as well as the opening to the West on the part of key Arab states, served to somewhat dampen his enthusiasm for Israel. Multifaceted relations grew in place of a one-sided interest. In the meantime this has become typical of all West German parties.

The SPD parliamentarians in the Bundestag supported the Restitution Agreement without reservation, but in the provinces and at the grassroots the feelings were not so unanimous. Like Minister of Justice Dehler and Vice Chancellor Blücher (both FDP), Bavarian SDP leader Högner feared that restitution to Israel would mean the sacrifice of individual recompensation. Mayor Kaisen (SPD) of the port city of Bremen welcomed the Luxembourg treaty in principle but made his support contingent on Israel permitting the transport of German restitution goods on German ships. Kaisen and his Bavarian colleague Ehard thus presented an obstacle to ratification by the Bundesrat in 1953. Adenauer personally assuaged Ehard's doubts and Hallstein persuaded Israel to accept the demands of the German shipping interests.

The SPD gave unconditional support to the assumption of diplomatic relations with Israel and the suspension of the statute of limitations on National-Socialist crimes. Nevertheless, even the Social Democrats had their problems with Israel in the 1950s, especially with Israel's military policy of preventive strikes and drastic retaliation against Palestinian guerrilla actions, with their enthusiasm for Israel on the one hand and the Third-World romanticism personified by Egyptian President Nasser on the other, and with the SPD's interest in ideological issues which their friends and comrades in Israel treated with polite indifference at best.

As the dominant party in the governing coalition, the SPD found it difficult to maintain its traditional unconditional friendship for Israel. The SPD leaders were forced to consider financial, economic and, since the late 1960s, factional political interests within their own party. The SPD sought to integrate the youth of the 1968 generation into the party—and thus into the larger political community. Many young people were, in fact, attracted to the party, but they tended to be critical of Israel and friendly to the PLO. The Middle East policy pursued by Helmut Schmidt, flanked by plans for the sale of weapons to the region, was torpedoed by his own party, partly because of German-Jewish sensitivities, but mostly because of party grassroots objection to increased arms exports.

The Free Democrats' initial approach to Israel was characterized by internal reservations, which were at least sometimes also given public expression. Under the leadership of Thomas Dehler, the FDP exhibited strong nationalist tendencies until the mid-1960s. Adenauer's restitution policy and diplomatic relations were rejected but the suspension of the statute of limitations was supported. As the party's social-liberal elements achieved ascendancy, the FDP continued to maintain its close identification with business interests, and this was reflected in the Middle East policies pursued by both FDP Foreign Ministers Scheel and Genscher. In the 1980s, the FDP's Jürgen Möllemann, as president of the German-Arabian Society, was at the forefront of German-Arab relations. (In contrast to the German-Israeli Society, the German-Arabian Society and its president refused to let us examine any of their internal minutes or documents.) Nevertheless, even the FDP had its pro-Israel faction, including Burkhard Hirsch, Detlef Kleinert, and Hildegard Hamm-Brücher.

In Israel there was and is really only one pro-German party, the Mapai, now known as the Israeli Labor Party. Although not unchallenged, the spirit of Ben-Gurion continues in his party. Relations were deepened and strengthened early on by the close cooperation between Mapai and the Histadrut, the Israeli union organization on the one hand and the German Labor Federation, and thus also the SPD, on the other.

Following the rise to power of Menachem Begin's Herut Party in 1977 the previously much feared German-Israeli clash at first failed to materialize. The collision finally came in May of 1981 (see chapter 2) and was all the more vehement. The scorched earth eventually brought forth fruit once again, and even in Begin's party there is increasing evidence of a pragmatic attitude toward Germany. Then came the fall of the Berlin Wall and the re-ideologization of bilateral relations—at least on the official level. The Gulf War further promoted this process.

The Independent Liberals and their predecessors, in other words the old *jeckes*, Israelis who immigrated from Germany and who, despite everything, still identify with the culture of their homeland, never succeeded in weighing in with sufficient political influence in Israel to influence the thrust of policy toward Germany.

The religious parties exhibit a friendly disinterest in Germany. Joseph Burg, a veteran of the National Religious Party and for many years Israel's Minister for Religious Affairs, often served as a German-Israeli-Jewish bridge builder.

In both states, antipathies toward the other side are chiefly to be found among the parties of the extreme left and right, in Israel among the Communists, the left-wing socialist parties, and the extreme nationalists.

2. Cultural Institutions

Cultural and scientific institutions deserve much more attention than we are able to give here. There is, first of all, the Goethe Institute and its predecessor, the German Cultural Institute. In the beginning, it was only the old *jeckes* who appeared. Now, more and more *sabras*, many of whom are not of German extraction, frequent the courses and cultural events sponsored by the Goethe Institutes in Israel. A third of the current library users are immigrants from Germany or Austria, and if one includes all immigrants from central Europe, the number is about half. The same applies for the participants in the German-language courses of the Goethe Institute.

The numbers indicate that, despite the Holocaust, the German-Israeli Jews and their descendants identify with German culture. They differentiate between the Germany of Goethe and Schiller and that of Adolf Hitler. There is no assignment of "eternal guilt" in this everyday mode of dealing with history. Nevertheless, we do find a contradiction between expressed opinion and actual behavior, between the political confrontation with history and the everyday life of the citizen.

Germany has become increasingly attractive to those parts of Israeli society without any historical connection. What is new about this new Germany is constantly being emphasized in the cultural programs of the Goethe Institute, the goal being to document the changes in Germany and thus overcome German-Israeli dis-synchronism: New German art, new German films, new German literature, new German music, new, new, new. The number of visitors has been steadily increasing. The products of the new Germany are in demand.

According to a poll conducted in 1974, fewer Israelis took offense at the presence of uniformed West German military officers in Tel Aviv than at the public performance of works by Richard Wagner. The anti-Semitic, old-German composer provoked a more emotional response among Israelis than new-German military officers! Times have, indeed, changed since the fifties, when the plan to stage Lessing's *Nathan the Wise* provoked a heated controversy and when it was debated whether the Israeli public would tolerate showings of the romantic, tear-jerking films about the nineteenth-century Austrian empress "Sissy" (Elizabeth)—not because of the movies' third-rate quality, but because of historical sensibilities. In 1990 another plan to perform works by Wagner was advanced, but opinion within the Israeli Philharmonic Orchestra and the Israeli public was sharply divided over the proposal, which was dropped.

One significant indicator of the interest on the part of Germans for Israeli culture is that in the last forty years about a third of the peace prizes awarded by the German booksellers at their annual book fair have gone to Israeli authors. In 1992 the recipient of this prize was Amos Oz, who had sharply criticized the German peace movement in connection with the 1991 Gulf War.

It is highly informative to take a look at West Germany's universities. Until 1967, German students were mostly friendly toward Israel. Then came a turnabout. A number of public appearances by Israel's ambassador, Ben-Nathan, were disrupted. Whistles, shouts, rotten tomatoes, and bags of paint were substituted for arguments. Among the 1968 generation, Israel was "out," Palestinians "in." On the other side of the spectrum, the conservative right began to discover its sympathies for Israel during the period of the student revolt, some of which were lost again in the course of the battle of the historians in the late 1980s. The conservatives' later withdrawal of sympathy for Israel, however, involved considerably less of an uproar. It also ought to be mentioned that the present atmosphere of research and publication on the Middle East is strongly imbued with the spirit of the 1968 generation, which exhibits few historically conditioned inhibitions in its analysis of Israel.

3. Research Institutions

A strong desire for atonement and reconciliation can be recognized in the substantial support for Israeli research institutions by their counterparts in West Germany. Under the leadership of Otto Hahn and Wolfgang Gentner, preparations for the Minerva Program of the Max Planck Society were already underway before the outbreak of anti-Semitic graffiti in the winter of 1959–60. Early in 1960, Konrad Adenauer personally joined in the effort, and by the time of his meeting with Ben-Gurion in New York in March of that year, the first phase of the program between the Max Planck Society and the Weizmann Institute was ready to be launched. Before the meeting with Ben-Gurion, Adenauer placed a high priority on informing the Israeli government through his foreign minister that "it is a special satisfaction that the government of the Federal Republic of Germany can be of service to the Weizmann Institute." A special program sponsored by the Max Planck Society continues to support German-Israeli research in the natural sciences.

In the year 1976 about 90 percent of all the funds supplied to non-German institutions by the Volkswagen Foundation went to Israel. This proportion declined in the following years, averaging about 25 percent and reaching a low point of 6 percent in 1986. This, too, is a sign of normalization. Applications from Israel are now treated like any other; well-founded requests are funded, the others not. The total sum of funds made available to Israel by the government-sponsored research society, *Deutsche Forschungsgemeinschaft* (DFG), was always somewhat higher than the sums provided by the Volkswagen Foundation.

Hardly anyone involved in the management of research institutions would deny that the now sometimes smaller, but still very considerable overall volume of grants to Israel has to do both with the highly respected achievements of Israeli researchers and with West Germany's political efforts to confront the legacy of the past. The degree of entanglement between politics and academic research is indicated by Adenauer's personal involvement in 1960 as well as by the German-Israeli Foundation for Scientific Research and Development founded in 1986 by Chancellor Kohl and Prime Minister Peres with an annual budget of about 75 million dollars.

The shock waves generated by the so-called *historikerstreit* also carried over from the ivory towers of academia and the DFG into the sphere of international politics. Ernst Nolte, the main figure in the controversy, was seen as a roadblock which required removal before Israel's President Chaim Herzog could make his 1987 visit to Bonn.

4. German Business and Industry

West German business and industry has viewed Israel less as a partner than as an obstacle to better trade relations with the Arab world. This is confirmed by the internal documents of the *Bundesvereinigung der Deutschen Industrie* (BDI), the national organization representing West German industry. The German-Israeli business council founded in April 1967 altered the picture little, even though this organization was led by Walter Hesselbach of the trade-union owned *Bank für Gemeinwirtschaft*. The leading circles of the BDI seldom concerned themselves with Israel itself, but all the more frequently with Israel as a potential obstacle to improved Arab-German economic relations.

This tradition began with the conclusion of the Luxembourg Agreement. In September 1952, Adenauer's foreign policy adviser Herbert Blankenhorn reported "strong resistance" particularly from "German high finance." This is confirmed by other documents both from Blankenhorn's period in the Bonn chancellery as well as from the archives of the Bonn Foreign Ministry.

German business circles nevertheless proceeded with great caution. The Near and Middle East Club, a focal point of West German business interests in the region, held a conference for businessmen interested in the Arab countries, at which the "obligation to make restitution" was described as "a matter of course." Nevertheless, the complaint was registered that the discussions with the Arab League delegation, which had traveled to Bonn in order to protest the Luxembourg Agreement, had been conducted "exclusively" by the Foreign Ministry, without the participation or representation from the "practical economy." The club was always careful to add to its warnings about an impending threat of losses in the Arab markets the caveat that the remarks were "in no way politically motivated," and in particular not intended to be "critical" of the German-Israeli treaty.

In the Arab world, however, German businessmen appear to have permitted themselves some sharper remarks concerning the restitution agreement. In a letter authored by an anonymous "Arab personality from Jeddah" (Saudi Arabia) in September 1952 we read: "The Germans here face a very difficult task in making clear that the German people cannot be identified with a measure that was forced on them by the victors" and that Adenauer was not comfortable with the agreement but that he feared "the Jews of America."

Despite all the threats of impending disaster, German-Arabian business went very well. In December 1956, following the British-French debacle at Suez, the Near and Middle East Club found, to its satisfaction: "The restitution deliveries have clouded the attitude toward the Federal Republic, but if measured against the attitude toward England and France, there is a small positive balance." As measured by statistics, the balance was in fact considerable.

From 1957 on, business circles in Germany began to see Israel in a more positive light, whereas the Arab world, especially its would-be leader, Egypt's President Nasser, was viewed less favorably. This was due in no small degree to the series of nationalizations in Egypt.

In contrast to the later weapons deals with Saudi Arabia and other Arab states, which were loudly and energetically defended, German business chose to either ignore (in 1957–1959) or criticize (in 1964–65) German-Israeli arms transactions. Very little interest was shown regarding the activities of the German rocket experts in Egypt, much more for the issue of diplomatic relations: "The political damage inflicted can hardly be estimated; the German East Zone and World Communism are the undeserved beneficiaries in the Near and Middle East." In 1965 the Club complained of the advances of World Communism. In 1967 the Club identified what it considered to be a relapse into the thinking of the nineteenth century, and criticized the "West German mass media and even Christian organizations, which for years have given welcome support to supra-national thinking" for having taken Israel's side in the Six Day War, "as though it were a 19th century war . . . and a nation state has to be assisted in achieving its rights, the decisive basis of which must be regarded as largely antiquated in our European region."

The Club wanted to avoid lending its support to either the world communist revolution, or Israel's nation-state anachronism. It is hard to imagine greater historical-ideological obtuseness.

The new dawn of German-Arabian trade relations arrived with the oil shock of 1973–74. The great trade offensive was flanked by attempts on the part of the Schmidt–Genscher government to make the great leap forward in the areas of Middle East and weapons export policy. Once again, the praises of the "traditional German-Arabian friendship" were sung, and, of course, it was once more necessary to counter "growing Soviet pressure," to secure peace in the region and, last not least, guarantee the free flow of oil.

The offer of German-Saudi-Arabian economic cooperation was, according to the reassurances given at the high tide of the debate over the proposed delivery of German arms to Saudi Arabia "not a question of weapons exports." Such cooperation, however, would be possible only with a partner "prepared to deliver proof for the seriousness of its engagement." In other words, no deal without weapons, as whoever wants to supply civilian must also deliver the military goods. In the view of the Near and Middle East Club, the entire discussion over German weapons exports to Saudi Arabia had become much too "emotionalized" and ignored the "real interests of the Federal Republic."

Much of the elan of the early 1980s has in the meantime dissipated. Both the price of oil and the buying power of the Arab states have decreased. In view of the empty purses, the loud pronouncements of the Near and Middle East Club were toned down to a cautious optimism, its economic-strategic-ideological advice was dispensed more quietly and, although the Club's advice continued to be ignored, World Communism failed to take over the Near and Middle East.

The activities of certain German enterprises and businessmen in Libya and especially in connection with supply, development, and production of rockets, biological, and chemical weapons in Saddam Hussein's Iraq produced a spate of negative publicity in the late 1980s that escalated into an international outcry in the wake of the Gulf War in 1991. Neither the responsible government ministries nor the judicial system appeared to be able to deal with these violations of German law in a consistently convincing manner. When in 1991–92 the Bonn government proposed a dramatic tightening of export controls on military and dual-use technology, numerous German business organizations protested vigorously. Although Economics Minister Jürgen Mölle-mann (FDP) had served as President of the German-Arabian Society for many years, he credibly led the government effort for tighter restrictions.

In the face of the rising incidence of anti-Semitic and xenophobic violence in 1992, the German political and business communities once again found themselves in general agreement. Apart from the histori-cal and moral dimensions of the issue, German business, industrial, and financial leaders attempted to educate the public on the depen-dence of the German economy on exports—and thus on the good will of customers in other countries—and argued that the self-anointed patriots of the extreme right were in fact inflicting serious damage to the interests of the nation.

5. The Churches

In connection with the fiftieth anniversary of the *reichskristallnacht*, the Synod of the Evangelical Church of the Rhineland passed a reso-lution in January 1988 calling upon Germans to learn "to recognize the elements of guilt entailed in our national identity and to assume our responsibility rather than fleeing into a supposed normality and thus separating ourselves from the past."

The Evangelical Church of Germany has come a long way since 1945. The "Stuttgart Confession of Guilt" of 1945 stated that Germans had inflicted "immeasurable suffering on other peoples and countries" but the document contained no statement concerning the Holocaust. The same was true of the otherwise self-critical "Fulda Declaration" of the Roman Catholic bishops, also issued in 1945. As late as March of 1949, Evangelical Dean Grüber complained "that up to now no official [Evangelical] church authority has uttered an official word concerning restitution."

In 1952 Swedish churches took up a collection for Israel and sug-gested similar action be taken by the German Evangelical Church. The church authorities replied: "Israel is a state, but not identical with the Jews. If the Evangelical Church in Germany were to ask for an offering of restitution, the recipient would have to be a religious or social institution of Judaism, but not the state of Israel."

In 1953, in the year in which the Luxembourg restitution agreement was ratified, the official German Evangelical *Church Yearbook* noted that the church had taken "no clear position on restitution," a fact that ought to be explained in the "need of our own people" and that "honest restitution," described as a "special matter for the German people" was by no means limited to the fulfillment of the material "demands of Jewry."

As cautious as one was in the question of restitution, there was no restraint regarding the issue of missionizing among Jews: "As long as Jews continue to live in Germany we in all unworthiness have the obligation to preach to them of Jesus of Nazareth" was the statement to be found in the same 1953 *Church Yearbook*. As Helmut Gollwitzer noted in this context (in 1960): "Nowadays, the concept of a mission to the Jews sticks in one's throat."

The Evangelical Church also did not hesitate to advance its own material claims against the Jewish State. The Roman Catholic Church, too, demanded the return of religious properties expropriated by Israel after the founding of the Jewish State. Both churches wanted to see the conclusion of the German-Israeli treaty made contingent on the fulfillment of their claims, but were unable to get either the Israelis or the German government to heed their demands. Both churches also sought to bolster their positions with aid from abroad. The Evangelical Church turned to the Lutheran churches of the world and the Catholics to the Vatican.

In contrast to the Evangelical Church, the first conference of German Catholics after the Second World War, held in Mainz in 1948, expressly recognized the obligation to make restitution and to return illegally confiscated property. This did not include Israel as a state, but it did encompass the principle of individual restitution to the victims.

Before March 1953 neither the official Evangelical nor the Catholic media concerned themselves to any noteworthy extent with the issue of restitution. But exactly two weeks before the commencement of the ratification debate in the Bundestag, Cardinal Frings of Cologne published an article welcoming the fact that at least the economic side of the Nazi crimes would be dealt with. In a reference to the concept of "collective shame" advanced by (Protestant) Federal President Theodor Heuss, Cardinal Frings wrote of the *beschämung*, the abashment or shame of the German people over the Nazi crimes. The Cardinal also emphasized that many Germans had also worked to save Jewish lives, thus, like Adenauer, rejecting the concept of collective guilt. Without specifically saying so, Frings used a Jewish argument against the collective guilt thesis, reminding his readers that Abraham, the progenitor of the Jews, begged God not to destroy Sodom and Gomorrah if only a few righteous men could be found there. In Hitler's reich, as Frings indicated, these righteous were to be found. It was perhaps too optimistic to expect that a largely secularized Jewish-Israeli public, which was anything but well-grounded in its religious heritage, would understand such a reference, even if such a figure as Ben-Gurion surely did.

In the late fifties and early sixties a fundamental change took place in both German churches as their role in the Third Reich became a focal point of discussion. The impulses came both from outside and from within. One important internal impulse was the decision to support *Aktion Sühnezeichen* (literally: Action Sign of Atonement) at the 1958 Evangelical Church Conference. External factors included the wave of anti-Semitic incidents in the winter of 1959–60, the Eichmann trial in 1961, and the debate unleashed in 1963 over Rolf Hochhuth's drama *The Deputy*. We must also not overlook the Second Vatican Council, which met between 1962 and 1965 and on October 26, 1965, issued the declaration *Nostra Aetate* intended to put an end to two thousand years of Christian-Jewish tensions.

The anti-Semitic incidents of 1959–60 caused the Synod of the German Evangelical Church to express its "horror and shame," but an amendment proposed by Helmut Gollwitzer stating "Whoever strikes at them [at Jews] strikes at us" was voted down. At the latest it was reaction to the Eichmann trial that led to a process of rethinking in the churches. The national assembly of the Evangelical Church in Germany referred to Romans 11:2 in emphasizing that God has not rejected his chosen people, that Evangelical Christians were "involved" in the guilt for Eichmann's crimes and therefore obligated to do their best to ensure the well-being of their Jewish countrymen and the "development and peace of the State of Israel and its Arab neighbors."

Despite (or because of?) Romans 11:2 Bishop Kurt Scharf, some eight years later, encountered problems with "Israel's role in history of salvation": Like the famous "Synagogue" figure of the Strasbourg cathedral, Israel's eyes, according to the bishop, remained "blindfolded" to Jesus Christ. But "Israel in the theological sense" is "not simply identical with the present State of Israel" and therefore one ought to speak of "the Jews of the whole world" rather than of Israel. The Jews of the world represent a special "sign and instrument" of God. The recipient of Bishop Scharf's theologically accurate as well as finely spun thoughts was probably an inappropriate partner, namely the Lebanese Pastor Chemayel, who promptly inquired as to whether, in the light of such an interpretation, "Adolf Hitler should be declared the executor of God's will toward Israel in Germany." To this Scharf replied: "Certainly he was a scourge of God's judgment against Israel and Christianity. Not only the angels, but also the demons, even though they may gnash their teeth, carry out the will of God."

No, these remarks by Bishop Scharf are truly not anti-Semitic; they merely document his view of history, which for him, as well as for Orthodox Jews, can only be the history of salvation. Scharf's interpretation of the Holocaust does not differ fundamentally from that of Jewish Orthodoxy, which we have already described.

"In the spirit of atonement" the spring conference of the Catholic Bishops of Germany in 1961 begged God for "forgiveness for the sins committed by our fellow countrymen." In June 1961 all those attending mass united in "prayer for the murdered Jews and their persecutors."

In October 1964, the Evangelical Church of Germany addressed an energetic appeal in favor of the assumption of diplomatic relations with Jerusalem to the West German Chancellor, President, and Foreign Minister. In December 1964 Evangelical Church authorities heard a rumor that Cardinal Frings had expressed support for diplomatic relations with the Jewish State. Upon inquiry the Cardinal replied that he "had never thought" of contacting the federal government with regard to this matter.

Before, during, and after the Six Day War, German Catholics and Protestants unhesitatingly took Israel's side. During the October 1973 Yom Kippur War the usually reserved official church demanded that the West German government and the United Nations "do all in their power to end the military conflict as soon as possible and to peacefully resolve" the issues at conflict. Munich's Cardinal Döpfner went further and called on the Arab states to recognize Israel's existence, while also urging that Jerusalem "not make the problem of its security exclusively dependent on the question of borders." The Central Committee of German Catholics went still further. Perceiving a threat to the "existence of the Jewish people" (meaning, of course, Israel), the Central Committee called for a peaceful solution guaranteeing the "right to exist and the security of the State of Israel."

In November 1975 the General Assembly of the United Nations passed a resolution in which Zionism was equated with racism. The Synod of the Evangelical Church of Germany reacted promptly: "Old or new forms of enmity toward Jews must not be awakened or tolerated via the detour of anti-Zionism." Cardinal Döpfner, Chairman of the German Bishops' Conference, expressed deep disappointment over the UN resolution: "In our country we must do everything to ensure that the spirit of this resolution is unanimously rejected." The Central Committee of German Catholics, which has always tended to make its political position clear, reacted with even greater indignation. In the name of the Committee, Bernhard Vogel expressed shock at the "senseless equation of Zionism and racism" which happened to coincide with the thirty-seventh anniversary of the *reichskristallnacht*.

A month later, Pope Paul VI adopted a much more reserved tone. Avoiding any direct reference to the November UN resolution, the Pope appealed to the willingness of the "responsible authorities of the differing parties" to negotiate. Paul VI expressed understanding for the desire of the "people of Israel" to seek "protection in a sovereign and independent state" but invited the "children of this people" to "recognize the legitimate expectations of another people, who have also suffered for a long time—namely the Palestinians."

The determination of the German Catholics to pursue their own, so-to-speak "national" course was once again demonstrated in November 1978. In numerous declarations and commemorations of the fortieth anniversary of the *reichskristallnacht* the self-critical trend among Germany's Roman Catholics went further than ever before: "The churches and Christian communities also kept silent in the face of the public injustice," declared a statement by the vicar-general of the Cologne diocese and its Cardinal Höffner personally added that the church had begun to reflect on "the Jewish roots of its faith." That these words were followed by actions was demonstrated by the April 1980 declaration of the German Bishops concerning relations between the Roman Catholic Church and Judaism: "The Jews must not be labeled as the people of the murderers of Christ" and: "The anti-Semitism still more or less alive among Christians must be replaced by a dialogue borne by mutual understanding and love." This spirit also imbues the "Suggestions for the Correct Presentation of Jews and Judaism in Sermons and in the Catechism of the Catholic Church" published by the German Bishops Conference in June 1985.

While the Catholic Church concerned itself almost exclusively with Judaism and avoided the Arab-Israeli conflict, from the early 1970s on the Evangelical Church of Germany has concerned itself with the question of how to achieve "peace in the land of the Bible." The results of the "Deliberations of the Evangelical Middle East Commission" were published in 1985. While unambiguously recognizing Israel's right to existence, the "Deliberations" also call for a "realization of the right of the Palestinians to self-determination" and refer to the "conflict over Israel/Palestine," the slash documenting the shift from the one-sided pro-Israeli sympathies proclaimed in 1967 to a new, two-sided view.

The Evangelical Commission did, however, fall into the trap of one old legend: "We Christians in Germany are affected by the situation in the Middle East . . . because we . . . as a result of the mass murder of the Jewish people contributed to the escalation of the conflict between Jews and Arabs in Palestine and thus . . . are involved in the guilt." In this case, good will substituted for good analysis. We have already mentioned that such well-known politicians as Chancellor Helmut Schmidt also accepted and spread this false interpretation.

The shift in accent on the part of the Evangelical Church also had to do with the fact that the Church was actively seeking to open itself to the 1968 generation and the peace movement, and thus consciously accepting the risk of an increasing politicization. This can be seen in the development of *Aktion Sühnezeichen*, most obviously in the addition of the word *Friedensdienste*—peace services—to the organization's official name and in its active involvement in the peace movement. Israel is no longer the nearly exclusive focus of *Aktion Sühneze-*

ichen activities. Poland has become an additional area necessitating a simultaneous historical-political high-wire act, as until well into the 1980s there was strong evidence to support Shalom Ben-Chorin's observation (in 1968) that "the Nazis eradicated the Jews and the Poles the memory of it." Instead, memories of the mass destruction of the Jews were revived in Poland. This has a great deal to do with the domestic political revolution in Poland, but credit is also due to the activities of *Aktion Sühnezeichen–Friedensdienste*.

■

A lion's share of the credit and praise for bringing down the East German communist regime must go to the protest, opposition, and (here, at last, the word fits) resistance of the Protestants of the former GDR. Anyone who has seen but few examples from the mountain of documents accumulated by the Bureau for Religious Affairs, which was part of the office of the Prime Minister of the GDR, realizes that the leaders of the religious communities of the former East Germany were forced to walk a sometimes impossibly fine line between opposition and resistance on the one hand and involvement and corruption on the other. Some representatives of the Evangelical Church, also, of course, of the Roman Catholic Church and the Jewish community, fell into the abyss of involvement with the regime, others landed in the resistance, and still others, many others, ended up walking both sides of the line.

While prominent officials involved in the East German regime's relations with the churches, such as Willy Barth, complained that the majority of East German churchmen, Catholic and Protestant, sympathized with Israel and refused to join in the SED regime's condemnations of Israel and Zionism, a number of individual church leaders eagerly followed the party line, including a Mecklenburg official who volunteered that "Zionism is nothing more than racism in action."

Who are we to issue praise or condemnation? As a Jew I gladly follow Jesus' admonition about casting the first stone. Precisely because these not-only-resisters of the religious communities in East Germany were able to accomplish such an impressive feat with purely peaceful means, I can only express my gratitude and respect.

Nevertheless, we must ask the question: Was the resistance of the

Protestants of the GDR not symptomatic of a larger crisis in the Evangelical Church of Germany? The more heretical question arises: Has the Evangelical Church since 1945 evolved into a political party: Christian and democratic, Christian and socialist, the best of the CDU-CSU-FDP-SPD? If so, the church is digging its own grave by attempting to compete on the political stage. The church leaders are political amateurs. In a contest with the professionals they can only lose. They have, in fact, already lost.

The proof: Before the successful outcome of the "gentle revolution" the churches in the GDR were full to bursting, thereafter empty. Apparently the people of the former East Germany were more interested in the political message than that of Jesus Christ. Polls have confirmed this repeatedly.

Were the East Germans really as ungrateful as it would appear? No, they are, in fact, consistent and realistic. It is not that the supposedly heathen East Germans did not or do not confront basic questions about the purpose of life. Indeed, the environmental consciousness so prominent in Germany today extends beyond environmental politics, technology, and physics into the realm of metaphysics. But that is precisely where modern-day German Protestantism has so little to offer— because it has become a political movement. The empty churches thus mirror the crisis of current Protestant dogma. (We choose here not to pursue the crises of the Roman Catholics and the Jews.)

The German Protestant churches, both East and West, paid too much attention to politics and history, to the material well-being of the people and not enough attention to their spiritual salvation.

Yet, just before and during the Gulf War, the people, especially the young, packed the churches. True, but they went into the churches because they thought that politics had failed. They went into the churches seeking better politics. The church leadership preferred a different interpretation, but they were soon confronted with their error: After the war was over, the churches were as empty as before.

■

Are we to imagine the Protestant church as an institution for secular morals? As the great awakener, admonisher, and excoriator of war? Why not? Especially, why not in 1991, during the Gulf War? In an otherwise secularized world, the church would thus serve as a bridge between the history of salvation and the history of the world and thus contribute to the salvation of human life.

From my German-Jewish-Israeli perspective, this particular salvation of human life in the year 1991 appeared somewhat suspect, not least of all precisely because the Evangelical (like the Catholic) church came out on the side of the "good Germans."

These "good Germans" appear to follow a selective moral code. Did they fail to read the newspaper reports about the involvement of German companies in the production of Iraqi chemical weapons in 1987 and 1988? In the summer of 1988, Saddam Hussein, a self-proclaimed mortal enemy of Israel, gassed not only Iranian soldiers but also Kurdish civilians in his own country. Where were the demonstrators then? The political parties remained largely indifferent, the churches silent and the good citizens of the Federal Republic enjoyed their summer vacations.

Following the end of the summer season, the good Germans and their churches commemorated the anniversary of the *reichskristall-nacht* on November 9. Tears were shed over the dead Jews, but the acute danger to the living Jews in Israel was studiously ignored. Nevertheless, the self-righteous children and grandchildren once more put their parents and grandparents on the historical witness stand, demanding: "What did you know?" and "What did you do about it?" The Protestants of 1988 went about in sackcloth and ashes for the sins of 1938 and thereafter, but once again became guilty of the sin of omission—and failed to recognize this until 1991. One might also ask where and when the churches protested the Khmer Rouge massacres in Cambodia, the war in Afghanistan, or the Iran-Iraq war started by no lesser figure than Saddam Hussein. Yes, some German Protestant voices were raised and tears of sympathy shed, but there was nothing comparable to the outpouring of protest over the Gulf War of 1991.

On January 20, 1991, the Synod of the Evangelical Church of Germany passed a resolution condemning the Gulf War and Bishop Forck (of the former East Germany) gave the main speech at the peace demonstration in the center of Bonn on January 26. Forck criticized the Iraqi dictator, but also claimed that the United States and the United Nations had responded to "one injustice with an even greater one," namely the war. Although it is meet and just, moral and honorable to condemn war and the resultant ecological catastrophes in the Persian Gulf area, one must question the sort of self-righteousness that chose not to confront the probability of the even greater catastrophe the region would have faced a few years later once Saddam Hussein's arsenal of biological, chemical, and nuclear weapons had been fully developed.

This is the same Evangelical church leadership which, just before the gentle revolution began in East Germany, called on the Bonn government to strike the supposedly anachronistic first article from the West German constitution on the grounds that there would never be a German reunification.

■

On the other hand, when it came to the problem of Russian Jewish immigration, Bishop Forck and the Evangelical Church of Germany stood on the side of the "good Germans." On page one of the Christmas edition of *Die Zeit* Forck posed the question: "Do we not have the obli-gation, as a result of our history, to take in Jews from the Soviet Union [. . .]?" Manfred Stolpe, a key lay leader of the East German Evangelical Church and later Minister-President of the state of Brandenburg, found "moving" the trust displayed by the Jewish immigrants, despite German history. Stolpe was wrong. This trust is *because of* German history, namely the history of *West* Germany, since 1945. Because of this history, the Jews of the former Soviet Union see no reason to fear Germany.

Those who, like Forck, Stolpe, and their church, call for unrestricted Jewish immigration into Germany thus hurt the Jewish State. Whether they know it or not, in the final analysis their message is "Jews yes, Israel no." Solidarity with the dead Jews (who also do not talk back) is much more simple. It is thus no surprise that the "Working Group of Jews and Christians" sponsored by the German Evangelical church came apart shortly after the Gulf War.

To put it somewhat heretically, with all its political involvement and activism, German Protestantism must take devilish care that it does not lose sight of heaven.

10

TRIANGULAR RELATIONSHIPS

In the analysis and discussion of bilateral relations, multisided relationships are often neglected or ignored, although this does not do justice to the complexity of political relations. Let us take a brief look at three triangular relationships important to German-Israeli relations, namely: German-American-Jewish/Israeli, German-Israeli-Jewish, and German-Arab-Jewish/Israeli relations.

1. Israel as an Irritant in German-American Relations?

Israeli-Jewish issues have repeatedly led to unease in German-American relations. We need only to remind ourselves of some of the examples already cited in previous chapters, in particular the American fears in the period 1951–53 that West German restitution payments to Israel could interfere with the rearmament of the country.

The Truman administration expressed moral sympathy for Israel's demands, but made it clear that there were priorities between these demands and the necessity for a West German contribution to Western defense. "We want action, not sympathy," protested representatives of the Diaspora-Jewish Claims Conference. Despite personal efforts in April 1952, not even Truman's influential Jewish friends succeeded in extracting from the President the public statement they hoped would increase the pressure on Adenauer. The Claims Conference did not hide its disappointment at the friendly but noncommittal public comments by U.S. High Commissioner for Germany John McCloy.

The State Department repeatedly informed its Israeli interlocutors that, in face of the demands of rearmament, Bonn could not be expected to undertake additional large financial commitments. Ben-Gurion and his diplomatic representatives countered that the people of Israel must not go hungry in order that the Germans make a contribution to the defense of the Allies. In a conversation with Secretary of State Acheson in May 1951, Ben-Gurion considered it "unthinkable" that the Germans should be permitted to have a higher standard of living than the Israelis. His appeal went unanswered.

In chapters 2 and 8 we have already mentioned that in 1956–57 Adenauer chose not follow Washington's lead in imposing economic sanctions on Jerusalem in order to force an Israeli withdrawal from the Sinai. We have also already pointed out that this decision to continue rather than suspend restitution payments was a turning point in (West) German-Israeli relations.

The debate over the statute of limitations for National-Socialist crimes, the issue of German-Israeli diplomatic relations, and German arms deliveries to Israel all led to German-American irritations. As Franz Josef Strauss reported to a meeting of the CSU party leadership on June 30, 1967, just after the Six Day War, "The Americans were the first to protest" the decision by Adenauer and Strauss to extend German military aid to Israel "[. . .] with the argument that it would only create unrest. The Israelis already had an American security guarantee and that would suffice completely. A year later, however, the Americans were telling us we had to continue deliveries, they now had a different evaluation of the situation." In the mid-1960s the U.S. strongly pushed for increased West German arms deliveries to Israel in order to keep Washington's hands free in the Arab world. Strauss went on to ask rhetorically, "But what would have happened later, if, in the face of the country's militarily hopeless situation, an opponent of even half-ways equivalent strength would have dealt a lethal blow to Israel?" Strauss's answer: "Nothing. President Johnson would have given the Chief Rabbi of the United States permission to conduct a solemn funeral service in the Washington synagogue. [. . .] The asinine behavior of the Americans can only fill one with deepest apprehension if things ever came to a head in Europe."

From the other side of the Atlantic, the Nixon-Kissinger administration apparently viewed as asinine the efforts on the part of the West German government to at least publicly distance itself from American efforts to reinforce Israel during the October 1973 Yom Kippur War. President Nixon addressed a sharply worded letter to Chancellor Brandt.

This pattern was not repeated by the Kohl government during the Gulf War. With no objections from Bonn, Washington used its bases in Germany as the primary conduit for the transport of troops and supplies to the Gulf.

President Carter was angered by West German Chancellor Helmut Schmidt's severe criticism of the American-Egyptian-Israeli balancing act that finally led to the Camp David accords of 1978 and, in 1979, to the first peace treaty between Israel and an Arab neighbor. Chancellor Schmidt favored a "comprehensive solution" to the Arab-Israeli conflict over a bilateral Egyptian-Israeli agreement, even though a multilateral approach requires as many partners prepared to make compromises and at that time there were only two such parties: Egypt and Israel. Bonn's indirect recognition of the PLO and its active role in the EC declaration in support of negotiations with the PLO met with little understanding and a great deal of annoyance on the part of the Carter and Reagan administrations, both of which insisted that the PLO must distance itself from terrorism and recognize Israel's fundamental right to exist as preconditions for negotiations.

The attempts on the part of the Schmidt/Genscher and then the Kohl/Genscher governments to mix *geschichtspolitik* with weapons exports ultimately led to the dispute over the program for President Reagan's 1985 visit to West Germany and thus to the resurrection of a past thought to be long dead and buried (see chapter 2.5).

The role of American Jews in the German-American-Israeli triangle consists of more legend than substance. It has already been pointed out that Chancellor Adenauer almost demonized the influence of the American Jewish community. Adenauer not only spoke of this supposed influence, but also included it in his political calculations, but he did not complain about it, as did his and his successor's official government spokesman, von Hase, at the high point of the debacle over German Middle East policy in February 1965 (see chapter 2). To a small circle of editors from CDU-associated newspapers von Hase complained about the anti-German "emotions" to be found "not only in Israeli newspapers, but in almost all newspapers in which world Jewry has a large influence." The unspoken reference was, of course, to the Jewish ownership of or influence with leading U.S. East Coast papers, especially the *New York Times* and the *Washington Post*. This was nothing more than a replay of the old record about Jewish dominance of the Eastern establishment press, and von Hase was automatically presuming an identity of interests between Israel and the American Jewish community. Although both of these highly influential U.S. newspapers were in Jewish hands, what von Hase apparently did not know was that both papers had tended to be anti-Zionist before 1948 and after that had continued to be only reservedly pro-Israel, always emphasizing the independence of the Diaspora and the American Jewish community in particular. They were never Israel's journalistic mouthpiece in the United States.

Finance Minister Schäffer and Foreign Minister von Brentano were better attuned to Israeli-American-Jewish dissonances. As already mentioned (in chapter 2), in 1952 Schäffer sought to turn the oversaturation with Israel on the part of no small number of American Jews to the advantage of West German restitution policy. During the controversy over the rash of anti-Semitic incidents in 1959–60, von Brentano took special pains to make sure that, in addition to positive statements about the new Germany from Israel such as Ben-Gurion's, Diaspora Jewish voices were also given prominence. Von Brentano pointed out that not all Jews and Jewish groups accepted the government of Israel as their legitimate voice. "Under certain circumstances we would lose favor among these circles, which have an open mind toward to the Federal Republic" von Brentano wrote to Adenauer in January 1960.

There is a great deal of sympathy and understanding for Jewish sensitivities in the United States. This has more to do with general American feelings toward history than with the American Jews themselves. Nearly three-quarters of the Americans polled in a May 1985 survey agreed that Jews were justified in their anger over President Reagan's (originally announced) intention to visit the German military cemetery at Bitburg but not the Bergen-Belsen concentration camp. In contrast to public opinion in West Germany, an equal number of Americans agreed that the Jewish anti-Bitburg campaign was not "too aggressive." As the polls have demonstrated over the last decades, the American public has consistently ranked Israel highly as a strategic partner in the pursuit of global American interests, and this is so regardless of transient shifts in sympathy. Israel has been viewed on a par with the British, French, Japanese, and German allies. Thus, even without the "large influence of World Jewry" on the American press, German-Jewish or German-Israeli storms also tend to cloud the German-American sky.

It is wrong to cast the American Jewish community in the role of moral prosecutor against Germany. The large and influential American Jewish Committee (AJC) did pioneer work in promoting German-American understanding and reconciliation. In doing so, the AJC calmly weathered storms of Jewish and Israeli criticism, especially in the early 1950s. The AJC and other Jewish organizations have built, not demolished, German-American bridges.

2. Without Identity—With a Future? Germany's Jews Between Diaspora and Israel

Hitler won, so it seems. Once upon a time there was a German Jewry, but no more. Jewish museums such as in Frankfurt am Main or Braunschweig, Jewish departments such as in the Berlin museum, or exhibitions on the former life of Jews in Germany, the wonderful reconstruction of the Raschi House in Worms and parts of the former Jewish quarter of that city, the building of new synagogues which are much too large for the existing Jewish community, superb, large Jewish community centers generously financed with public funds and well-organized Jewish communities such as those in Berlin and Frankfurt am Main—despite all such cultural maintenance there appears to be little left of German Jewry.

To be sure, the Federal Republic of Germany is not *judenrein* as the Nazis intended. In the German Democratic Republic it was a different story. In its final years the East German state registered a mere four hundred Jews, a quarter of them over eighty years of age. Viewed in quantitative terms, even the 40,000 registered members of the German Jewish community are of little significance in either the European or global Jewish context. It also changes little to point out that there are almost as many Jews living in Germany who are not registered members of the official community.

German Jews share their quantitative and also qualitative inner-Jewish insignificance with their brethren in almost all western and eastern European countries. Only France and Great Britain have not only large and well-organized but also, for at least the last decade, spiritually revitalized Jewish communities.

The number of Jews living in the former Soviet Union is large, their Jewish consciousness revived, but, despite the vast changes that have taken place since the advent of Gorbachev, the chances for the revival of a Jewish community appear dim, as classic Russian anti-Semitism has been reawakened and hundreds of thousands of Jews have chosen to seek safety in immigration. Until the United States severely restricted immigration in 1989, America was the goal of the vast majority of Jewish immigrants. It has been reported that the German consulates in the successor states of the former Soviet Union received more than a hundred thousand applications for immigration but, under pressure from Israel, Germany also severely restricted the number of Russian Jewish immigrants to about 5,000 in 1990 and 1991. By the end of 1992 the total had reached 12,000. Of these, some 3,000 had settled in Berlin.

The particular situation of the German Jews is, of course, a result of the Holocaust. But the German Jewish community must also be viewed in the larger European setting. It is, indeed, necessary to regard the German-Jewish community in the global Jewish context of the polarity of forces between the Diaspora and Israel. Upon closer examination, many problems of the West German Jews turn out to be problems of the Diaspora as a whole, which, since the founding of the Jewish State, has found itself forced to seek a new identity.

Much has been written about the Jewish citizens of the Federal Republic of Germany, and the German Jews themselves have not been miserly in terms of publications. Many of the presentations and self-portraits have been impressionistic, subjective, frequently aggressive, and more judgmental than descriptive in nature. Let us attempt to approach this delicate subject more from the analytical than the polemical side. In order to avoid misunderstandings, permit the author to state that he describes inner-Jewish troubles as an eager but not zealous observer, and more in sorrow than in anger.

The Demographic Situation: Quantity and Quality

A brief look at the regional distribution of the world Jewish population suffices to demonstrate the insignificance of both the German and even the larger European Jewish community. A consensus of estimates placed the world Jewish population at about 13 million in 1988. Of these, some 6 million were living in North America alone with a further half-million in South America. Thus almost exactly half of the total Jewish population was to be found in the Americas. Israel accounted for 3.6 million, or nearly a quarter of the total; Europe for 2.7 million (21%). Of these, 1 million (8%) were living in Western Europe and 1.6 million (13%) in Eastern Europe, including the Asian parts of the Soviet Union, the Balkan countries, and Turkey. Germany counted 28,000 Jews in 1988, a number that grew until 1992. Officially registered members of the German Jewish community thus represented 0.002% of the world Jewish population. The largest Jewish community in Western Europe was to be found in France with 530,000 Jews, followed by Great Britain with an estimated 322,000. The Jewish communities in Belgium, Italy, the Netherlands, and Sweden were all just slightly larger or smaller than that of West Germany.

With the exception of Israel, the world Jewish population has stagnated or is shrinking, mostly as a result of mixed marriages—a symptom of crisis in the traditional Jewish view.

One might be tempted to advise incorrigible anti-Semites that the best way to solve the Jewish "problem" would be to provide them with the most comfortable Diaspora life possible. If we take a longer view of Jewish history, however, we find again and again, to our surprise and relief, that this people has somehow managed to survive both the worst and the best of times.

A brief comparison with the demographic distribution of the world Jewish population in 1939, before the Second World War and the genocide of the death camps, documents the fundamental shift brought about by the Holocaust and the founding of the State of Israel. In 1939, 58 percent of all Jews lived in Europe, including the Asian parts of the Soviet Union, 33 percent in the Americas, and only 3 percent in what was then Palestine. The focal point of the Jewish population has thus shifted from Europe to North America and Israel. Expressed in percentages, Europe lost more than half of its proportion of the world Jewish population and the Jewish population in Germany dropped from about 3 percent of the world total in 1933 to the present 0.002 percent. Even before the Holocaust, the German Jewish population was not quantitatively significant.

It ought also to be mentioned that the Jewish communities of North Africa and the Near East were drawn into the Zionist-Arab conflict. Here, too, little remains of what were once large and proud Jewish communities. What the Holocaust did to European Jewry the Arab-Israeli conflict did to the tradition-rich Oriental Jewish communities, which have all but disappeared.

In other words: the demographic structure of today's world Jewish population is essentially bipolar: 73 percent of all Jews live in the Diaspora, 27 percent in Israel. The Diaspora population has stagnated or is shrinking, but in quantitative terms it remains significantly larger than the Jewish State. The future may belong to Israel, but in the present, if only by virtue of sheer numbers, the Diaspora Jews ought to have their say. The quantitative structural shift in Jewish demography and geography raises a question that is both new and more than two thousand years old: Can—and should—Jews living outside the Jewish community survive both materially and spiritually as Jews?

Let us take a closer look at the data regarding the present Jewish population of Germany. With about 10,000 members, Berlin has the largest Jewish community, followed by Frankfurt am Main with 7,000, Munich with 6,000, Düsseldorf with 4,000, Hamburg with 3,000, and Cologne with 4,000. These numbers have fluctuated considerably since the beginning of Jewish immigration from the Soviet Union.

As was the case before the Second World War, the German Jewish population—as the Jewish population in general (including Israel)—is largely urban and well-educated. Now, as before the war, the internal structure of the German Jewish community is characterized by tensions between Jews born and raised in Germany and so-called Eastern Jews. As before the Holocaust—one will not and cannot believe it—the "genuine" German Jews look down on their co-religionists whose origins lie in Eastern Europe. What is different is that today the Eastern Jews and their descendants dominate. Even before the most recent wave of Jewish immigration from the Soviet Union and its successor states, Eastern Jews represented about 70 percent of the registered Jews in Germany. Today they represent more than 80 percent. Despite their numerical superiority, they have, however, accepted the political and normative dominance of the "native" German Jews. This can be seen in the composition of the leadership of the German Jewish organizations, where about 90 percent of the "elite" consists of Jews of "genuine" German backgrounds. Ignatz Bubis, who succeeded Heinz Galinski as Chairman of the Central Council of Jews in Germany in 1992, is the first German-Jewish community leader from an Eastern European background. The official representative is thus truly more representative.

This leadership role did not automatically fall to the Jews of German origin among the survivors of the Holocaust in Germany after 1945, and their leadership was not uncontested. In their bastion in Munich, the Eastern Jews under the leadership of Maurice Weinberger maintained their dominance into the 1950s, but surrendered their demographic and democratic chances to ideological goals. In contrast to the later dominant German Jews, the Eastern Jews' long-term intention was to dismantle (i.e., transplant to Israel) rather than to (re)build Jewish communities in the "land of the murderers."

With their goal of eventually dissolving the Jewish community in Germany, the Eastern Jewish leaders disqualified themselves in the eyes of both the German Jews and those Eastern Jews who chose to remain—with a more or less bad conscience—in Germany. The Eastern Jews intent on immigration were also anything but ideal partners for the German authorities.

The German-Jewish leaders of the nation-wide Jewish organization, the "Central Council of Jews in Germany," exploited their advantages over their Eastern-Jewish rivals in the Munich leadership—and they did so in a gloves-off manner. In a dispute over appropriations for the Jewish welfare office in Munich in 1952 the Central Council blocked the funds, giving as their reason that a large part of the "persons supported" in Munich were "former black marketeers" who refused "to go to the German welfare authorities because they are in good health and would have to perform compulsory labor." In other words, these work-shy, questionable figures—"black marketeers," also described as "unpopular" or "dubious elements"—were enriching themselves at the expense of the German taxpayer. "Since the community requires precisely these circles—it is these same circles which aided the community leadership to its dubious election victory—they receive full support payments." Mentioning only the support payments apparently connected to election promises and expectations, the Central Council claimed that it was only "under the worst terrorist pressure" that the Munich leadership retained control of the local community and the Bavarian organization. The Central Council stated further: "We cannot accept responsibility for allowing persons who in large part have only been in Germany for a few years to head social institutions and to make available to them funds which are used neither in the German nor the Jewish interest. The present representatives of the Jewish community neither understand conditions in Germany nor the duties involved in maintaining an orderly welfare system." As a precondition for the release of funds the Central Council demanded the election of a new community leadership, unmistakably indicated its preference for the opposition group consisting "of German Jews" and went so far in its inner-Jewish xenophobia as to demand that the new welfare committee must be composed of "German citizens [. . .] and not of foreigners."

It is revealing that this shocking document is to be found in the archives of a non-Jewish authority, namely the city of Munich, among the documents pertaining to "mayor and council." It bears the signature of Karl Hefter, who in 1952 and 1953 repeatedly provided Munich's Mayor Thomas Wimmer with information about the Bavarian organization of Jewish communities and the president of the Munich Jewish community, noting that the city government had to deal with Herr Weinberger. Needless to say, the "German Jews" prevailed in the struggle for power.

The geographical and cultural heritage of the majority of Jews living in the Federal Republic is non-German. Politically, the German Jews are dominant. Socially, the groups of various origins are largely isolated from one another. One visible indication of this are the different Jewish lodges active in Berlin, one with a predominantly German-Jewish, another with a Polish-Jewish and yet another with a Russian-Jewish membership.

■

It is almost impossible to believe, but since the 1960s the Federal Republic of Germany has been a goal of Jewish immigration. If it were not, the total membership of the otherwise predominantly elderly Jewish communities would never have remained stable. As far as the Israeli and official-Jewish *geschichtspolitik* with regard to Germany is concerned, increasing numbers of Jewish immigrants have chosen to vote with their feet. The numbers are not large, some ten thousand in all, but still a remarkable total. Once again we see a gap between Jewish ideology and actual behavior.

This gap had, for example, led to a significant structural change in the West Berlin Jewish community, which took in about 2,500 immigrants from the Soviet Union between 1973 and 1980 and some 4,000 between 1990 and 1991. These Jews chose to take up residence in Hitler's former command center rather than immigrate to Israel. This is historically grotesque and a historical-political failure for Israel and the Diaspora Jewish organizations but at the same time an indication that (even the Jewish) man cannot live by principles alone.

A similar structural shift has not taken place in other Western European countries with the exception of France, where 45 percent of the Jews are of French background, 39 percent of Algerian, Moroccan, or Tunisian descent, and 7 percent from other countries.

One qualitative consequence of the quantitative shift just described is the almost unavoidable danger of the exaggerated, almost exclusive preoccupation with one's own group.

The German-Jewish, indeed the Diaspora communities in general, are shrinking as a result of a clearly discernible trend toward mixed marriages. In terms of actual behavior toward their non-Jewish environment, German Jews have proven themselves more pragmatic than their ideological worldview would appear to permit. Among German Jews, the proportion of mixed marriages has long been significantly higher than in other Western European countries or the United States. In Scandinavia about half of all Jews marry non-Jewish partners; in France, too, about 50 percent of the inactive and even 35 percent of the active community members marry non-Jews. In the United States the proportion of mixed marriages grew from 5 percent in 1948 to 9 percent in 1964 and in 1985 reached a level of 55 percent, which has obtained since then. In West Germany the proportion was 68 percent in 1951, reached 77 percent in 1985, and rose to a record 81 percent in 1987. Since then, about three-fourths of German Jews continue to marry non-Jews.

We can only conclude that there is a vast gap between the publicly expressed opinion and the actual behavior of German Jews. If we are not to believe that they marry for masochistic reasons, German Jews would appear to feel much more comfortable among their non-Jewish countrymen than they are willing to admit.

The stronger the sense of Jewish community identity, as indicated by active participation in Jewish community affairs, the lesser the inclination to mixed marriages. This sense of community identity can be religious, purely social, or a mixture of both. It is in any case reinforced by normative pressures: whoever is prepared to marry a non-Jew is branded as something akin to a traitor to his people. Such behavior may be understandable from a collective, but certainly not from an individual, point of view.

A basic structural conflict is thus evident: On the one hand, as a community, Jews depend on the tolerance of a liberal society. On the other hand, the foundation of the liberal society is the individual, not the collective. The kind of society desired by Jews in the present brings with it undesired threats to the future of the community.

In order to confront such dangers more aggressively than before, the Diaspora Jewish communities have, among other things, taken on the role of match-making institute, organizing all sorts of national and international Jewish weekend activities for "singles."

Another method of avoiding mixed marriages is voluntary withdrawal into the ghetto, reducing the supposed risk by avoiding contacts with non-Jews. Doris Kuschner collected valuable data on this approach in the late 1960s and early 1970s in West Germany. At that time 51 percent of the Jewish respondents had no non-Jewish friends. The larger the community, with the thus larger selection of Jewish partners, the less frequent the contacts between the two worlds. It comes as no surprise that "Jews without German culture," i.e., Eastern Jews, had fewer private contacts with non-Jews. It is also no surprise that neither the Jews of German nor of Eastern European extraction felt any "love of country," although the degree of disaffection was astoundingly high: 77 percent of the Jews of German and 100 percent of the Jews of Eastern European backgrounds said they felt no "love of country." Younger German Jews were even more disaffected (95 percent) than their parents and the younger Eastern Jews were as unanimous in denying "love of country" as their parents. This lack of identification among the young is both surprising and depressing, as nearly two-thirds stated they maintained social contacts with non-Jews. While tensions were thus on the rise among German Jews of the second generation, research by Renate Köcher indicates that their non-Jewish contemporaries evidenced much more relaxed attitudes toward Jews. Judging from the data, it is easy to imagine the deep spiritual affliction of the majority of German Jews who find themselves living in a land in which they do not feel at home.

■

An important instrument in the creation of an active Jewish sense of community identity, both in Israel and in the Diaspora, is the Holocaust. In connection with our discussion of German and Israeli strategies of *geschichtspolitik* we have already described the political mechanics involved and the concomitant dangers of a loss of Jewish contents in the process of creating identity on this basis. We also spoke of an ultimately un-Jewish view of humanity and the world and of political biology. With the Nuremberg Laws of 1935 political biology became an instrument of the National-Socialist criminals. Now, in a complete reversal, it serves the victims.

There are other alternatives to maintaining the continuity of Jewish life and ensuring the survival of Judaism. One possibility would be the increased cultivation of Jewish religious and philosophical traditions and contents, but efforts in this direction soon come up against the narrow limits of a religiously and intellectually disinterested community.

Typical for the choice of the path of least resistance, for the negative definition of Judaism by means of the Holocaust rather than positive, traditionally Jewish contents was the reaction of the Central Council of Jews in Germany in the December 23, 1987, issue of the Council's weekly newspaper to British Chief Rabbi Immanuel Jakobovits's criticism of Israeli and Diaspora-Jewish Holocaust politics. The spiritual leader of British Jews and member of the House of Lords had given an address in November 1987 in Jerusalem on the topic "The Religious Response to the Holocaust," in which he explained that all leading rabbis agree on the singular horror of the Holocaust but reject with equal unanimity the notion that the Holocaust was historically unique in comparison with previous catastrophes. Jewish history, Jakobovits emphasized, consists of cycles of the most horrible of catastrophes followed by survival and renewal. Thus, in the period following the Holocaust, it is essential to concern oneself less with the survival of Jews and more with the survival of Judaism. Without Judaism, Jakobovits stated, Jewish survival is dubious and without meaning.

In the first three chapters we repeatedly returned to the Jewish-religious understanding of history, particularly because it must appear incomprehensible to secular, non-Jewish readers. According to Jakobovits, the religious-rabbinical view is more important than ever, especially in the face of a "profitable branch of industry for writers, researchers, film-makers, memorial architects, museum planners and even politicians" involved in the marketing of the Holocaust. Even some rabbis and theologians are "partners in this big business" (*Jerusalem Post*, international edition, December 5, 1987).

The Central Council of Jews in Germany, the members of which are almost all nonreligious, at least nonrabbinical, came up with no better response to the carefully reasoned remarks by the Chief Rabbi of Great Britain than to register "sharpest objections" that were not further explained. The official organ of the Central Council chose to avoid confrontation with the contents of Jakobovits's arguments.

Immanuel Jakobovits's inner-Jewish warning represents anything but a whitewash for the old or a declaration of sympathy for the new Germany, much less an Orthodox-Jewish contribution to the inner-German *historikerstreit* (the context in which the Central Council chose to regard it). Jakobovits was born in Germany but has broken with the land of his birth and refuses to speak the German language "which was spoken by millions of murderers." He refuses to set foot on German soil, which he describes as "soaked with the blood of millions of Jews."

Of the more than twenty books concerning the so-called *historiker-streit* that have been published by non-Jewish historians, not one deals with the traditional Jewish view of history in this context. This, of course, can come as no surprise when not even the German Jews discuss this perspective. Although the Jewish-religious worldview belongs more to the realm of the history of salvation than that of historical science, it ought not to be neglected entirely in the context of the issues raised by the *historikerstreit* in Germany.

From an Israeli viewpoint, the identity problems of the German and the Jewish Diaspora as a whole are hardly unwelcome. According to the Zionist axiom, Jews in the Diaspora can expect assimilation at best. In the worst, and, in the Zionist view, the more likely case, they must face anti-Semitism. Both assimilation and anti-Semitism spell the end of Judaism over the long term.

As we have seen, however, the Jewish State finds itself in the same identity crisis as the Diaspora. The Diaspora crisis therefore does not strengthen Israel. Nonfundamentalist, religious Jewish contents are thus little in evidence, either in Israel or in the Diaspora. Does that leave the Holocaust as the only means of combatting assimilation?

The assimilation that presents such a danger to the Jewish collective and of which mixed marriages are the clearest indicator is also a sign that the non-Jewish environment is well-disposed toward its Jews, that the Jews are doing well. It is precisely this subjective sense of wellbeing on the part of the Jewish individual that is all but impossible to reconcile with the priorities of the Jewish collective, which, like any collective, seeks to survive as such. The perception of not belonging is a function of the internalized Jewish superego, while the sense of security with a Christian partner is a function of the ego in everyday life. Collective norms and individual experience collide in the souls of Diaspora Jews, resulting in internal conflicts, divisions, and unease.

Self-Image, Worldview, and Behavior

Three fundamental factors have shaped the self-image, worldview, and behavior of German Jews since 1945: First, a view of the world that only takes into account victims on the one hand and persecutors on the other. This is simplified, but not falsified, into a juxtaposition of Jews and non-Jews, into a we-versus-them perspective. Second comes the change in biological and political generations; third are the changes in the internal structures of the community itself.

First of all, which Jews are we talking about? Not the individualists, not those who swim against the prevalent currents in the community. And not those who are largely or even completely integrated into the larger German community, who feel at home there and who identify with the state, a party, or one of the political groups in the country. We also do not include deeply religious Diaspora Jews or the Zionists who truly intend to immigrate to Israel but have not yet made their intention public. To borrow from Max Weber, the Jews we are speaking of here fulfill the "ideal type" of the community Jew to whom the above-mentioned traits do not apply. It is this German Jew we shall attempt to briefly describe.

All Jewish survivors of the Holocaust have had to directly or indirectly face the question: "Why did I survive and others didn't?" While there are many rational explanations both for the survivors among the camp inmates and those whose fates were less horrible, there always remains something of what is known as "survival guilt," the feeling on the part of the survivor that he is somehow guilty, simply for having survived. What is involved is a metaphysical perception of guilt both toward the murdered individuals one knew as well as toward the Jewish collective.

At the same time, the survivor is a part of the formerly persecuted collective. Whether one was actually in the grip of the machinery of mass murder or not, as a Jew one belonged to the group of the victims, and thus to the powers of light and goodness. The others, the non-Jews, are branded as belonging to the powers of darkness and evil, whether or not they were among the architects of or served as mere cogs in the genocidal machine. This is a historically understandable view of the world. The insecurity stemming from the guilt of the survivor was at least partially compensated by the security of belonging to the world of the good.

This, of course, is true of the Auschwitz generation by virtue of their experience, but because of the previously described political mechanisms and the political biology of anti-Germanism as well as the Israeli-Jewish Holocaust fixation, this also applies to the children and even the grandchildren of the survivors. They regard themselves as second or third generation Holocaust survivors, even though they themselves did not experience its horrors.

Such patterns of thought and subsequent behavior can be considered typical for Israeli and Diaspora Jews, and most especially for those living in Germany. These are the Jews living in the "land of the murderers." As Jews, and doubly so as Jews in Germany, they view themselves as Holocaust survivors, even in the second and third generations. It is thus no surprise that they feel as strangers in their own country.

This view of the world must also lead to increased tensions in relations with the non-Jewish environment, as the overwhelming majority of non-Jewish West Germans—57 percent according to Allensbach survey data gathered in the mid-1980s—only recognized a German responsibility for the Jews directly affected by the Holocaust. Only 23 percent were prepared to extend this responsibility to all Jews as a matter of principle. An EMNID poll conducted in December 1991 produced a similar picture: When asked if the German people have a special responsibility toward Jews, even if the younger generations bear no direct or personal guilt, 33 percent of the respondents agreed, whereas 42 percent said they tended to disagree and 24 percent expressed no opinion. Even though the EMNID survey, in comparison with the earlier Allensbach data, appears to show an increase in the percentage of Germans accepting a special historical responsibility toward the Jews, the results were generally received as bad news, both in Germany and internationally. In any case, the gap in perceptions of responsibility could prove to be politically explosive.

Direct and indirect guilt was not limited to the Germans alone. The Allies, too, must bear a certain portion. They proved unwilling to take in Jews fleeing from persecution, would not allow them to immigrate to Palestine, or did nothing to slow or stop the Nazi death machine. Thus the we-versus-them, victim/persecutor dichotomy is character- istic of the worldview of all Jews, not just German Jews. But because the authors of the Holocaust were German, this basic perception shared by all Jews is held more intensely by German Jews.

This view of the world determines patterns of thought and behavior in the political arena, where chosen or self-appointed spokesman for German Jewry present themselves in the role of schoolmaster to the non-Jewish world about them. For example, at the beginning of the 1983 "brotherhood week" a leading representative of Germany's Jews explained that he believed that the still young German democracy was making progress in the field of basic human rights but at the same time criticized what he termed the "German moral custodians" (refer- ring to "representatives of Christian churches") who had not hesitated to compare Israel's treatment of the PLO in Lebanon with National- Socialist concentration camps.

The role of admonisher, moral custodian, and schoolmaster for the subjects of tolerance and democracy in German society is under- standable with regard to the Auschwitz generation, but even the sur- vivors of this hell do not hold a monopoly on morality. The attempt on the part of the second or third Jewish generation to continue in this role is founded on political biology. One belongs to the forces of light and goodness by virtue of birth. Democracy and political biology are, however, mutually exclusive, as roles in a democracy must be earned, not inherited. The more democratic German society becomes, the greater the tendency will be to reject the Jewish role as moral custodi- an and schoolmaster. The likely result will be an increase in Jew- ish–non-Jewish tensions.

■

The outside world has not remained entirely unaware of the not always totally democratic, sometimes more authoritarian decision- making processes within the German Jewish community. The very fact that many Jewish communities have been—quite successfully—

led by the very same personalities for decades nurtures the well-founded suspicion that the Jewish communities resemble other organizations in Germany in which we find, in addition to numerous institutional interests, permanent functionaries, lifetime representatives, and other fat cats; but not necessarily a great deal of substantive content. Germany's Jews are in danger of degenerating into an interest group just like many others with similar authoritarian leadership. It is only the weight and burden of the past that distinguishes the Jewish community from other organizations in non-Jewish eyes. Konrad Adenauer spoke of this openly. On the occasion of a state dinner a search was conducted for an appropriate representative of West German Jewry to be seated next to Cologne's Cardinal Frings. The search turned up no one and the suggestion was made that an official representative of the Central Council be invited. Chancellor Adenauer, however, refused to have a "functionary" placed next to the Cardinal and other spiritual leaders.

We have already pointed out the contradictions in tolerant behavior and demands in connection with the 1952–53 power struggle between the German Jewish leadership of the Central Council and the Eastern Jewish leadership of the Jewish community in Bavaria. This domestic dispute, which was certainly not guided by the spirit of tolerance, extended, as we know, beyond the Jewish community.

Over the course of the last decades, Jews and non-Jews have acted out—at least to the outside world—the roles of admonisher and admonished with almost ritual regularity. Often enough the roles were internalized, but only rarely were they subjected to earnest reflection. Whenever the non-Jewish side dared to break out of its assigned role, the resulting scene was usually played to what one took for a closed house, the general public excluded. In reality, what happened can be easily reconstructed with the aid of innumerable internal documents. Over the long term this represents a potentially acute danger for the Jewish side, as it forces patterns of conduct that are anything but open and honest upon sincere and well-intended non-Jews.

The Jewish admonishers and custodians, as a rule the official representatives of the German Jewish community, are predominantly active in the political arena. They do not regard themselves as foreign

TRIANGULAR RELATIONSHIPS   173

to, but rather as an integral part of, German society. There are, of course, still a number of incorrigibles from the past who continue to attempt to stir up public ire against what they label as the "self-appointed Jewish custodians of democracy." As irritating and inconvenient this role of the Jewish representatives may be for some non-Jews, it must not be misunderstood as a sign of Jewish alienation. It is, to the contrary, the not always successful attempt to share and to communicate identity, concern, and political ideas and suggestions to non-Jews.

In everyday German-Jewish life, alienation can be recognized in a number of behavioral patterns which, although extreme examples, are not unusual and which hold the potential to create great tensions. Among the Jews living in the Federal Republic there are many who managed to survive the horrors of the Holocaust and who remained in the country, often out of sheer exhaustion, rarely out of conviction. Ever since, these Jews have had a bad conscience. Both within their own personalities and with regard to their non-Jewish, their German-Jewish, Diaspora-Jewish, and Israeli-Jewish environment they feel alienated, insecure, persecuted. They feel guilty for having remained in Germany. They do not trust non-Jewish Germans. Many Diaspora Jews defend the Diaspora as such, but not in Germany, and Israel expects these Jews in particular to immigrate to the Jewish State.

"Many of them were motivated by the understandable desire to 'pay back' their tormenters. The manner in which this was occasionally done—black marketing, speculation, pimping, and similar criminal pursuits—was not a glorious chapter in Jewish ethics, even if the motives were psychologically more than understandable." This description by Yohanan Meroz, Israel's ambassador to Bonn from 1974 to 1981, shows considerable sensitivity for the situation and extremity of anguish among many West German Jews.

The intention to "pay back" the tormenters or their progeny nevertheless remained a personal, individual "business" matter. The word of such affairs, of course, spread among affected as well as unaffected non-Jews, often enough in whispered tones, and thus, inaudible for Jewish ears, acquired a political dimension.

Such tensions surfaced in the summer and fall of 1985 in the controversy over the Fassbinder play *Garbage, the City and Death*. The critical protests were dominated not by the familiar extreme-right tones of old, but rather by the new-German leftist-alternative scene, but the sound was anti-Semitic not only to Jewish ears. The picture of the Jew presented by Fassbinder's play was not lacking in resemblance to the caricature of Nazi propaganda, but the comparison would be misleading. The picture and sound belonged more to the anticapitalist mindset and were aimed at criticizing a basically non-Jewish system which happens to include some unfortunate Jewish souls alienated from themselves and from the rest of the world.

The drama extended beyond the anticapitalist-alternative scene in Frankfurt and became the object of a Jewish-German debate, the first of its kind concerning the worldview of the Jewish victim determined to "pay back" his tormenters. What was intended as an object on the stage became the focal point of public discussion outside the theater. This was not, as some claimed, the "end of the closed season" but it did mark the beginning of a public discussion over the sins of omission committed by both sides.

The reaction of German Jews to the Fassbinder play was much more vehement than that of Jews in other Western countries or in Israel. This is indicative of the particular situation and isolation of the German Jews within the Jewish world. In the Netherlands, however, the protests were also strong, and not without grotesque and embarrassing aspects, and a judicial aftermath as well. In Denmark, the Copenhagen Jewish community came out in favor of staging the production, which attests to their political rather than their literary acumen. The Jewish businessman, developer, and Frankfurt community leader Ignatz Bubis, who played a prominent role in the German protest, succeeded Heinz Galinski as Chairman of the Central Council of Jews in Germany in 1992.

The successful author Lea Fleischmann also ought to be mentioned in the cultural context of German-Jewish alienation. "In my childhood," she wrote, "the world consisted of two kinds of people. Jews and Nazis." It is hardly possible to find a more graphic documentation of the good-versus-evil worldview. The same is true of some views expressed by Henryk Broder. Before immigrating to Israel, Broder claimed that his one-time "leftist friends" in Germany remained the children of their parents and had "inherited" their racism. This is political biologism in its purest form. Broder, born in 1946, asserted in

Speigel that "Auschwitz will grow stronger in the Jewish consciousness the further away it is in time."

But Auschwitz as a political argument is used in an inflationary manner, and will therefore lose its effect over the short or the long run.
One need not be a prophet to make this prediction. Once the unique
event becomes an everyday affair, the emotional response is blunted.

The non-Jewish contemporaries of the first post-Auschwitz Jewish
generation must bear exactly the same portion of guilt as their Jewish
contemporaries of the second generation experienced suffering in the
camps—namely none. It must, however, be noted that many Jews of
the second generation have indeed experienced the continuing spiritual sufferings of their parents, and such experiences cannot be simply
laid aside.

The patterns of thought and behavior of Lea Fleischmann and Henryk
Broder are also indicative of the change of biological and political generations among German Jews. By "political generation" I mean an age-
group shaped by the same political events and developments. The decisive formation usually takes place between the ages of 17 and 25. Fleischmann and Broder thus belong to the political generation of the student
revolt of the late 1960s and early 1970s. This is confirmed by their behavior, choice of vocabulary, and their published experiences. Broder and
Fleischmann are anything but typical "community Jews," but the term
"political generation" does not imply that all who belong to the same generation exhibit the same opinions and behavior. The extreme example of
a type displays its chief characteristics most clearly.

Bernard-Henry Levy, born in 1949, is also not typical of the French
"community Jew" but does embody the 1968 generation. In his sensational and controversial book *L'Ideologie française*, Levy fires a broad-
side at his non-Jewish environment: chauvinism and xenophobia, the
cult of the body and of youth, the celebration of order, technology, and
progress, anti-Semitism and anticapitalism, contempt of America and
democracy, are the building-blocks of French ideology, according to
Levy.

Apart from the differences between Fleischmann and Broder on the
one hand and Levy as a representative of the so-called New Philosophy
on the other, the basic phenomenon is the same: a Jewish 1968 generation which is politically conscious, active, and sometimes aggressive,

at least verbally. Of course, there is also a similar Jewish political generation to be found in the United States. The development is thus not limited to Germany or Europe, and the adjective "Jewish" refers more to family background than to religious beliefs.

The shift in the structure of Jewish society in Germany has not yet resulted in any basic changes in the patterns of behavior already described. The Russian Jews are as yet new arrivals in Germany. Nevertheless, here and there, some small changes can be detected; the first buds of an independent German-Jewish intellectual revival are forming, especially in the field of journalism, at the universities, in the professions, and even in politics.

This second generation indicates a new type of German Jew, more conscious of Jewish heritage and thus both more self-conscious and self-confident than their ancestors of the German Empire or the Weimar Republic. They publicly, sometimes demonstratively, avow their Jewishness. They are accepted by, integrated, and successful in their non-Jewish environment. But they are not practicing Jews. Their Jewishness is more related to history and the community of a common fate than to religion. They can thus at best solve the dilemma of a future independent Jewish identity as individuals, but not for the collective. And they are by no means atypical. One interesting attempt, begun in 1982, to build bridges between Jewish traditions and the modern age, between "Eastern" and "German" Jews, and between Jews and non-Jews is the Munich bookstore "Literaturhandlung." This second generation is also well represented among the politicians of Jewish background to be found in prominent positions in the democratic parties in Germany, including the CDU, FDP, SPD, Greens, and also the PDS.

The quality of life in the Federal Republic of Germany will probably alter the German-Jewish mentality over the long run without being able to assist in the formation of a specific Jewish identity. Will future German Jews live in a country providing state financial support but no religious-traditional identity? If so, their Jewishness will stand only on one leg; the historical and religious leg will have been long amputated.

In France the demographic trend in favor of the Jews of North-African descent has produced a stronger inclination toward the values of the Jewish-religious community, as the Jews of Morocco, Algeria, and Tunisia are generally more traditional. What is more, they are affected neither by classical nineteenth-century French anti-Semitism (as embodied by the Dreyfus affair) nor by twentieth-century French anti-Semitism of the Vichy era and the Holocaust.

It is only in France, but therefore in the largest of Europe's Jewish communities, that a process of psychological weaning away from the Holocaust has begun—as a result of the influence of the North African Jews. Much the same is also true for the Jews of Israel, where the proportion of the Jewish population of Oriental heritage has steadily increased over the years and now forms a majority. We have already pointed out the consequences of this demographic process in previous chapters.

■

Political events sometimes set off "political cycles," or at least encourage them. The term "political cycles" is used here to refer to middle-term political trends of a cyclical nature. As in business, in politics, too, there is a market for certain products. The increase in attacks and assaults on Jewish institutions and individuals in recent years confirms the interconnection between political events and political cycles. Of course, these attacks are largely, if not exclusively, related to Israel's conflict with its Arab neighbors and with the Palestinians. But their effect is also of significance for German as well as West European Jews in general. Such incidents reawaken memories of persecution and generate fear of anti-Semitism. Certainly, criticism of Israel, even when vehement, is not to be automatically equated with anti-Semitism (even if the opposite case is often argued). But because of their experience and their view of the world, many Jews react as if this were so. People who are afraid cannot think and act with detached rationality.

Political cycles involving Jewish fears of renewed anti-Semitism can only further cement already set ideas and patterns of behavior and produce a sort of substitute Holocaust experience among the post-Auschwitz generations. In France this could inhibit or even reverse the slow process of movement away from the Holocaust syndrome made possible by the increasing North African influence in the French Jewish community. In that event, the inflationary use of the charge of anti-Semitism may in turn so anger the non-Jewish environment that even those well-disposed toward Jews may prefer to distance themselves from the Jewish community and thus unwittingly contribute toward a Jewish self-ghettoization.

One must also note that the attacks on Jewish institutions and individuals, despite their Middle Eastern origins, also exhibit political, ideological, and operational links to organized and militant West European anti-Semitic groups. A brief examination of the annual reports prepared by the West German Bureau for the Protection of the Constitution during the early 1980s suffices to give a picture of the cooperation between elements of the terrorist right in Europe (such as the *Wehrsportgruppe Hoffmann*) and the PLO (Al-Fatah). To this extent, the relevant incidents did, indeed, have an anti-Semitic background. The purely Palestinian acts of terror against Jewish institutions and individuals are chiefly directed against Israel, and only to a lesser degree against the infrastructure of the Jewish Diaspora, but they awaken deep-seated Jewish fears for which the term "Holocaust" is the chief abbreviation.

With the opening of the East German archives, more and more light is also being thrown on the involvement of the GDR regime in this unholy anti-Israel and anti-Semitic alliance. It has also been revealed that in 1988, one year before the fall of the Berlin Wall, the GDR authorities were aware of—but took no active role in combatting—the activities of at least 800 skinheads in East Germany. The SED-regime could not bring itself to face the existence of neo-Nazis in the German state that claimed in its propaganda to have eliminated fascism at its very roots. By late 1992 the ranks of right-wing radical and violence-prone skinheads had swollen to more than 4,000 in all of Germany, of which 3,000 were to be found in the area of the former GDR.

3. Diaspora and Israel. Or: The Double Dilemma of German Jews

Before the Holocaust, the Zionist movement had considerable problems legitimizing itself in the eyes of the Jews of the world. Zionism had to justify not only its goals but also the necessity for its very existence, and it remained a minority movement among Jews worldwide. Asylum-seeking Jews, by voting with their feet, provide sufficient proof. The majority of Jews forced to leave their homeland in the course of the nineteenth century immigrated to the United States, not to Palestine.

Zionist ideologues skirted their legitimacy deficit by understanding and presenting themselves as the embodiment of the "general will" of the Jewish people. One hears the voice of Rousseau speaking through Mosche Beilenson, a pioneer of socialist Zionism: "We are of the opinion that the Zionist ideal meets the needs of the Jewish people and thus we regard the Zionist movement as truly democratic, independent of whether or not the Zionist ideal is supported by the majority of the people." In other words: quantity is not quality, and Zionism knows what is good for the Jewish people. Zionism is always right.

In the aftermath of the Holocaust it was no longer the Zionist movement, but the Diaspora that was in need of justifying its existence. The course of history, as interpreted by Zionists and largely accepted throughout the Jewish world, had proven the Zionists right. Apart from the feelings of guilt for having survived, Diaspora Jews were now forced to justify themselves for not immigrating to Israel.

For the German Jews there was an additional dilemma: They were living not merely in the Diaspora but actually in the land that had brought forth the Holocaust. German Jews had to justify their country of residence not only to themselves, but also to the remaining Diaspora and to Israel.

Why did the majority of Diaspora Jews nevertheless choose not to immigrate to Israel? The most disarming answer was provided a few years ago by a young French Jew who had just shortly before been observed shouting "Down with assimilation!" and "Long live Israel!": "Israel is a wonderful country, but the food there is bad."

As far as France was concerned, the rest of the Jewish world seemed to have accepted this sort of argumentation, as it did with regard to the Jews of Great Britain and the United States. But for a considerable time there was no understanding shown for those Jews who chose to remain in Germany, especially in the years immediately after the Holocaust. And the reaction was not limited to words alone: In August of 1950 the Jewish Agency presented the Jews in Germany with an ultimatum. They were to all leave the country within six weeks. Whoever remained in Germany after this time would no longer be regarded as a Jew and in the case of a later decision to come to Israel could not count on the normal assistance provided Jewish immigrants. In October of the same year the chairman of the General Council of the World Jewish Congress demanded that all of the world's Jewish organizations cut off all relations with the German Jewish communities. In consequence, the "Claims Conference," which represented the Jewish Diaspora in the restitution negotiations with the West German government, at first excluded the German Jews.

The chairman of the Jewish community of Berlin, Heinz Galinski, who battled much more intensely for recognition than did the majority of his colleagues, informed the Claims Conference in November 1951 that the Central Council of Jews in Germany was not willing to allow itself to be excluded. Rather, it was insisting that the Jews living in Germany were an integral part of all of Jewry. In early January 1952, the Central Council was invited to send a representative to the guidelines committee of the Claims Conference.

Institutional recognition was thus achieved. Moral recognition, however, was not—and has not to this day. In order to blunt moral condemnation on the part of Israel and the Diaspora, as well as their own bad conscience, the Jews of Germany took a number of steps. No longer did they call themselves "German Jews," as before the Holocaust, or "German citizens of Mosaic faith" (an expression from earlier decades that was designed to avoid use of the unpopular term "Jewish"). They called themselves "Jews *in* Germany," thus defining a locality but not a political identification and thus also abandoning any sense of independent, German-Jewish identity. This was to pre-program an existence without content. By distancing themselves from the earlier sense of community of the German Jews, the "Jews *in* Germany" unwittingly permitted Hitler's *judenpolitik* a final triumph. In 1935 the Nazi authorities decreed that the "Reich-Representation of German Jews" be renamed as the "Reich-Representation of the Jews in Germany."

In the course of their intensive survey of West German Jews in 1990, Silbermann and Sallen found that more than 78 percent thought the existing name"Central Council of the Jews in Germany," with its indication of separate identities, to be more appropriate than the designation "Central Council of German Jews," which implies assimilation and integration and was favored by only 20 percent of the respondents.

The German Jews also sought to free themselves of the ban imposed upon them by Israel and the Diaspora by means of zealous fund drives for Israel. Relative to its size, the German Jewish community ranks among the leading financial supporters of Israel.

In their self-chosen role as "bridge-builders" between Israel and the Federal Republic, the German Jews aimed to achieve inner-Jewish recognition. In Israel, however, their efforts met with little applause. As already mentioned, the Jewish State considers itself the embodiment of the "general will" of the Jewish people. Only political realism forced Israel to accept the vital bridge-building function of American Jews, but the intentions of the German Diaspora were treated as presumptuous. As then Israeli Foreign Minister Dayan told leaders of the German Central Council in late 1977, Israel takes care of its contacts itself and has no need for the "ghetto customs of middlemen."

Sympathy for and sensitivity toward Israel are constantly exhibited by German Jews. In early 1987 the city theater company of Haifa toured the Federal Republic. One of the plays scheduled for performance was a controversial piece that was nevertheless staged in Israel. Entitled *The Palestinian*, the drama, written by a Jewish Israeli playwright, concerns the love between an Arab woman and a Jewish man, a love doomed to failure by the Israeli social environment. The Jewish community of Düsseldorf blocked the performance of the premiere scheduled for that city with the argument that the piece could provoke "anti-Semitic reactions." In Munich the Jewish community deemed it necessary to distribute pamphlets to the theater-goers explaining and lauding the play as proof for democratic pluralism in Israel.

Apart from their protest against "ghetto customs" Israeli politicians are also fearful of Diaspora Jews being used against Israel as Jewish alibis. The resentment on the part of Israeli officialdom against Nahum Goldmann, who for many years presided over the World Zionist Organization and the World Jewish Congress, must be seen against this background. Goldmann gradually came to personify the role of the Diaspora Jew who regarded himself as a middleman, but who was viewed in Israel as an "alibi Jew" or, even more spitefully, as "court Jew."

This "type" was to be found among the Jews of West Germany as well, and each and every one of them claimed to be performing a vital "bridge-building" function between Israel and the government of the Federal Republic of Germany. Highly prominent among them was Karl Marx, the publisher of the *General Jewish Weekly*. In numerous published articles Marx publicly expounded on Germany's good intentions toward Israel, which he exhorted to moderate its claims. Behind the scenes he not infrequently encouraged West Germany not to give in to Israeli demands. This behavior, both at the time of the negotiations leading to the Luxembourg Agreement as well as later, did not endear him to the Israeli government. In a private conversation in the Bonn Federal Chancellery in July 1964, in the midst of the storm over the activities of German rocket experts in Egypt, Marx suggested that the German government take a "clear and well-founded stand" with regard to Jerusalem's demands, claiming that he had repeatedly endeavored to "explain to Jewish and particularly Israeli circles that their demands for legislative action on the part of the West German government were unjustified." Marx did not neglect to add that the missile experts were not "Nazis" and that their presence in Egypt was "far less dangerous than if scientists from the East block were active there." Not only Israelis were irritated by this sometimes obvious, more often suspected "alibi function." Diaspora Jews well-disposed toward the new West Germany, including such organizations as the American Jewish Committee, were critical of this kind of "court Jew" behavior.

Tensions have repeatedly arisen between American Jewish organizations and the Central Council of Jews in Germany, which was intent on maintaining its monopoly position regarding Jewish issues in Germany. Interventions by American Jewish leaders with the German government and parties have proven a mixed blessing, lending international pressure to support Jewish interests in Germany on the one hand but weakening the position of the internal Jewish lobby on the other. The activities of Edgar Bronfman, described in section 7 of chapter 2, are a case in point.

■

In contrast to the uncommon type of the "alibi" Jew, the phenomenon of Israelism, i.e., an Israel-centered fixation, is highly visible and deeply entrenched among both West German and Diaspora Jews. The idea that the Jewish State embodies Judaism, or at least its "general will," has apparently been unquestioningly internalized not only by the majority of Diaspora Jews, but also by numerous non-Jews. How else are we to explain the phenomenon that the adjectives "Israeli" and "Jewish" are used as interchangeable equivalents in European media reporting about the Middle East? The "Israelism" of Diaspora Jews, including German Jews, is a virtually automatic assumption.

This "Israelism" has two chief characteristics, the first of which is more superficial in nature but—at least in the United States—not irrelevant in terms of foreign policy. The second aspect is more substantial and deep-seated. The superficial component consists of support for Israel in its conflict with the Palestinians and the Arab states. At least until the Sadat initiative of 1977, support among Diaspora Jews, especially in the United States, was unbroken, and still continued at a high level thereafter. This dimension of Israelism, the *identification with* Israel, is taken as virtually axiomatic by the non-Jewish world.

The more substantial component of Israelism is the tendency to equate Israel and Jewry and is thus ultimately the issue of Jewish *identity*. In the original sense of the word, identity means the total equivalence of two objects. To thus equate Judaism and Israel is to narrow the scope of Judaism. Regardless of whether one is pro-Zionist or indifferent toward Israel, and although Zion is a concept central to the spiritual world of Judaism, Zion is only part of the whole. Israelism as the Jewish identity entails, in the final analysis, the total secularization of Judaism. If God is "dead," at least one still has an idol. The anti-Zionist orthodox recognized this danger early on and combatted Zionism as a form of blasphemy, pointing out that is it not for man to interfere with God's handiwork, i.e. with the course of history.

Among German Jews, the Diaspora in general and Israel as well, Jewish substance has not been in great demand. Jews avoid the synagogue just as many of their non-Jewish fellow citizens avoid the church. In recent years, however, there have been signs of a new interest in the Jewish religion in the United States, Great Britain, France, and even in West Germany. It is being slowly recognized that Jewish identity does not consist exclusively of Jewish solidarity.

Chief Rabbi Jakobovits was among the first to discern the danger to the Jewish Diaspora identity inherent in Israelism. Jakobovits warned as early as 1976, well before criticism of Israel came into vogue with the Sadat initiative, against too much enthusiasm for the overenthusiastic Jewish settlers in the West Bank, pointing out that the issue of the quality of life in the Jewish State was more important than the question of its borders. In February 1980, he would not exclude the creation of a Palestinian state on the West Bank and in Gaza with its capital in East Jerusalem as a potential solution to the conflict. Such statements from leaders of the Jewish community in Germany would have been unthinkable. What the Chief Rabbi of Great Britain recognized was that extreme Israelism could drag the Diaspora into Israeli extremism, or at least involve it in Israel's domestic quarrels. This was amply illustrated in 1987 when both Foreign Minister Peres and Prime Minister Shamir mobilized their supporters among American Jews in order to strengthen their positions in the domestic political struggle over Israel's policy toward the Palestinians.

Since the 1977 Sadat initiative, more precisely since the controversy over the proper approach to peace negotiations, Israel itself has been divided, and Israel's domestic polarization has spilled over into the Diaspora. This, in turn, has generated more criticism of Israel. In West Germany, however, this applies only to fringe groups, not to the majority of the community and its leadership. This comes as no surprise, as Israel's supporters in the Diaspora, and most certainly Israel's hawks, are all but certain to respond to German-Jewish criticism of Israel with the reproach: "How dare you who live in the land of the murderers . . . ."

The present polarization in the Diaspora communities is reminiscent of but not identical with the widespread and constant tensions between Zionists and anti-Zionists before the Holocaust. Today the confrontation is not between pro and anti, but rather between community Jews more and less critical of Israel. Nor would the majority of Jewish critics of Israel want to be considered anti-Zionist. Nevertheless, as a result of the Sadat initiative and subsequent events, especially the 1982 war in Lebanon against the PLO and Israel's policies in the occupied territories, the question of Diaspora Jewish identity has been recast for the first time since the founding of the Jewish State. In search of lost Judaism, Jews are looking less to Israel and more to and within themselves. The Diaspora is in the process of emancipating itself from Israel.

The particular position of West German Jews between Israelism and national German-Jewish identity is illustrated by the responses to statements presented by Silbermann and Sallen in their 1990 survey. More than 96 percent of the respondents agreed with the proposition that "Every Jew must decide for himself whether he feels closer to Israel or to Germany," whereas only 43 percent agreed with (and more than 56 percent rejected) the statement that "All Jews should regard Israel as their true homeland." More than 66 percent agreed that "Despite being a part of Jewish culture, German Jews are still Germans first."

In the overall context of Jewish history, problems of identification and identity between the Diaspora and the Jewish State are nothing new. In the period of the Second Temple (516 B.C. to 70 A.D.), for example, two centers of Judaism existed outside of Zion: one in Babylon, the other in Egypt. In contrast to the present, especially the Western European, and most particularly the German Diaspora, the Jewish communities of the past had their own, individual identities.

■

Quite clearly, Judaism today stands at a crossroads. New paths will have to be explored, but the perennial question remains: What constitutes Jewish existence? The follow-up question to this is, of course: Where can, where should, this Jewish existence be located? The two and a half millenniums of Jewish Diaspora history, in which, despite everything, Jews have continued to exist as Jews, prove that the answers to these questions are anything but certain. Whatever the future answer, it will determine whether Judaism will follow the cosmopolitan traditions of the Diaspora or that of the zealots of Zion, i.e. the nationalist tradition.

If the decision is in favor of the nationalists, the Jews will ultimately and finally become what the Zionists have always sought to promote and the Orthodox to avoid: a people like any other. For the religious sector, which, in Judaism, is all but inseparable from the political, the question will then be: How can the religious claim of a chosen people be maintained? Orthodox Jews are understandably upset at the prospect of such developments. As Rabbi Jakobovits argued, the realization of the ideology of the Zealots in the rebellion against Rome (66–70 A.D.) resulted not only in the destruction of the Jewish State but the end of the Jewish people—"national euthanasia," as Jakobovits put it, nationalism as a form of euthanasia for the Jewish religion, state, and people. The fact that numerous Jewish settlement activists in the occupied territories are Orthodox Jews does not disprove this thesis. It merely demonstrates that these zealots are not fully aware of the consequences of their actions. The irony is that, if it had not been for the ultra-nationalists, Israel would probably not have survived—certainly not on the basis of cosmopolitanism.

For the traditional leadership of the West German Jewish community, Israelism represents a challenge from the outside. This leadership must now also face a challenge, at the very least an opposition from within, an opposition originating mainly among younger university-educated representatives of the 1968 and the eco generations. Many of their attitudes and opinions with regard to Germany are reflected in the book by Broder and Lang: *Fremd im eigenen Land—* Stranger in One's Own Country. What is most striking is their criticism of Israelism, of the lack of democratic and intellectual-spiritual legitimation on the part of the official Jewish leadership, its lack of understanding for activist "grassroots" politics, its orientation to Israel one the one hand and its obsequiousness toward German politicians on the other. Anti-intellectual attitudes within the Jewish communities and leadership are also criticized, and anti-intellectualism among the "people of the book" certainly represents a break with Jewish tradition. Nevertheless, anti-intellectualism has a certain tradition in the Jewish communities. We are reminded of Spinoza and the Amsterdam Jewish community which, in effect, excommunicated the great philosopher. It remains to be seen if and how long such a small Jewish community as that in Germany can continue to afford the luxury of anti-intellectualism.

Many of these younger Jews find the constant Jewish self-adulation revolting and launch polemics against the "we-the victim" versus "you-the-perpetrator" worldview. They perceive less anti-Semitism in their environment than the traditional community Jews.

In France the gap between the leadership and its supposed or potential followers has grown to the point that only a third of all French Jews are registered members of the community. The proportion in Germany is about half. The situation in Great Britain, where about two-thirds formally belong to the community, is much better.

The younger generation is putting pressure on the leadership to initiate actions and policies to mobilize the people and get things done—for example to organize demonstrations against the European Community's Middle East policies. Extraparliamentary opposition and mass demonstrations are techniques learned from the non-Jewish environment. Guy de Rothschild, a representative of the old leadership, dismissed such demands in 1980 with an incontrovertible argument: "One does not play with mass actions when one doesn't have any masses."

The West German Jewish version of mass action without masses was demonstrated in Frankfurt in 1985 with the controversy over Fassbinder's purportedly anti-Semitic play. In the eyes of their organizers, the actions were a great success, but in the opinion of their opponents they represented proof of "enormous Jewish influence." Polls showed that the supposed "mass actions" were approved of by only a quarter of the West German public. The greatest portion of sympathy (54%) was expressed by supporters of the Greens, who are generally more open to this sort of politics. The polls also indicated that the basic position of the Jewish protesters nevertheless enjoyed general support: only a third of the respondents thought that Fassbinder's play ought to be staged. The Jewish activists had thus zealously squandered sympathies and given nourishment to the ancient legend of Jewish omnipotence, a legend that has often served as an excuse for anti-Semitic excesses.

On closer examination, the group of Jewish intellectuals—which also includes this author—offers, instead of an alternative of their own, a Jewish rewarming of non-Jewish recipes from the younger generations. They are on the whole more concerned with actions and identifications than with traditions, not to mention religion. They thus avoid the central problem of the Diaspora: the issue of Jewish identity.

Nevertheless, we must not underestimate the regenerative capacity of German Jewry. Considering the starting point, the organizational accomplishments are impressive. It was simply not possible to do everything at once. Perhaps there will some day be a spiritual renewal of German Jewry akin to that which took place in the eighteenth and nineteenth centuries. Perhaps.

■

Both Germans and Arabs frequently refer to "traditional German-Arabian friendship." If the praises of this traditional friendship are so highly sung, then we must presume that it is based on happy memories, as memory is the only paradise from which humanity cannot be driven. On closer examination, however, traditional German-Arabian friendship necessarily evokes some rather unpleasant historical memories, at least on the German side. But a cursory examination of the history of German-Arab relations in the twentieth century is sufficient to make the dimensions clear.

Before the First World War, Germany's policy toward the Middle East was oriented toward the Ottoman Empire. It was pro-Turkish and thus automatically directed against Arab efforts to achieve independence from their Turkish-Ottoman overlords. This was not the foundation of German-Arab friendship.

After the First World War, the Weimar Republic was faced with many more pressing foreign policy problems than the Middle East. German-Arab relations were dominated by silence. Hitler's rise to power at first resulted in little change, despite the efforts of the National Socialist party's "Foreign Office" and especially those of its chief, Alfred Rosenberg, to enlist the support of the Arabs as allies in the battle against "Bolshevism and World Jewry" and in the effort to weaken the position of the British Empire in the Middle East. But the government Foreign Office and Hitler himself applied the brakes.

Until 1939 Hitler clung to the hope of establishing a form of partnership with the "Germanic blood brothers" on the British isles. Hitler did not hold a high opinion of the Semitic Arabs: "Let us think as lords and regard these peoples [the Arabs] as, at best, veneered apes who want to feel the rod," as he put it to a gathering of German officers at the Obersalzberg on August 22, 1939.

Nevertheless, once war with Great Britain became reality in 1939, Hitler was prepared to cooperate with the "apes" against the British. He lent his support to the Palestine national movement under Amin el-

Husseini against the common Jewish enemy, declared his willingness to supply arms to the Saudis and to render assistance to the anti-British movement in Iraq. Hitler attempted to mobilize the Arab world against British power in the Middle East. By 1941, he was describing Amin el-Husseini as a man of "aryan physiognomy, blond hair and blue eyes." How the "race" had changed in but two years' time!

From the perspective of actual tradition, i.e., history, the "traditional German-Arabian friendship" is certainly no crown jewel for either side.

We are reminded of the Arab arguments against the German-Israeli restitution agreement. The fact of the Holocaust was sometimes denied, as well as the Jewish, and most particularly the Israeli, right to receive compensation.

We are reminded of Saudi King Khalid, who, on the occasion of an official and public state banquet on April 27, 1981, called upon visiting German Chancellor Helmut Schmidt, who listened in silence, to return to the German-Arabian tradition of the 1930s. We can be certain that the Saudi King was not referring to biological observations concerning primates, but rather to Hitler's planned weapons deliveries, which never actually materialized. Hitler's promise was given in June of 1939 and transport between Germany and Saudi Arabia became impossible soon thereafter.

We are reminded of the Saudi newspaper *Al-Riyad*, which, following the gruesome September 1986 terrorist bombing of the synagogue in Istanbul, accused Israel of having carried out this massacre: "The Zionist groups which, to further their higher aims, contributed to the attacks upon the Jews in the Nazi period," according to *Al-Riyad*, did not hesitate to attack synagogues in the present.

To conjure the spirit of "traditional German-Arabian friendship" is thus to plunge into one of the deepest pitfalls of history. This potential means of escaping German-Jewish via German-Arabian history is clearly a dead end.

As long as the attitude of the Arab states toward Israel remains inflexible (and there are increasing signs of change), German policy toward the Arab states runs the risk of encouraging anti-Israeli and anti-Jewish sentiments and thus returning to the starting point of "traditional German-Arabian friendship," namely the Third Reich.

German policy, *geschichtspolitik*, toward the Arab states or Iran provides no better way of escaping German history than German policies toward Israel. That the history of the years 1939 to 1945 is cited as a common tie is an embarrassment to the new, democratic Germany. German policy toward Israel involved a painful but necessary process of confronting the nation's past. The decision is between embarrassment and painful catharsis. This should not and cannot be a practical-political alternative, as German policy toward the Arab states is frequently purely pragmatic in nature. It is no longer so, however, when the praises of "traditional German-Arabian friendship" are sung. It is best not to conjure such spirits.

11

IMAGES AS A SOURCE OF
INFORMATION AND DANGER

Or, Germans and Jews in Search of Reality

L et us turn to images, namely the pictures of Jews created by Christians, especially in German Central Europe, and the images of themselves and their environment presented by Jews over the centuries. Such images were—and are—highly political.

For historians, images are an important source of information, and this holds particularly true for the history of German-Christian-Jewish relations. Images are a source in a double sense: a source of information and a source of danger. As a source of information, images have much to tell us about continuity and change in opinions and attitudes of and toward Jews. When used not only to represent but also to propagate opinions and attitudes toward Jews, i.e., when misused as propaganda, images present a source of danger.

Images can, of course, be a literal pictorial representation or, in a more abstract sense, a picture of "the" Jew or "the" non-Jew. My contention is that, in the course of Western and thus of German history, the image of Jews has alternated between caricature and idealization, but a realistic picture was rarely if ever painted and thus remained without historical effect. A comparable lack of realism is to be found today on the Jewish and Israeli side.

Whether the tenor of the times was more religious or secular, at no time were the Germans able or willing to deal dispassionately with the Jews living within or outside their borders. As is documented by numerous surviving works of sculpture in and on the facades of churches and cathedrals, the church saw itself not only as the rival but also as the supplanter of the synagogue. This image applies to nearly two thousand years of relations between Germans and Jews. Particularly in times of increased religious fervor, German Christians could not adopt a neutral stance toward Jews. For centuries, the political mechanics of anti-Judaism were directed against the people supposedly responsible for the murder of Jesus Christ.

Since the beginning of the historical process of secularization, many reasons have continued to prevent the development of a more detached and objective basis to German-Jewish relations. There is no need to repeat this long and complicated history here, as it is self-evident that, in the wake of the Holocaust, Jews and Germans are both unable and unwilling to be indifferent toward each other.

Germans, Germany, indeed the whole of Western Christianity has never been indifferent toward Jews, and this continues to apply to the Jewish State. The sometimes excessive attention paid to the State of Israel can be better understood against this Occidental Christian— and thus German—tradition. Granted, this is a greatly simplified generalization, but it nevertheless applies to all phases of the nearly two-thousand-year-old history of German-Jewish relations from Roman times to the present. Especially after the convolutions of recent history, it should come as no surprise that, despite all individual differences, present-day collective attitudes and perceptions continue to be distorted by centuries of hubris and humiliation.

Of course, all of us, Jews and non-Jews, are insecure and inhibited as a result of the past. How can we be certain that we at long last see the true picture? We should begin by carefully examining the distortions and the idealizations in the images handed down to us. We must then evaluate these images both intellectually and emotionally, shedding at least a symbolic tear where appropriate. Of course, the emotional confrontation with the past is not enough. Actions must follow. We must also proceed to create a new image. This, in German newspeak, is what we call *vergangenheitsbewältigung*, overcoming the past.

The generations born after the Holocaust, both Jewish and non-Jewish, need not make atonement. For purely biological reasons they bear no guilt. Their responsibility is to prevent a recurrence, and in this both Jews and non-Jews can come together in pursuit of a common goal.

First, however, we must know the past. We must know why we have arrived at where we are. In doing so, we automatically and unavoidably form images of ourselves and of others. But what is the accurate, the real picture? We must embark on a search for reality.

Why a search? Again, the answer has two sides. First, to arrive at the German-Jewish, indeed the Western-Christian-Jewish, reality is much more difficult than one might anticipate. Often we must look for the seemingly apparent, and it is anything but certain that we will discover it, especially when we consider that over a period of nearly two thousand years Jews and non-Jews proved incapable of forming realistic images of each other.

Second, to "search for reality" may involve looking for something which has been lost. This is, in fact, the case. In the years between 1933 and 1945 Germany destroyed this German-Jewish reality, drowned it in the blood of millions. Granted, there are survivors, but the German-Jewish life of the present bears neither quantitative nor qualitative comparison with the past.

Further, to describe this reality would be tantamount to presenting German-Jewish history in its entirety. Let us therefore concentrate on the distortions and idealizations of the images in the past and present. Between them, we may find the reality we are searching for. We have every reason to be skeptical.

■

The "ugly Jew" was certainly not the invention of Julius Streicher's Nazi propaganda mouthpiece *Der Stürmer* (The Stormer). One of the oldest representations of the "ugly Jew" in Germany is to be found in the so-called "Christ window" in the Church of the Friars Minor in Regensburg, where the "ugly Jew" is portrayed whipping the bound

Christ. This fourteenth-century image is little different from that presented in the twentieth-century *Stürmer*.

The image of the *judensau*, literally: the Jewish sow, is certainly the most horrid, although not the oldest, historical distortion. It is well-known that this epithet was hurled at Jews in Germany from the thirteenth century on. What is not so widely known is that, also from the thirteenth century on, there are numerous pictorial representations of the *judensau*. Some of these are highly elaborate, but that does not by any means make them works of art. The *judensau*, in fact, is to be found on the facades of numerous churches in German-speaking locations: in Freising, Magdeburg, Salzburg, Regensburg, Frankfurt am Main—and also in Milan. These sculptures were by no means tucked away in a corner. Quite to the contrary, they are clearly visible.

One of the most revolting descriptions we have flowed from the pen of Martin Luther. His sensitivity toward Jews was not very pronounced, even before 1523, when he abandoned his futile attempts to win over the Jews to the Reformation. His disappointment turned into hate. Luther described the *judensau* prominently displayed on the south facade of the church at Wittenberg since 1305 with the following words (minus the untranslatable color): "Here on our church in Wittenberg a sow is sculpted in stone. Young pigs and Jews lie suckling under her. Behind the sow a Rabbi is bent over the sow, lifting up her right leg, holding her tail high and looking intensely under her tail and into her Talmud, as though he were reading something acute or extraordinary, which is certainly where they get their Schemhamphoras."

What a magnificent, honorable, and exemplary picture is presented by Lessing's *Nathan the Wise*, which was first staged in 1781. This Nathan is the personification of Enlightenment and tolerance, a wonderful human being. A human being? A superman!

With the Enlightenment, the ugly, distorted image of the Jew as symbolized by the *judensau* was contrasted with the idealized image of the Jew. This was and is praiseworthy, but also unrealistic. Hardly any human being, Jew or Gentile, can live up to such an ideal. Such an image thus at best leads to disappointment, more often to sharp counter-reactions. That is exactly what happened to the Enlightenment idealization of the Jew. "This is the Jew?" scoffed the old and new anti-Semites, and promptly began drawing a new counter-image, a new portrait of the enemy with old, familiar traits. Julius Streicher's *Stürmer* was not without its predecessors in the nineteenth and competitors in the twentieth century, but it was certainly the most extreme expression of a centuries-old tradition of anti-Jewish distortions.

Since 1945, the efforts at re-education and the earnest attempts at offering more than merely financial and political "restitution" led to a new image of Jews in Germany, an image which, on second look, proves familiar: it is once again Nathan the Wise.

That the contempt bred by propagating images of an enemy can lead to mass murder is a lesson of history. What was the reaction? The image of the subhuman Jew was reversed into that of a Jewish superhuman. At least until after the Six Day War of 1967 and the oil crisis of the 1970s, official Germany imbued Jews with a sort of halo. Only in private was a more realistic picture discussed.

One of the high points of this beatification of the German Jews was reached at the funeral service for Werner Nachmann, the late chairman of the board of the Central Council. Many of the most prominent representatives of the Federal Republic of Germany found only the highest words of praise. Soon afterward, however, Nachmann's misdeeds were uncovered. As a result, the image of the fallible Jew was revealed. Throughout the country the sensationalistic press proclaimed the discovery that the saint was a sinner; the angel had become a normal human being.

Why had the Jewish human being been elevated to a kind of sainthood in the first place? And why did so many speak with a different voice in public than in private? Once again, it was deemed necessary to combat the distorted with an idealized image. Only realism can confront reality, but it was this reality that was feared. Good intentions are not enough; only realism can overcome the burdens of the past, and good intentions lead to terrible results when a gap grows between public and private pronouncements.

There has been a great deal of discussion about this fact in German-Christian circles, but this has remained behind closed doors, for fear of furnishing the anti-Semites with arguments. This is unhealthy, both for the individual as well as the collective. My fear is that constantly swallowing frustrations can lead only to a build-up of pressures that will eventually break out, all at once, in a massive storm.

The image of the Jews has undergone cyclical changes in the course of the centuries. Elements of that image have appeared and disappeared—and reappeared again. The mechanisms related to the political use and abuse of these images have remained largely the same, not just before and after the Holocaust, but for centuries. Because I am convinced of the cyclical character of history, I fear the return swing of the pendulum. The more extreme the movement in the one direction, the more violent the reaction. Moderation is the desired historical virtue.

■

Uncritical idealization and beatification of the other side is no substitute for historical knowledge, and can produce acute embarrassments. For one example, let us take a closer look at the term *reichskristallnacht*, usually translated as the "night of broken glass." From today's perspective it is legitimate to question whether this term, which was used at the time, does not serve to render harmless the shameful and murderous actions on the part of the Nazis on the night of November 9th and 10th, 1938. If so, we must search intensely for a more appropriate term. However, we should not, as has been suggested, simply substitute a Russian word, namely "pogrom." The atrocities were committed in Germany, not in Russia.

Those who reject the term *reichskristallnacht* with the claim that this was the euphemistic label invented by the National-Socialists themselves are simply wrong. The Nazis always spoke in terms of the "big Jewish action" or "the spontaneous wrath of the German people," which allegedly broke out without any organized assistance from state or party organs. Many Berliners were not deceived. By using the prefix *reich*, the Berliners documented that they were well aware of who had instigated these events, namely the leadership of the *reich*. And because everyone was also well aware that a great deal more was broken that night than mere glass and crystal, because everyone knew that Jews had been kidnapped and murdered, their houses of worship put to the torch, the reference to *kristall* was, to contemporary ears, an obvious derision of the Nazi party and regime. This note escapes our ears today.

The term invented by the Berliners of the time is thus an indication of the revulsion they felt, but it is not, on the other hand, a symbol of resistance. Unfortunately, there is little evidence of publicly expressed revulsion, and even less of resistance toward the Nazis. We should therefore think twice about blowing out the last trace of one of the few faint candles that glowed in that dark time.

Just because Heinz Galinski, the leading representative of the official Jewish community in Germany, chose to repeat the claim that the term *reichskristallnacht* was coined by the Nazis does not lend it any truth, and those who choose to parrot the argument only open themselves to ridicule. The good intentions of politicians, journalists, and their followers is one thing, the political effect is another matter. The examples of good political and educational intentions producing undesired effects because the initiators got their facts wrong are legion. We will briefly describe but two:

In the fall of 1988 a praiseworthy citizens' initiative in Munich led to an examination of the names of the city streets in order to expunge any remaining vestiges of the Nazi era. The search was not in vain. For example, the *Treitschkestrasse* turned up. An editor of the prestigious Munich daily, the *Süddeutsche Zeitung,* expressed indignation that a city street should still bear the name of "a spokesman of anti-Semitism in the Third Reich" who was the author of the then popular saying: "The Jews are our misfortune."

In addition to being a much admired historian in his own day, and one whose role is still frequently overrated, Heinrich von Treitschke was truly a horrible anti-Semite. It is certainly repugnant that a street should be named after him, but Treitschke was not a "spokesman" of the Third Reich. He was in no position to be. The quote in question was from the year 1869 and Treitschke died in 1896.

The second example: Many newspaper articles and magazine features recalling the fiftieth anniversary of the *reichskristallnacht* in November 1988 were accompanied by photographs of the ruins of the New Synagogue in Berlin, which, it was reported, had been set on fire by the SA on that night in 1938.

The facts were the following: The New Synagogue in the Oranienburger Strasse, which had been dedicated in Bismarck's presence in 1866, had been designated a legally protected monument in the nineteenth century. Wilhelm Krützfeld, the officer in command of the local police station in November of 1938, was aware of this. Neighbors who observed the brown-shirted mob attempting to enter the synagogue alerted the police. Krützfeld and his men rushed to the synagogue and drove away the mob with pistols drawn. In addition, he summoned the fire department, which extinguished several minor blazes. The synagogue was actually destroyed by a British air raid on February 23, 1943. The famous photographs were from the year 1943, not 1938. Krützfeld received a reprimand from the Berlin Police President, but apparently nothing further happened to him, although he was retired from the force "for reasons of health" in 1942. Krützfeld died in Berlin in 1953.

The German post office had selected the motif of the burning Berlin New Synagogue for a commemorative issue on the *reichskristallnacht*. Happily, the Jewish magazine *Tribüne* learned of and was able to stop the post office's plans in the nick of time. How eagerly the old and new incorrigibles would have seized upon such a mistake to distract from the facts: the murder of nearly a hundred Jews, the arrest of 30,000 others, most of whom ended up in concentration camps, and the arson of some 1,350 synagogues during the night of November 9–10, 1938. On that night there were very few who, like Police Lieutenant Krützfeld, demonstrated more than the mere verbal revulsion that the people of Berlin gave expression to with their term *reichskristallnacht*.

The incorrigibles of the past and present are quick to pounce whenever someone has their facts wrong. In triumphant derision they argue that if what we are told about the term *reichskristallnacht* and the New Synagogue is wrong, then all that about Auschwitz and the millions of murdered Jews can't be right either.

In the fall of 1988 I shared these thoughts with a West German politician, a man of intelligence and absolute integrity. I pointed out the gap between intent and knowledge that was apparent in his statements about the *reichskristallnacht* and was characteristic of speeches by numerous other politicians across the political spectrum. His reply: "Please don't consider me an opportunist. In most speeches there is this tension between perception and profession. And when both are legitimate it is hard to strike a balance." In discussions with other politicians, also from other parties, I heard very similar, albeit less convincingly formulated statements. I thus link my criticism with a sincere and high regard for the motives and convictions of these men and women. They desire only the best, but inadvertently also give impetus to the undesirable.

When numerous politicians contribute to widening the gap between knowledge and intent they also increase the general credibility gap between politics and society. They thus play into the hands of those whose influence they seek to weaken, namely the incorrigibles.

■

Early on in the cultural life of the new West Germany, considerable efforts were made to overcome both the distorted and the idealized clichés of the Jew. These efforts were both more open and more energetic, but not always more successful. Understandably, the first moves were made on secure ground. Productions of Lessing's *Nathan the Wise* were an honorable and easy way to deal with the Jewish question and the issue of tolerance in general.

With Shakespeare's *Merchant of Venice* it was much more difficult. Could the rejected and revengeful Shylock, the figure of a Jew who both suffers and inflicts suffering, a character representing both good and evil, be presented before a German public?

"One sits in the audience with a racing heartbeat, feels the pulse of the play rise and fall, waits for reconciliation and wonders: Will it be possible this time to make the whole complex richness of this play palpable so that no blemish will remain?" asked the drama critic of the *Frankfurter Allgemeine Zeitung* on the occasion of the Düsseldorf premiere of the *Merchant of Venice* in September 1957, the first production of the play in West Germany since the war. That the critic was able to breathe a sigh of relief was really not surprising, as the main role was played by a truly outstanding actor, Ernst Deutsch, who happened to be Jewish. Nevertheless, at that time it was still a high-wire act.

This became even more apparent in the early 1970s in West Berlin, where the Freie Volksbühne staged a new production. Again, a lively discussion broke out over the familiar issue: Was it still too soon for this play? Especially in Berlin, where the *endlösung* had been planned and directed? The doubters were encouraged by official Jewish spokesmen whose judgment it was that this play could not be staged, not yet, and perhaps not at all.

The production went ahead nevertheless. First, the suffering rather than the evil-doing Shylock was emphasized. And second, the actor in the main role provided the best alibi. Fritz Kortner was not only Jewish, but also highly sensitive to anti-Semitism. Kortner did not require the help of official representatives of Jewish and non-Jewish interest groups to decide what was anti-Semitic and what wasn't.

The struggle over the distorted and the idealized images could also be observed during the 1980s. A production of *Nathan the Wise* was all but a certainty during the annual "brotherhood week," but *Ghetto* by the Israeli dramatist Joshua Sobol presented formidable problems, not just for the spokesmen of the official Jewish community.

In this play, some of the Jewish victims become guiltlessly guilty as accessories to the National-Socialist murderers. A true tragedy was staged in the seemingly relaxed form of a semi-musical. In the ghetto of the Lithuanian capital of Vilnius, as in many other cities in Eastern Europe, the Germans had instituted a sort of Jewish self-administration, a so-called Jewish Council. Jews who strove to preserve their co-religionists from being kidnapped and murdered were forced into cooperation with the Germans. The Jewish Council was forced to decide how to distribute the few remaining medical supplies in the ghetto. Was it better to aid the old and the sick, or attempt to help the younger and the productive to live longer? This is the question faced not by dyed-in-the-wool Nazis, but by Jewish representatives. Should every third child be sent into the gas chamber so that at least the other two might remain with their father and mother? Terrible questions and a terrible answer, as the Jewish Council decides, so to speak, for the "positive" solution. The ghetto leader stands before a blood-red sun and recites the two-by-two rhyme of death: "Father, mother, child, end." An astounded SS officer remarks: "Looking into your Jewish faces is like looking into a distorted mirror. Our own caricature stares back at us."

The entire ghetto is such a mirror. The persecuted take on the methods of their executioners. But, no, more than just but, for this is the central point: the motives are totally different. The Nazis seek to exterminate the Jews, the Jewish Council seeks to survive.

The European premiere of Sobol's play was staged by the Freie Volksbühne in West Berlin. In Berlin! In Germany of all places! This was the reaction on the part of many, very many.

Following the world premiere in Israel (also in 1984), Israeli writer Boaz Evron wrote: "*Ghetto* by Joshua Sobol is the first of the many plays I have seen over the years about the mass murder of the Jews that is of true intellectual and artistic value. Here there is no idealization and no demonization. Here people are presented with all sorts of characters and political views, all in a hellish situation. [. . .] This is a realistic play." Exactly that is the point: it is realistic.

Another Jewish critic agreed that the play was magnificent, but added without hesitation: "Staged in Germany, it is the right play for the wrong audience." The German public, so the critic contended, "cannot help but misunderstand this play."

Here, I cannot and will not understand: Why *the* Germans? All? Young and old? Guilty and innocent? Are Germans incapable of understanding this play because of their birth, for biological reasons? This is reminiscent of the worldview of the imperial powers of the past century, who thought that independence and self-determination could be granted to the peoples of Asia and Africa only when they were judged "ready." Especially in the era following the genocide of the Holocaust, the historical lesson that collective prejudice can have catastrophic consequences ought to apply universally, for Germans and non-Germans, Jews and non-Jews. Democracy, freedom, tolerance, and human rights are indivisible.

As already stated, Sobol's play was produced in West Berlin. This was due in no small measure to the efforts of the Jewish producer, Peter Zadek, who was so disappointed by the arguments and behavior of the official Jewish community that he left it in protest. Zadek wanted more German-Jewish realism, which was precisely what the joint Christian-Jewish actions aimed at preventing.

Peter Zadek was neither the first nor the last Jewish intellectual to decide to leave the organized Jewish community in protest over illiberal and thus un-Jewish cultural policy, a policy aimed at a closed rather than an open society. The main actors in Zadek's production, Ester Ofarim and Michael Degen, were also Jewish. After they broke the ice others could follow. Of course, other scandals also followed, with other plays by Sobol. The pattern was repeated: Realism was not desired and the official representatives of the Jewish community expressed their doubts over the maturity of the German public. This was the defensive tactic. The offensive approach was also attempted: massive efforts to block the productions.

Both approaches demonstrate that massive prejudices with regard to *the* Germans obtain on the German-Jewish side. Such clichés with regard to Germans and Germany are also to be found in Israel. The already discussed verbal assault by Menachem Begin against Germany and Chancellor Helmut Schmidt in 1981 is indicative of the intensity of the still existing, although no longer predominant, prejudices against Germany in Israel. As late as 1988, the newly elected President of the Knesset, Dov Schilanski, had nothing more pressing than to announce that he, in contrast to his predecessor, would refuse to receive any delegations from Germany.

In contrast to Sobol's plays, which are hard-boiled but realistic, Fassbinder's previously mentioned *Garbage, the City and Death* is equally rough, but by no means realistic. What makes this play disturbing is that Fassbinder picks up the tradition of the distorted image. In this play we meet not with Jewish people but with *the* Jew.

Realism with regard to both Jews and Germans is still not in demand, neither among the official representatives of the Central Counci, nor among many Germans, whether they hold public office or not. German individuals and institutions tend to look for Jews willing to say for them what they do not dare to say openly themselves, at least when it comes to criticizing other Jews. It is, of course, safer to leave the job to other, i.e., one's "own" Jews. Should we say "court Jews"? Despite the differences between the parties and newspapers, the pattern is much the same.

One thing this does make clear is that there is a spectrum of Jewish opinion in Germany. By means of such detours, Jewish pluralism might also lead to more realism. The problem is that such detours usually lead only to certain sections of German society, that is, to the diverse interest groups and subcultures. Conservative Jews tend to reach only a conservative non-Jewish audience. The same applies to socialists, environmentalists, the alternative scene, and so on. This is the position of the "court Jew," and the distorted image is displaced by the idealized but not by the realistic image. Very few among the well-meaning but ill-informed realize that they are moving in an old vicious circle.

■

The search for German-Jewish realities must not stop with the German Jews alone. It must also include German-Israeli relations. After a period of initial inhibitions and hesitations, a great majority of Germans entered into a phase of enthusiasm for Israel lasting from about 1967 to 1981. Almost everything about Israel was good, right, and nearly ideal: Jews and Arabs, Oriental and Euro-American Jews all seemed to live together in harmony. Even the occupation of the territories taken in the Six Day War was long considered a model of peaceful and enlightened policy. The idealized image of the Jew was also projected onto the Jewish State. This was well-meaning and historically understandable, but it had little to do with reality and did not serve the interests of either side; nor was it helpful in the context of the Palestinian-Israeli conflict.

From 1967 on, predominantly among the so-called New Left and later among the Greens and the alternative scene, a counter-image to the idealized picture was developed, but it was not more realistic. Israel was described as "fascistic," compared to the Third Reich and to the apartheid regime of South Africa, and portrayed as a killer state. It was soon considered "in" to boycott not only South African but also Israeli products.

From 1981 on, all political and ideological groups in the Federal Republic began to increase their distance from Israel. Not only Begin's verbal barrage against Germany, but also his government's settlements policy and its treatment of the Palestinians were contributing factors.

■

It would be both wrong and unjust to attribute the described lack of realism with regard to Jews and the Jewish State to the Germans alone, or even to non-Jews in general. Jews and Israelis also are subject to this lack of realism—with regard to their own self-image.

There is, first of all, the already described oversimplification and division of the world into the Jewish and the non-Jewish, the spheres of light and darkness. Although its roots are historically and psychologically understandable, this worldview no longer corresponds with reality.

In Israel, this view leads to a clichéd view of the international community. In oversimplified terms: "The whole world is against us. This was always so and it will always be so." This perspective corresponds at best to only a part of the larger picture.

But Israelis and Jews have not only the outside world to contend with. They have problems of their own. After centuries, indeed millenniums of persecution and suppression, the Zionist fathers and mothers swore that, after all the suffering, they would create a better, more humane, and more just society in Zion. The standard was held deliberately high, too high. The German-Jewish-Israeli philosopher Gershom Scholem recognized this earlier and more clearly than others. Zionism, according to Scholem, developed a pseudo-messianic message in that it promised freedom and salvation in this world. Every messianic movement, he pointed out, awakens unfulfillable expectations. For both Jews and their non-Jewish supporters disappointment was unavoidable from the start. Even the greatest moral, political, economic, social, and cultural achievements on the part of Israel could not measure up to hopes that had been raised. The ideal was predestined to shatter upon the shoals of reality.

This may provide an explanation for Israel's tendencies toward self-absorption and its bent for self-criticism, as well as for the frequent and often acid criticism emanating from abroad. At least some of this outside criticism can be traced back to the well-intended but ultimately unrealistic, pseudo-messianic expectations raised by Zionism. Because it set its own goals so high, the outside world frequently measures Israel with the most demanding and thus unrealistic moral yardstick. The root of such criticism is actually flattering to the Jewish State. Israel, in turn, was not always able to respond to this basically positive disposition because it was often enough not recognized. This, too, is a consequence of a lack of realism toward oneself as well as others.

The objective criticism of Israel, including that originating in Germany, once again demonstrates that human rights are indivisible. It also, unfortunately, shows that the victims and the descendants of victims can also become perpetrators. No one is immune.

12

RELAXATION BUT NO RELIEF?

Is anti-Semitism about to run rampant in reunited Germany, or can we confidently predict that the wave of incidents that swelled so suddenly and horrifyingly in 1992 will once again subside? In any case, anti-Semitism is far from being the most pressing disorder in the new Europe. For example, throughout Europe there is the issue of relations between natives, foreign residents, and refugees. In Germany, the prime worry is how to help the two parts of a country that had been divided for more than forty years grow together in harmony. There are more than five million foreign residents in the Federal Republic of Germany, but fewer than fifty thousand Jews, who thus represent less than one percent of the "minority" problem, at least in terms of sheer numbers. In qualitative terms, however, there is a significant, double difference: First of all, the Jews of Germany (despite their carefully cultivated doubts) are Germans. Second, in the entire Christian-Occidental culture, the history of the relations between Jew and non-Jew has always involved the true (and frequently failed) test of tolerance. This is all the more true in the aftermath of the Holocaust, especially so in Germany.

For purely quantitative reasons, relations with the Jews are no longer a problem concerning the entire society. Granted, it concerns me and other Jews. But (contrary to rumor and our own perceptions) we are really not all that important. The state of relations with the Jews represents a qualitative signal for the will and capacity for tolerance. Nothing more, nothing less.

Especially in Germany one encounters much discomfort toward Jews among people who are above suspicion of anti-Semitism. One reason is that these non-Jews are no longer willing to put up with almost constant Jewish moralistic finger wagging. This may have to do with the personality of one or the other representative of the German Jews, but personalities do not explain the problem, and they are not the problem, at least not the only one.

The constant Jewish moralizing has begun to grate on non-Jewish nerves. This is truly a new development. In the decades immediately following the Holocaust, many Germans and other Europeans (and Americans as well) had a bad conscience because they bore criminal, political, or moral guilt, or felt guilty in a metaphysical sense for not having offered sufficient resistance or assistance. The result was a widespread and far-reaching trend of self-questioning and self-criticism that left only the hard-core incorrigibles unmoved and unaffected. As victims, Jews were not only the objects of sympathy; they were also welcomed as moral healers. Sympathetic attention from Jews, in turn, was received—and used—as a form of moral or political "clean bill of health."

With the best of intentions an inverted version of the false theory of collective German guilt has been applied to the Jews. As the collective victims of the Nazi atrocities, Jews are viewed as collectively innocent and moral. This is all very beneficial for the subsequent generations of Jews born in the West. We Jews of the following generations have profited from the Holocaust in the sense that we have "inherited" a position of moral superiority without having had to experience the martyrdom of our forefathers. And the Holocaust survivors? They were imbued with moral "credit" as survivors, not on the basis of their personal moral qualities or qualifications. That we Jews, too, were human, all too human, was a fact that could not remain hidden indefinitely, even if there had been no Nachmann in Germany and no Maxwell in England—and without the Israeli settlements and policies in the occupied territories.

The story was, of course, quite different in Eastern Europe, where Jews today are faced with special difficulties arising out of the collapse of communism. The Jewish collective is accused of having provided a disproportionately large number of early communist revolutionaries. It is (deliberately?) forgotten that most of these revolutionaries of the first generation were later liquidated, the Jewish collective persecuted, and the Jewish State caricatured in communist propaganda as a Nazi monster.

The Jewish moral credit has been exhausted. This should not be shocking, as every such advance in credit is eventually used up. The problem is that many Jews proceed on the assumption that this moral credit reserve is unlimited, and that irritates many non-Jews who are not anti-Semites. This irritation is understandable as, for purely biological reasons, there are sufficient representatives of the politically and morally unencumbered outside the Jewish camp. This development is natural and presents no cause for anger or anxiety. What does provoke anger and fear is the deliberate, snotty contemptuousness of some of the new left and the "alternative" crowd. The low point thus far was reached by the Greens' Ströble who, as a member of a delegation of Green parliamentarians visiting Israel in 1991, informed his hosts that they had only themselves to blame for the Iraqi rockets falling on the Jewish State. At the party convention the following November Ströble received ovations from the "grassroots" delegates. Other less political Germans also hit upon the strangest ideas. Consider a university professor whose political hue would be more accurately described as pink rather than brown who distributes posters announcing that he will be staging a reading from *Mein Kampf*. Perhaps the professor meant no anti-Semitism, but his actions are certainly tasteless and lacking in historical sensitivity.

The results of recent polls on German-Jewish relations in Germany have given rise to numerous expressions of concern. Granted, there is no acceptable level of anti-Semitism, but if we compare the 1992 surveys with the data from previous years, we recognize a dramatic decrease in anti-Semitic opinion. The data for Germany are not any more disappointing than for other West European countries or the United States.

Why do we react to the successes of Le Pen in France, the Fascists in Italy, and the Flemish Bloc in Belgium with apparent equanimity but yet get most upset over the much smaller parties of the extreme right in Germany? According to conventional wisdom, the former East Germany has become a new hotbed of neo-Nazism. This, it was contended, was made possible by German unification. But the polls reveal more positive opinions of Jews—and of foreigners—in the east than in the west of Germany.

Perhaps it is time we take note of reality: Jews like to come to Germany—tourists and, for example, the musician Daniel Barenboim. Jews like to live in Germany—Russian Jews, for example, and I. German Jews hold the "world record" for mixed marriages. Is this masochism? Jews have experienced very little discrimination in West Germany, but since the rise in anti-Semitic incidents in 1992, German Jews feel less secure than before. Now more than ever, more sensitivity is what is needed—on all sides.

■

As early as the 1950s, Israel's David Ben-Gurion was prepared to recognize the Federal Republic of Germany as a new Germany. At that time, most Israelis and Diaspora Jews, politicians as well as nonpoliticians, disagreed with the Israeli Prime Minister. Their attitudes and behavior were determined by a perception of "eternal guilt" on the part of Germany. In Germany itself, the application of new political paint had not fully succeeded in covering up the former political colors. Polls taken in the early 1950s revealed that about 10 percent of the West German population still considered Adolf Hitler a "great statesman" and failed to recognize that, as Sebastian Haffner pointed out, Hitler was actually responsible for two "final solutions": the Holocaust and his betrayal of the German people, whom he mercilessly led into the slaughter of the Second World War. The lack of sensitivity toward the sufferings of others, especially the Jews, was complemented by blindness with regard to this betrayal.

In the intervening years much has changed, both in Germany and

the Jewish world. Despite the efforts of those on either side whose fixations are on the sufferings or the ideologies of the past, the wall of
mutual taboos is being slowly, albeit far from completely, dismantled.
In the realm of international *geschichtspolitik*, the barriers remain considerably more formidable than in everyday relations (*tagespolitik*).

In contrast to the realms of *geschichtspolitik* and ideology, routine
relations on both sides are less subject to the tensions of anti-Semitism
and anti-Germanism, political mechanics and political biology. More
and more Israelis display relaxed attitudes toward Germany. This is
demonstrated by public opinion surveys, the steady stream of Israeli
tourists visiting Germany, and the rising number of mixed marriages.
This poses a problem for the Jewish collective, but it represents a sign
of greater openness on both sides. At least on the private level, practical coexistence has replaced ideological confrontation.

To the extent that day-to-day policy (*tagespolitik*) dominates and the
de-historization of Jewish-Israeli society continues, German-Jewish-
Israeli relations become more oriented to the present and are increasingly taken for granted. The German public continues to recognize the
special character of these relations, but does not automatically extend
this recognition to the Jewish and Israeli generations born since the
Holocaust. For Germans, Israel is in the process of becoming a state
"just like any other."

The state of German-Israeli political relations does not, however,
correspond to the developments on the social plane. West German
political leaders have been forced to accept that a "normalization" of
relations on the basis of the present, on *tagespolitik*, continues to meet
with strenuous objections on the part of Jews as well as non-Jews. In
describing the mechanics of anti-Germanism we have attempted to
explain the reasons for this: when it comes to differences of opinion
between Germany and other countries, be it on the level of everyday
tagespolitik or in the realm of *geschichtspolitik*, the Holocaust has
proven an effective instrument against Germany. No one, and especially not politicians, willingly surrenders such a useful tool.

This does not mean that lamentations, much less a reversion to the
politics of yesteryear, are called for on the German side. The former is
unproductive, the latter counterproductive. It must be remembered
that the German economy is dependent upon imports and exports;

German prosperity requires the good will of other countries. The Western nations certainly did not make it difficult for the young Federal Republic of Germany to rejoin their exclusive circle and, contrary to legend, restitution to Israel was not demanded as the price of admission. German rearmament was considered a higher priority and the legend of the bowed head is just that and nothing more. Konrad Adenauer stood tall and erect. While remaining true to himself, Adenauer demonstrated a genuine willingness for atonement and thus earned for himself and his country a new dignity. This behavior garnered snide smiles in Austria—back then—and the East Germans responded with sharp polemics, until, in the context of German-German and foreign relations in the mid-1980s, East Berlin was forced to realize both the necessity and effectiveness of the policy initiated under Adenauer. West Germany's first Chancellor continued to steer a steady course in his relations with Israel and the Jews, even when this caused waves in German-American relations. Israel was to prove a frequent source of turbulence in German foreign relations, especially with the United States.

That Israeli and Diaspora Jewish politicians resist a relaxation in historical tensions and, despite Ben-Gurion's warnings, continue to insist on erecting barriers and maintaining taboos is not due to anti-Germanism. These politicians require the Holocaust and thus Germany as an instrument in the formation of Jewish solidarity, identity, and identification. Since "God is dead" also applies to the majority of Jews, religion and tradition no longer suffice as the means of Jewish bonding. The history of Jewish sufferings, for which the Holocaust and Germany serve as abbreviations, are substitutes for Jewish religion. This process of historization has the unintended consequence of emptying Judaism of content and meaning. This is precisely what Jewish Orthodoxy and Ben-Gurion had so often warned would happen. Gradually, the loss is being recognized, and this is one of the reasons why more and more Jews are turning away from the functionaries in Israel and the Diaspora and embracing Orthodoxy. Whether the Orthodox-Jewish alternative can solve the identity crisis in Israel and the Diaspora remains to be seen, as the good solutions of the past are not always applicable and productive today or tomorrow.

In the meantime, the Holocaust and anti-Germanism remain key

Jewish fixations. The next German-Jewish collision is thus pre-programmed, and the political conflict can easily spread to the social level. Germans and Jews thus remained tightly bound to each other and each attempt to escape these bonds only makes the chains cut deeper.

The politicians and functionaries on both sides appear to have run out of new ideas. Instead they practice rituals which, although correct in principle and even necessary, degenerate into empty shells by virtue of their thoughtless and inflationary misuse: German politicians make their pilgrimages to the Yad Vashem Holocaust memorial in Jerusalem, their Israeli and Diaspora colleagues to Bergen-Belsen or Dachau—all of this between airports, cocktail parties, official negotiations, small talk, and state banquets. Macabre and tasteless! In January 1988 West German Foreign Minister Hans Dietrich Genscher set a German-Israeli-Jewish record, accomplishing the entire program in only twenty-eight (or was it just twenty-six?) hours. Whoever performs rituals in such a manner distorts them into farce, makes a caricature of the memorial, and dishonors the victims.

In contrast: How thoughtful and sovereign was the awareness of history shown by Boleslaw Barlog, then director of the Berlin Schiller Theatre, who, in 1965, refused to stage Peter Weiss's dramatization of the Auschwitz trial. Asked by the critics for his reasons, Barlog replied: "Auschwitz on the stage and then in all likelihood sausages during intermission!"

The rituals revolve around keywords and slogans: Normality? Special relations? Special normality? Guilt? Duty? Responsibility? Uniqueness? Singularity? And so on and so forth. Contents? No, more often empty phrases!

The events of 1991–92 appear to have filled the phrases with content again. Temporarily? Permanently? Will reunited Germany prove able to continue the example set first by the leadership and later on by the society of the new, West Germany? A sign of hope: in late 1992 the no longer silent majority and the political leadership of both the government and the democratic opposition began to demonstrate a determination to reassert their moral and governmental authority.

Selected Bibliography

Auswärtiges Amt. *Die Bundesrepublik Deutschland und der Nahe Osten. Dokumentation.* Bonn: Reihe Berichte und Dokumentationen, 1987.

Balabkins, Nicholas. *West German Reparations to Israel.* New Brunswick, N.J.: Rutgers University Press, 1971.

Bendelac, Jacques. *Les fonds exterieurs d'Israel.* Paris: Economica, 1982.

Black, Edwin. *The Transfer Agreement. The Untold Story of the Secret Pact Between the Third Reich and Jewish Palestine.* New York and London: Macmillan, 1984.

Broder, Henryk M. *Der Ewige Antisemit. Über Sinn und Funktion eines beständigen Gefühls.* Frankfurt am Main: Fischer, 1986.

Broder, Henry M., M. R. Lang eds. *Fremd im eigenen Land. Juden in der Bundesrepublik.* Frankfurt am Main: Fischer, 1979.

Brumlik, Micha, D. Kiesel, C. Kugelmann, J. H. Schoeps eds. *Jüdisches Leben in Deutschland seit 1945.* Frankfurt am Main: Jüdischer Verlag bei Athenäum, 1986.

Cohen, Michael J. *Palestine and the Great Powers 1945–1948*. Princeton University Press, 1982.

Deutschkron, Inge. *Israel und die Deutschen*. Köln: Verlag Wissenschaft und Politik, 3d ed., 1991.

Dittmar, Peter. "DDR und Israel. Ambivalenz einer Nicht-Beziehung." *Deutschland-Archiv*. 1977, Part 1: p. 736ff., Part 2: p. 848ff.

Feilchenfeld, Werner, Dolf Michaelis, Ludwig Pinner. *Haavara-Transfer nach Palastina und Einwanderung deutscher Juden 1933–1939*. Tubingen: Mohr, 1972.

Feldman, Lily G. *The Special Relationship Between West Germany and Israel*. Boston: George Allen & Unwin, 1984.

Fleischmann, Lea. *Dies ist nicht mein Land. Eine Jüdin verläßt die Bundesrepublik*. Hamburg: Hoffmann und Campe, 1980.

Gerlach, Frederick H. "The Tragic Triangle. Israel, Divided Germany and the Arabs, 1956–1965." Dissertation, Columbia University, 1968.

Greschat, Martin ed. *Die Schuld der Kirche. Dokumente und Reflexionen zur Schulderklärung vom 18.,19. Oktober 1945*. Munich: Kaiser, 1982.

Herbst, Ludolf ed. *Westdeutschland und die Wiedergutmachung, Schriftenreihe des Instituts für Zeitgeschichte*. Munich: Oldenbourg, 1988.

Historikerstreit. Die Dokumentation der Kontroverse um die Einzigartigkeit der nationalsozialistischen Judenvernichtung. Munich: Serie Piper, 1987.

Jena, Kai von. "Versöhnung mit Israel? Die deutsch-israelischen Verhandlungen bis zum Wiedergutmachungsabkommen von 1952." *Vierteljahreshefte für Zeitgeschichte* 34 (4) (1986):457–471.

Knight Robert ed. *Ich bin dafür, die Sache in die Länge zu ziehen. Die Wortprotokolle der österreichischen Bundesregierung von 1945 bis 1952 über die Entschädigung der Juden*. Frankfurt am Main: Athenaum, 1988.

Kocher, Renate. *Deutsche und Juden vier Jahrzehnte danach*. Allensbach: Institut für Demoskopie, 1986.

Kuschner, Doris. "Die jüdische Minderheit in der Bundesrepublik Deutschland." Dissertation, Universität Köln, 1977.

Lichtenstein, Heiner ed. *Die Fassbinder-Kontroverse oder Das Ende der Schonzeit*. Frankfurt am Main: Athenaum, 1986.

Meier, Christian. *40 Jahre nach Auschwitz. Deutsche Geschichtserinnerung heute*. Munich: Deutscher Kunstverlag, 1987.

Meroz, Yohanan. *In schwieriger Mission. Als Israels Botschafter in Bonn*. Berlin-Frankfurt: Ullstein, 1986.

Neustadt, Amnon. *Israels zweite Generation. Auschwitz als Vermächtnis*. Bonn: Verlag J.H.W. Dietz Nachf, 1987.

Nicosia, Francis R. *The Third Reich and the Palestine Question.* University of Texas Press, 1985.

Nolte, Ernst. *Das Vergehen der Vergangenheit. Antwort an meine Kritiker im sogenannten Historikerstreit.* Berlin and Frankfurt am Main: Ullstein, 1987.

Pease, Louis Edwin. "After the Holocaust: West Germany and Material Reparation to the Jews—From the Allied Occupation to the Luxemburg Agreements." Dissertation, Florida State University, 1976.

Rabe, Karl-Klaus. *Umkehr in die Zukunft. Die Arbeit der Aktion Sühnezeichen, Friedensdienste.* Bornheim-Merten: Lamuv Verlag, 1983.

Rendtorff, Rolf ed. *Arbeitsbuch Christen und Juden. Zur Studie des Rates der Evangelischen Kirche in Deutschland.* Gütersloher Verlag, 1986.

Rendtorff. Rolf, Hans H. Henrix eds. *Die Kirchen und das Judentum. Dokumente 1945–1985.* Paderborn: Bonifatius-Kaiser, 1987.

Schauspiel Frankfurt: *Der Fall Fassbinder. Dokumentation des Streits um "Der Müll, Die Stadt und Der Tod in Frankfurt,"* 1987.

Schölch, Alexander. "Das dritte Reich, die zionistische Bewegung und der Palästina-Konflikt." *Vierteljahreshefte für Zeitgeschichte* No. 1 (1982): 646–674.

Schultz, Hans Jurgen ed. *Mein Judentum.* Stuttgart-Berlin: Kreuz Verlag, 1979.

Silbermann, Alphons and Herbert Sallen. *Juden in Westdeutschland. Selbstbild und Fremdbild einer Minorität.* Cologone: Verlag Wissenschaft und Politik, 1992.

Silbermann, Alphons. *Sind wir Antisemiten? Ausmaß und Wirkung eines sozialen Vorurteils in der Bundesrepublik Deutschland.* Köln: Verlag Wissenschaft und Politik, 1982.

Skriver, Ansgar. *Aktion Sühnezeichen. Brücken über Blut und Asche.* Stuttgart: Kreuz-Verlag, 1962.

Studienkreis fur Tourismus: *Urlaubsreisen 1954–1985. 30 Jahre Erfassung des touristischen Verhaltens der Deutschen durch soziologische Stichprobenerhebungen,* Starnberg, 1986.

Sykes, Christopher. *Kreuwege nach Israel. Die Vorgeschichte des jüdischen Staates.* Munich: Beck, 1967.

Wojak, Andreas ed. *Schatten der Vergangenheit. Deutsche und Juden heute,* Güterloher Taschenbücher, 1985.

Wolffsohn, Michael. *Spanien, Deutschland und die "Jüdische Weltmacht."* Munich: C. Bertelsmann, 1991.

—— *Israel. Geschichte, Wirtschaft, Gesellschaft, Politik.* Opladen: Leske & Budrich, 1991, 3d ed.

—— *Keine Angst vor Deutschland!* Munich: Straube, 1990.

———— "Globalentschädigung für Israel und die Juden? Adenauer und die Opposition in der Regierung." Ludolf Herbst and Constantin Goschler eds. *Wiedergutmachung in der Bundesrepublik Deutschland.* Munich: Schriftenreiche des Instituts für Zeitgeschichte, Oldenbourg, 1988, pp. 161–190.

———— "Das deutsch-israelische Widergutmachungsabkommen von 1952 im internationalen Zusammenhang." *Vierteljahreshefte für Zeitgeschichte* 36 (4) (1988): 691–731.

———— "Die Wiedergutmachung und der Westen—Tatsachen und Legenden." *Aus Politik und Zeitgeschichte (Das Parlament)* 16–17, 87 (April 4, 1987): 19–29.

———— "Deutscher Patriotismus nach Auschwitz?" Beiträge zur Konfliktforschung, No. 4 (1987): 21–36.

———— *Deutsch-israelische Beziehungen: Umfragen und Interpretationen 1952–1986.* Munich: Landeszentrale für politische Bildungsarbeit, 1986.

———— *German-Saudi Arabian Arms Deals 1936–1939 and 1981–1985. With an Essay on West Germany's Jews.* Frankfurt am Main: Peter Lang, 1985.

Zemach, Mina. *Through Israeli Eyes. Attitudes Toward Judaism, American Jewry, Zionism and the Arab-Israeli Conflict.* New York: Institute on American Jewish-Israeli Relations, The American Jewish Committee, 1987.

Zweig, Ronald W. *German Reparations and the Jewish World. A History of the Claims Conference.* Boulder and London: Westview Press, 1987.

Index

Weizsäcker, Richard von, 38, 40, 64
Wetzel, Dietrich, 53, 55
White Rose Foundation, 53
Wimmer, Thomas, 163
World Jewish Congress (WJC), 44–52, 180
World Jewish population, 160–161
World Zionist Organization, 6

Xenophobia, 101–102, 131–132, 144

Yad Vashem Memorial, 74–75
Yediot Acharonot, 52, 90–91
Yom Kippur War (1973), 29–30, 72, 115, 148, 156

Zadek, Peter, 201
Zemach, Mina, 90
Zionism, 3–7, 39, 92; East German churchmen, 150; goal of, 185; and the Holocaust, 82; messianic overtones, 80, 204; nationalism, 185–186; "new Jewish man" as goal of, 101; Orthodox Jews, 183; pre-Holocaust justification of, 178–179; secularization of Judaism and, 76; Soviet Union, 9–10; Transfer Agreement, 2; United States, 8; UN resolution, 72, 148. *See also* Revisionists, Zionist